WHERE TO WATCH
BIRDS IN
SPAIN AND
PORTUGAL

To Jane

HAMLYN BIRDWATCHING GUIDES

WHERE TO WATCH BIRDS IN
SPAIN AND PORTUGAL

LAURENCE ROSE

HAMLYN

CONTENTS

First published in 1995 by Hamlyn Limited,
an imprint of Reed Consumer Books Ltd
Michelin House, 81 Fulham Road,
London SW3 6RB and Auckland, Melbourne,
Singapore and Toronto

Copyright © Reed International Books Limited
1995

Text copyright © Laurence Rose 1995
Artwork copyright © Juan M. Varela 1995
Maps copyright © Reed International Books
Limited 1995

ISBN 0 600 58404 6

A CIP catalogue record for this book is available
from the British Library

Page design by Jessica Caws
Maps drawn by John Gilkes
Printed in Hong Kong

Introduction

In my teens I took a train from London to Tangiers. The memory of the two days spent looking out of the window as Spain passed by has survived the last two decades. I was struck by the vastness of the landscapes, with their few villages, and by the abundance of birds: a White Stork standing sentinel on its nest perched on a factory chimney; a dark-phase Montagu's Harrier quartering the vast fields of wheat; the vultures soaring over the gorges and *sierras*; and every 100 m or so, something on the cables by the side of the track: a shrike, a Stonechat or the occasional Bee-eater.

This first and all-too-brief glimpse of the Iberian peninsula has been followed by, so far, over 30 visits to Portugal and Spain, many of them for business reasons but always a trip or two a year for the pure enjoyment of the region's birds and countryside.

In 1989, many of the most important sites for birds were documented in a book which has proved to be of enormous value to the conservation community. *Important Bird Areas in Europe*, by Richard Grimmett and Tim Jones, was published by the then International Council for Bird Preservation – now BirdLife International. It describes nearly 2500 sites across Europe. Together they form the basis of an agenda for bird conservation in Europe and never a day goes by without my copy being lifted from its shelf in my office.

Almost all the sites described here are Important Bird Areas – IBAs. There are no fewer than 308 published IBAs in Spain and Portugal, and many more have been discovered since the IBA book was first published. This is a clear indication of the importance of the two countries for both birdwatching and conservation. In some of the site accounts I have drawn attention to some conservation problems – and opportunities. It is important that birdwatchers, especially visiting foreigners, are aware that many of the best areas enjoy only a fragile hold on existence. It is vital that the work of the conservation organizations, and in particular that of the Partners of BirdLife International, is supported if we, as birdwatchers, are to continue to enjoy our hobby.

Birdwatching is a pleasure that takes many forms, and different people will use this book in different ways. I have tried to include a representative selection of sites, covering all the regions, habitats and most interesting species. The species lists are by no means exhaustive, but contain a selection of what I feel should interest the foreign visitor most. Several species, rare or unknown at home, are abundant in Spain and Portugal. To save space and avoid repetition, I have mostly left out birds such as Yellow-legged Gull, Crested Lark, Black Redstart, Stonechat, Nightingale, Cetti's Warbler, Sardinian Warbler, Short-toed Treecreeper, Spotless Starling, Great Grey and Woodchat Shrikes and Serin, because in most mainland areas they are reasonably common, if not abundant. Most of the species listed should be new or unusual for anyone making their first trip to Iberia. As for those who are more familiar with the region, I hope this book helps them to discover some interesting new places, and to catch up with some species that may have eluded them in the past.

How to use this guide

The mainland area covered by this book is too large and too diverse for a single birdwatching trip to do justice to it. Furthermore, there are four distinct island groups, each justifying its own itineraries. The book is therefore divided geographically into what would seem to be the regions most likely to be covered in a single holiday by visiting birdwatchers. Each section has a map, which shows the sites in relation to the main towns. This should enable the reader to identify the sites that are convenient to their destination, or to plan tours based on a wider area.

In many cases, the site accounts cover more than one IBA. This is to enable itineraries covering whole days or longer periods to be drawn up. A word of caution when designing itineraries from this book: in some places, especially Portugal, Extremadura and Andalucía, it can take a lot longer to travel between two places than would at first seem likely. This is because the roads are often narrower or more winding than the maps might suggest; or because at certain times of the year they are crammed with holidaymakers, especially on the Mediterranean coast; or simply because of the frequent stops needed to identify soaring eagles *en route* and to enjoy the marvellous views. The road networks in both countries are changing at an extraordinary pace. Although this can mean dramatic cuts in travelling time, it also means that maps are inevitably out of date from the moment they appear. In any case many Spanish and (especially) Portuguese maps have annoying inaccuracies in them, especially in respect of the more rural areas. Notwithstanding this, the directions and maps in this guide cannot replace the need for up-to-date road maps and the reader is strongly recommended to have good maps to hand to use in conjunction with this book.

Acknowledgements

Since this guide takes its inspiration from *Important Bird Areas in Europe*, the work of Portuguese and Spanish colleagues who gathered the data in the first place is greatly appreciated, in particular Eduardo de Juana in Spain and António Teixeira in Portugal. Likewise Richard Grimmett and Tim Jones who compiled the data from all over Europe.

Many people have helped me by providing information and checking details and in particular I should like to thank Jane Binstead, Adrian del Nevo, Antonio Escandell, Peter Eden, Juan Antónío Gómez López, Graham and Carla Goodall, Peter Harris, Graham Hearl, Nuno Lecoq, Domingos Leitão, Francisco Moreira, Ivan Nethercoat, Jan-Erik Petersen, David Simpson, Malcolm Smith, Erich Streich, Jesús Valiente, Juan Varela and Frank Zino.

KEY TO MAPS

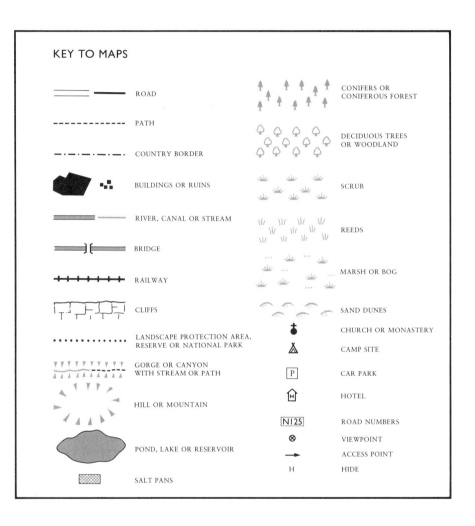

ROAD	CONIFERS OR CONIFEROUS FOREST
PATH	DECIDUOUS TREES OR WOODLAND
COUNTRY BORDER	SCRUB
BUILDINGS OR RUINS	REEDS
RIVER, CANAL OR STREAM	MARSH OR BOG
BRIDGE	SAND DUNES
RAILWAY	CHURCH OR MONASTERY
CLIFFS	CAMP SITE
LANDSCAPE PROTECTION AREA, RESERVE OR NATIONAL PARK	CAR PARK
GORGE OR CANYON WITH STREAM OR PATH	HOTEL
HILL OR MOUNTAIN	N125 ROAD NUMBERS
POND, LAKE OR RESERVOIR	VIEWPOINT
	ACCESS POINT
SALT PANS	H HIDE

BIRDLIFE INTERNATIONAL

BirdLife International is a worldwide partnership of organizations working for the diversity of all life through the conservation of birds and their habitats.

The partners in BirdLife International are like-minded national conservation organizations, which represent BirdLife in a country or specific territory. Where there is no Partner, an organization or individual may become a BirdLife Representative. BirdLife is represented in over 100 countries worldwide.

Birds are the entry point for BirdLife, providing it with a focus for all elements of its strategy. However, the organization recognizes broader environmental objectives. It adopts the rationale of shared responsibility for the global environment and the sustainability of the use of the world's natural resources.

BirdLife International pursues a programme of:

SCIENTIFIC RESEARCH AND ANALYSIS to identify the most threatened bird species and the most critical sites for the consevation of avian diversity, for setting global priorities for bird conservation.

FIELD ACTION to address these priorities, ranging from community-based integrated land-use and management projects to species recovery programmes, all benefiting wildlife and humans.

ADVOCACY AND POLICY DEVELOPMENT to promote sustainability in the use of all natural resources and the conservation of biodiversity, by targeting intergovernmental agencies, decision-makers, community leaders, non-government organizations and individuals.

NETWORK BUILDING to expand the global partnership of conservation organizations (especially in developing countries and Central/Eastern Europe) and promote worldwide interest in, and concern for, the conservation of birds and, through that, for wider environmental issues.

An example of BirdLife's work is the Important Bird Areas (IBA) programme. Sites of importance for birds throughout the world are being identified on strict, standardized criteria; IBAs in Europe and the Middle East have already been identified, programmes are underway in Africa, and currently being developed for Asia and the Americas. BirdLife's goal is to identify the world's Important Bird Areas by the year 2000. BirdLife also takes action for the priorities identified, as demonstrated by the successful programmes for the protection of Important Bird Areas in 31 countries in Europe.

BirdLife International has a headquarters in Cambridge (UK), and regional offices in Brussels (Belgium), Washington DC (USA), Quito (Ecuador), and Bogor (Indonesia).

SPAIN with Gibraltar

Spain is one of the largest countries in Europe, covering nearly 500,000 km². Much of the land is elevated, dominated by a huge central plateau, or *meseta*, and several high mountain ranges.

Although Spain is very largely an agricultural country, it has some industrial regions which are the traditional centres of the country's per capita wealth: the Basque country, Catalunya and Madrid. Extremadura and Andalucía are, by contrast, the traditional backwaters, with sparse populations and low income levels. The islands and the east coast have been revolutionized by the growth of tourism which has characterized much of the latter half of this century.

There are 17 autonomous regions in modern Spain, 15 on the mainland plus the two island groups. There are four Spanish languages and several dialects and variations, and six regions are officially bilingual. This means that many towns have two versions of their name. Maps and road signs now tend to use the local version in preference, so I have followed this convention, adding the *Castillano* version in brackets if there is a likelihood of confusion. This is a particular risk in the Basque-speaking areas of Euskadi and Navarra, where Basque place names are often completely unrelated to their *Castillano* equivalents.

Spain has a tradition of internal travel connected with the movement of livestock and with inter-regional trade. Most regions are therefore well served by a network of small, inexpensive hotels, complementing the large range of hotels of all classes available in the cities and resorts. The terms *Hostal* and *Pensión* are often applied to the smaller hotels, but this does not necessarily imply inferiority. Some of the better *hostales* are as good as any medium-range hotel. Generally, *hostales* and *pensiones* are cheaper than hotels, but this is not by any means universal.

There is a state-run (and soon to be privatized) chain of hotels, the *Paradores*, which are often found in some spectacular locations. They are usually converted castles or other buildings of great heritage value. They are towards the upper end of the price range but offer a guaranteed level of service and comfort.

Health care is to a high standard and EU citizens are entitled to free treatment, but the bureaucracy involved is such that the inexpensive insurance available through any travel agent is highly recommended. Doctors usually speak English, but if you have special needs it is worth learning the necessary vocabulary. Generally, English is widely spoken among young townspeople, but not among the older generation, who were discouraged from learning English during the Franco regime. French is more likely to be spoken by older educated people.

IMPORTANCE FOR BIRDS

Many first-time visitors to Spain are rightly captivated by the four 'gem' species, the Hoopoe, Bee-eater, Golden Oriole and Roller, which catch the eye as you flick through the pages of a field guide. They are generally common birds in most of Spain. Another popular group is the raptors. In all but the most industrial or intensively farmed parts of the country they abound. Four species of vulture, two great eagles and three smaller ones, three species of kite, three of harrier... it is difficult to spend a day in Spain without encountering a good selection of them.

On a world scale, Spain is important for several species. In the grasslands of central Spain live three-quarters of all the Great Bustards in the world, and half the Little Bustards. The Spanish Imperial Eagle is found nowhere else in the world, and numbers fewer than 150 pairs. These and 13 other species are deemed to be of the highest conservation importance, threatened with world-wide extinction or nearly so. Five such species are found on the Canary Islands, four of them endemic.

There are many species which are less threatened but for which Spain is outstanding. Almost the entire western population of Common Cranes, some 50,000 birds, winters in the wetlands and oak groves. The White Stork remains a common sight in towns and villages, having declined dramatically in much of the rest of Europe. The Balearic and Canary Islands hold important seabird populations, notably tens of thousands of pairs of Cory's Shearwaters.

CONSERVATION

Spain's government is very decentralized, with each region having substantial legislative powers, its own Parliament and Ministries. Conservation and the environment is largely handled at regional level, although National Parks and some overall coordination are managed in Madrid. Thus the quality of wildlife conservation and the degree of official commitment to it are to a large extent determined by local rather than national policies.

As with all southern European countries, the pace of change to fully developed status is quickening, and some arms of government clash with the attempts of others to meet the needs of conservation. On occasion, this has amounted to wilful disregard for the environment and the long-term pros-perity of a region in the interests of short-term gain. In both Spain and Portugal, this process is exacerbated by membership of the European Union, which has provided huge sums of money to speed up development. EU funds have been spent on destructive projects sponsored by one ministry inside the very Natural Parks set up by other government agencies; this despite the fact that the EU and its officials are bound by strict conservation laws and policies, and that often their collaboration in this destruction is in the face of viable alternatives.

However, EU membership offers certain opportunities to conservation. New incentive schemes make traditional farming systems more viable, and could promote conservation in agricultural areas. This has already started to benefit Great Bustards in Castilla y León. There are modest, but useful, funds available from Brussels for direct conservation action and a growing number of Spanish protected areas have benefited from this, through extended boundaries, improved management and better facilities for visitors.

SEASONS

Spring comes early to Spain. If the arrival of the first White Storks is anything to go by, then in Andalucía spring starts before Christmas! By early February vultures and eagles are on eggs and within a week or so swallows are flying over most of the country.

Late spring is a delight in all parts of Spain, in any habitat. In the south, May can be hot. Birds will be quiet and elusive around the middle of the day and there will be many young birds on the wing. North of Madrid and in the mountains, May is still a spring month, and June is marvellous for flowers, butterflies and birds.

July and August are, as elsewhere in Europe, less rewarding months for the birdwatcher. Most wetlands are naturally dry, the corn is high (too high to see bustards!) and nothing much is singing. Storks leave early, and have vacated their village nests by the time that, in mid-August, coastal migration has begun to pick up. September is marginally cooler, and the birds are becoming more active, having completed their summer moult.

The first flights of Cranes may reach northern Spain in October but are not common in the *dehesas* until late November. Then the wetlands begin to fill up again and attract thousands of Greylags, Pintail and Wigeon from the north.

GETTING THERE AND GETTING AROUND

Flying to Spain is straightforward, with daily flights to Madrid, Barcelona, Seville and Bilbao from most western European capitals and North America. The Balearics and Canaries are also well served, and, along with Málaga, Alicante and Girona are regular destinations for charter and package flights. Indeed, although a typical coast holiday may not be what you are looking for, a package based on the Mediterranean coast or the islands is a cheap way of getting to some good birdwatching regions if you are content not to travel too far. The ferries to Santander and Bilbao are interesting alternative ways into northern Spain and the Pyrenees, and afford good birdwatching at sea. There are several points at which you can drive into Spain from France or Portugal.

To reach most of the sites in this book, a car is essential. All the big international car hire firms have branches in Spain, and can be found in most good-sized towns. There are numerous smaller firms of variable quality which are often cheaper. Get a recommendation first. Never leave valuables on show in the car; Seville, in particular is notorious for theft from cars.

In the Canary Islands, it is likely you will want to visit more than one island, if you are interested in seeing all the specialities there. This is straightforward and ferry services link the islands, in some cases providing good birdwatching opportunities at sea.

NORTHERN SPAIN

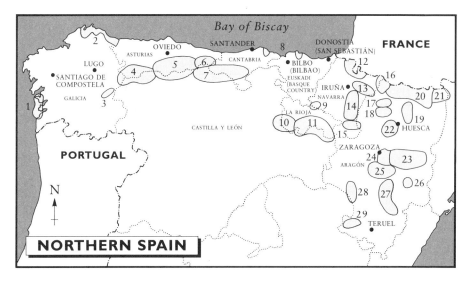

1 *Rías and headlands of south-west Galicia*, 2 *Rías and headlands of north-east Galicia*,
3 *Serra do Courel*, 4 *Cantabrian Mountains: West*, 5 *Cantabrian Mountains: Central*,
6 *Picos de Europa*, 7 *Riaño and Fuentes Carrionas*, 8 *Santoña and Guernica Marshes*,
9 *Laguna de las Cañas and the Logroño area*, 10 *Sierra de la Demanda*, 11 *Upper Ebro valley*,
12 *Roncesvalles area*, 13 *Sierras de Leyre, Orba e Illón*, 14 *Lower Aragón valley*,
15 *Bardenas Reales*, 16 *The Western Pyrenees*, 17 *Sierra de San Juan de la Peña*, 18 *Riglos*,
19 *Sierra de Guara*, 20 *Central Pyrenees*, 21 *Posets–La Madaleta–Entecada*,
22 *Wetlands and Sierras around Huesca*, 23 *Los Monegros*, 24 *The Ebro at Zaragoza*,
25 *Belchite and the Zaragoza Steppes*, 26 *Alcañiz*, 27 *Ríos Guadalope and Martín*,
28 *Gallocanta*, 29 *Montes Universales and Llanos de Pozondón*

In this section we visit green, lush Galicia, rugged Cantabria, the stormy Basque coast and hills of Navarra, the dry steppes of Aragón and the alpine regions of the Pyrenees. Thus there is a staggering variety of birds on offer. The three high mountain ranges, the Pyrenees, the Cordillera Cantábrica and the Sistema Norte, are home a great variety of raptors as well as mountain specialities that are found in few if any other parts of Spain: Alpine Accentor, Wallcreeper, Snow Finch, Tengmalm's Owl and Capercaillie.

The Atlantic coast has important seabird and wader populations, part of the great East Atlantic Flyway linking the Russian Arctic with the tropics. In the steppes of Aragón are to be found bustards, sandgrouse and Dupont's Lark.

Many people visit the Spanish Pyrenees and the North by driving over from France. There is a choice of crossing points all along the border. The sea ports of Santander and Bilbao are convenient for the Atlantic coast, the western and central Pyrenees, the Cantabrian mountains and on into central Spain.

Flying into the north is straightforward from Britain and most of Europe. Bilbao, Santander, Zaragoza, Barcelona and Santiago de Compostela are all served by scheduled or charter flights and are convenient starting points for the sites described in this chapter.

BIRDWATCHING SITES

RÍAS AND HEADLANDS OF SOUTH-WEST GALICIA

42°28N 08°51W

Galicia, in the north-westernmost corner of Spain, is very Atlantic in character: greener and wetter than anywhere else in the peninsula. Its estuaries, *rías*, are a vital link in the chain of wader and wildfowl feeding grounds that conservationists call the East Atlantic Flyway, stretching from Russia to South Africa.

The estuaries of the Miño, which forms the Portuguese border at this point, and the Arousa, are important during migration for tens of thousands of waders and hold good winter populations of Grey Plover (over 1000 on the Arousa), Avocet, Wigeon, Pintail, Red-breasted Merganser and Sanderling.

TIMING

In addition to passage waders, passerine numbers are also important, and falls of warblers, chats and flycatchers are often spectacular during poor weather in April, May, September and October. More attention from birdwatchers during October would almost certainly turn up transatlantic vagrants from time to time.

SPECIES
- *Resident* Cormorant, Shag, Shelduck, Red Kite, Marsh Harrier, Goshawk, Peregrine, Guillemot, Fan-tailed Warbler, Waxbill, Chough.
- *Breeding season* shearwaters, Nightjar, Alpine Swift.
- *Passage* Spoonbill, Osprey, waders, terns.
- *Winter* divers, Little Egret, Scaup, Common Scoter, Hen Harrier, Grey Plover, Purple Sandpiper, auks.

ACCESS

The Miño estuary can be appreciated from the Portuguese side (*see* page 163) or from the river mouth at A Guardia. There are bird hides north of Pasaxe, a small settlement on the east side of the headland. These are reached by taking the coast road for 300 m beyond Pasaxe where the hides – *observatorios ornitológicos* – are signposted to the right before and after the 'Santa Tecla' campsite.

The Ría de Arousa is north-west of Pontevedra. The southern shore of the estuary is best, between Cambados and O Grove, including Lanzada beach and the southern end of the Illa de Arousa. The C550 from this island southwards round the bay to O Grove, and the coast roads leading off it provide access.

There are also colonies of Shags on the west coast island groups such as the Islas Cíes and the Islas Ons. The Islas Cíes are reached by boat from Vigo, whence there are frequent sailings in summer (tel. 986 437777). The Islas Ons are also served by public boat-trips in summer, from Bueu, Sanxenxo and Portonovo.

RÍAS AND HEADLANDS OF NORTH-EAST GALICIA

43°40N 07°52W

The Rías de Ortigueira and Ribadeo are on the north coast, close to the towns of the same names. In the first case, the road from Cariño to Punta de Estaca de Bares (*see* below) skirts the estuary. In the second, the Ribadeo–Vegadeo road is particularly good for access and scenery. There is a *Parador* and other accommodation in Ribadeo, and plenty of choice all round the Galician coast.

Several of the rocky capes are good sea-watching and migration landfall points. Estaca de Bares, east of the Ortigueira estuary, for example, is good for passing Gannet, Razorbill, Common Scoter, Manx, Yelkouan, Cory's and Sooty Shearwaters and divers. There is a bird observatory there, where between August and November up to 100,000 passing seabirds are noted. About 14 km east of Ortigueira there is a local road leading off the C642 to the Punta, via Vila de Bares. Soon after this village there is a left turn to a wind energy installation (*estación eólica*). After 2 km there is a right turn then a left at a communications station. The observatory is a stone building along a footpath below the parking area. There is sleeping space and a fireplace, but no electricity or running water.

SERRA DO COUREL

42°15N 06°45W

One of the few mountainous areas in Galicia, the Serra do Courel lies to the south and west of the Cantabrian Mountains. The range reaches 1616 m at Piapaxaro, and has scattered pockets of deciduous forest. It is a small but complex area, comprising both Mediterranean-type *matorral* and Atlantic-type beech and oak forests, along with riverine woodland.

Typical northern birds such as Red-backed Shrike, Goldcrest and Bullfinch therefore rub shoulders, so to speak, with Dartford and Subalpine Warblers, as well as a selection of raptors that might be somewhat unexpected for a Galician bird list.

TIMING
Winter weather is usually very wet; late spring is the best time, although this is often rainy as well.

SPECIES
◆ *Resident* Golden Eagle, Goshawk, Hen Harrier, Grey Partridge, Woodcock, Crag Martin, Blue Rock Thrush, Dipper, Crested Tit, Cirl and Rock Buntings.
◆ *Breeding season* Short-toed Eagle, Montagu's Harrier, Hobby, Red-backed Shrike, Subalpine and Melodious Warblers, Rock Thrush.

◆ ACCESS
From Lugo, the C546 leads south to Monforte, 66 km away. From here the N120 Ponferrada road leads, after 31 km, to the small village of Quiroga. In the village there is a turning which leads along a minor road for 35 km through the *serra* to Seoane. From here there are interesting walks to Miraz, to the north-west, or Moreda, to the south-east, along the valley of the Río Pequeño.

CANTABRIAN MOUNTAINS: WEST

42°55N 06°30W

The Cantabrian Mountains lie roughly parallel to Spain's north coast and are probably the least well known of the high mountain areas. From the naturalist's point of view it is as a stronghold of the brown bear that the Cordillera Cantábrica is most famous, but birdwatchers have plenty to find here, too. The entire range contains no fewer than 13 Important Bird Areas, which I have divided into four groups.

The western four IBAs cover 1200 km² and include the Sierra de Rañadoiro, which contains the superb Muniellos Forest. This is the best preserved oak wood in Spain and one of the finest in Europe. Its 3000 ha are covered in virtually pristine stands of sessile and 'English' oak. Elsewhere there are good stands of beech. Capercaillie, Black and Middle Spotted Woodpeckers are common here, as are wildcat, otter and wolf. Bears are occasionally spotted here, but they are always elusive.

South of here, in León province, is the Sierra de los Ancares, a mountain massif with rugged hills, oak-covered valleys and lush meadows. Birds of prey are abundant, notably Short-toed Eagle and Goshawk. The threatened Spanish race of Partridge is also common. There are at least 20 breeding male Capercaillie. A third IBA comprises the Sierras del Coto and Gistreo, immediately to the east, in the largely unprotected area to the south of Villablino, where a similar range of species can be found.

The fourth Important Bird Area in the western sector is the more wooded Degaña, some 27,000 ha, of which one-third is protected as a national game reserve (hunting is permitted). There are particularly good stands of beech wood, where wolf and brown bear live. Again, it contains a good selection of species typical of the region, including the two woodpeckers already mentioned.

TIMING

Snow lies late into the spring on the north slopes of Ancares, but by the end of April the meadows are beginning to come into flower. From then until late June the mountains are perfect. Autumn is a time of spectacular colour.

SPECIES

◆ *Resident* Golden Eagle, Goshawk, Griffon Vulture, Peregrine, Capercaillie, Woodcock, Eagle Owl, Middle Spotted and Black Woodpeckers, Crag Martin, Blue Rock Thrush, Crested Tit, Cirl and Rock Buntings, Crossbill, Rock Sparrow, Chough.

◆ *Breeding season* Black Kite, Short-toed Eagle, Honey Buzzard, Hoopoe, Red-backed Shrike, Subalpine and Melodious Warblers, Rock Thrush, Ortolan Bunting.

ACCESS

Degaña and the Muniellos forest can be reached from Villablino, on the C623 north-west of León city. About 5 km west of Villablino, a small road leads off to the left from Caboalles over the Puerto Cerredo and on to Degaña village. About 8 km farther, at Larón, a right turn leads over the Puerto del Rañadoiro. From here much of the area is forested, and the road begins to follow the valley of the Río Narcea. A right turn before Ventanueva leads to the beech forests of Degaña and the Monasterio de Hermo. A left turn in Ventanueva to Puerto de Connio marks the northern edge of the Muniellos forest.

Sierra de los Ancares is north-west of Ponferrada. From this town a small road runs to Vega de Espinareda, of the C631 Columbrianos. From Vega a choice of roads leads into the reserve. Alternatively, 36 km along the NVI Lugo road is Ambasmestas, from where the small Galician sector can be explored, taking the road to the Castillo de Doiras and then turning right to Cela and beyond.

The Sierra de Coto is immediately south of the C631 Villablino–Ponferrada road, from which smaller roads head into the hills. From here, tracks lead on to the neighbouring Sierra de Gistreo, so this has to be reached from an entirely different direction, taking roads north off the NVI in the region of Bembibre.

There is plentiful accommodation in the larger villages such as Degaña.

CANTABRIAN MOUNTAINS: CENTRAL
43°10N 06°00W

Another four IBAs constitute the central portion of the Cordillera Cantábrica. These mountains are marginally higher, reaching 2417 m at Peña Ubiña and are therefore home to the Alpine Chough, which is less frequently seen farther west. The best population of brown bear in Spain is to be found in the Somiedo IBA, which is a very well-preserved area of mountains, woods, meadows and small villages. Honey Buzzards are found here, and Golden Eagles range over most of its 900 km^2 seeking out hares, chamois and roe deer. Otters, wildcats and genets are among the mammalian predators, and the little Pyrenean desman is common.

To the east are the Game Reserves of Aller in Asturias and Mampodre in Castilla y León, which between them cover two more Important Bird Areas. The beech woods here are some of the best in the country, and wolf and bear are again present. The fourth IBA links Somiedo to Mampodre, and comprises the small, high Sierra on the Asturias–Castilla y León border at Piedrafita.

TIMING
Snow in winter, morning mist followed by hot afternoons in summer and breathtaking colour in autumn; as elsewhere in the mountains, late spring and early summer are the best times for birds.

SPECIES
Birds are similar to the previous site, with the addition of Alpine Chough.

ACCESS
The whole area is conveniently crossed by good roads and tracks. The huge Somiedo reserve can be explored via the C633 road which runs north from the C623 east of Villablino to the C634 west of Oviedo. The busy A66 and C630 roads cut across the eastern end, and smaller roads run off into the interior, such as the local road from Pola de Lena west and south. The C630 also crosses the Piedrafita range, which can be explored by taking the right turn at Villamanín. After 8 km a left turn heads towards Puerto de Piedrafita, which is a dead end. Retracing to the turn, carry on heading east to the next left turn a couple of kilometres farther on. Another left at the junction after 12 km leads into the Mampodre reserve. A right turn instead would eventually lead, via Boñar, into the heart of Mampodre and into the Sierra Mermeja in the Aller game reserve.

Picos de Europa

43°10N 04°50W

The wild and rugged Picos de Europa take their name from the fact that they were often the first part of Europe to appear to whalers, fishermen and explorers on the return home from the Atlantic. For naturalists, their renown is well deserved, with over 40 species of orchid, countless endemic subspecies of flower and butterfly, and, for good measure, brown bears, wolves, Pyrenean desman, otters and wildcats. The area comprises the 17,000-ha Montaña de Covadonga National Park and a 7600-ha National (hunting) Reserve. There are plans to increase the size of the National Park considerably. There is a cable car from Fuente Dé, which, although crowded on summer weekends, offers some excellent views and probably the easiest birdwatching.

The three massifs that make up the Picos harbour a typical selection of Cantabrian birds, as well as three specialities: Wallcreeper, Alpine Accentor and Snow Finch. Other high altitude species include abundant Alpine Choughs and Rock Thrushes. Golden and Short-toed Eagles and Griffon Vultures soar over the limestone cliffs and gorges. There are extensive beech and oak woods where Middle Spotted and Black Woodpeckers are not uncommon.

Middle Spotted Woodpeckers, in fact, can be seen in several villages where they frequent the cherry trees that grow on the outskirts. Brez, between Potes and Espinama, is a good bet.

TIMING

In July and August accommodation can be very hard to find without prior booking. June is the ideal month for a visit to the Picos.

SPECIES

◆ *Resident* Golden Eagle, Goshawk, Griffon Vulture, Peregrine, Capercaillie, Grey Partridge, Woodcock, Eagle Owl, Middle Spotted and Black

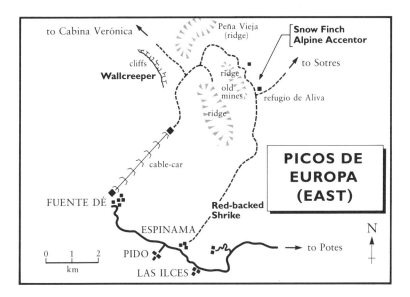

Woodpeckers, Crag Martin, Blue Rock Thrush, Crested Tit, Dipper, Alpine Accentor, Wallcreeper, Rock Bunting, Citril and Snow Finches, Rock Sparrow, Crossbill, Chough, Alpine Chough.

◆ *Breeding season* White Stork, Black Kite, Short-toed and Booted Eagles, Honey Buzzard, Egyptian Vulture, Hen Harrier, Bee-eater, Hoopoe, Water Pipit, Red-backed Shrike, Subalpine and Melodious Warblers, Rock Thrush, Ortolan Bunting.

ACCESS

There are excellent maps available locally and from good suppliers in the UK, which are highly recommended for anyone spending time in the Picos; they are essential for a serious walking trip.

There is an information centre and accommodation in Cangas de Onís, in the northern foothills of the Picos. This village is on the C6312, 108 km west of Santander. From Cangas a road leads to the village of Covadonga and on up into the National Park. The southern slopes of the Covadonga National Park are reached via the Riaño National Reserve (below): just south of the Puerto de Pontón, on the N625 there is a mountain road up to Posada de Valdeón, where there is another information centre and accommodation.

From Fuente Dé, where there is a *Parador* and other accommodation, a cable car runs up to the peak at the Mirador del Cable, where Alpine Accentors abound. Fuente Dé is on the southern face of the Picos, 20 km west of Potes which is on the N621. The cable car operates from about 10 a.m. in season, but it is necessary to arrive an hour beforehand at weekends and in high summer, otherwise there will be a wait of *several hours*. At the peak, there is well-trodden path which, after a kilometre, turns left into the heart of the Picos towards Cabina Verónica, where there are often Snow Finches and Alpine Accentors. The cliffs on the right should be checked for Wallcreeper.

Instead of turning left to the Cabina, there is a round trip of about 4 km to Espinama, on the road below Fuente Dé, which takes in meadows and scrub with Red-backed Shrikes, and beech woods that are good for Black Woodpeckers.

For the southern slopes, Fuente Dé, Potes and Espinama are good bases with a choice of accommodation and restaurants. Carreña and Las Arenas are good for the northern side, and allow access to the Sierra de Cuera.

RIAÑO AND FUENTES CARRIONAS

43°05N 05°00W

Riaño National Reserve is on the southern face of the Cordillera Cantábrica, with steep slopes covered in scrub and grassland, oak and beech woods and limestone cliffs. As well as having one of the most important Capercaillie populations in Spain, with at least 180 males, there is a rich forest bird community, with Middle Spotted and Black Woodpeckers and Short-toed Eagles. In the remoter parts, Eagle Owls call by night and Golden Eagles hunt by day. There is also a good population of brown bears, chamois and wild boar.

Immediately east of the Riaño national game reserve is another, Fuentes Carrionas. Many of the valleys in this 47,000-ha reserve are accessible only on foot, but in spring the pastures are covered in Lent lilies, meadow saxifrage and Pyrenean horned pansies. There are small colonies of Griffon Vultures and these magnificent birds can be seen thermalling anywhere in and

Capercaillie

around the reserve, with Booted, Short-toed and Golden Eagles also common. Above the tree-line here are Hen Harriers, relatively uncommon breeding birds in Spain. The longest river in Spain, the Ebro, rises to the east but is soon captured by a huge reservoir before being released on to the Mediterranean. The only significant White Stork population in northernmost Spain is in this area, and the reservoir itself holds a good post-breeding assemblage of around 2000 Red-crested Pochard.

TIMING
Similar to previous sites, but the existence of so many reservoirs in the area adds significant winter interest. Red-crested Pochard numbers peak in July.
SPECIES
◆ *Resident* Bonelli's and Golden Eagles, Goshawk, Griffon Vulture, Peregrine, Capercaillie, Woodcock, Eagle Owl, Middle Spotted and Black Woodpeckers, Crag Martin, Blue Rock Thrush, Crested Tit, Dipper, Cirl and Rock Buntings, Rock Sparrow, Chough, Alpine Chough.
◆ *Breeding season* White Stork, Red-crested Pochard, Black Kite, Short-toed and Booted Eagles, Honey Buzzard, Egyptian Vulture, Hen Harrier, Hoopoe, Red-backed Shrike, Subalpine and Melodious Warblers, Rock Thrush, Ortolan Bunting.
◆ *Autumn and winter* wildfowl.
ACCESS
The Riaño reserve is easily reached via the good C621 from León which joins the C625 coast road, passing by the Picos de Europa. Smaller roads come off these into the interior. For Fuentes Carrionas, it is necessary to take the local roads which cut through the reserve between Cervera de Pisuerga and Velilla del Río Carrión. There is a Parador in Cervera and other hotels here and in Velilla. The Saja reserve is served by several picturesque mountain roads. For example, the C627 north of Cervera runs over the Puerto de Piedrasluengas before a right turn heads into the interior and, eventually, to the coast west of San Vicente de la Barquera. To the east of this road is another running parallel from Espinilla, west of Reinosa, to Valle de Cabuérniga, before joining up with the San Vicente road.

East of Reinosa the C6318 skirts the north shore of the Ebro reservoir; a smaller, more winding road runs along the south shore. Accommodation can be found in Reinosa and several of the villages, as well as along the coast road.

SANTOÑA AND GUERNICA MARSHES

43°30N 03°30W

The extensive mud-flats, salt-marshes and coastal dunes along the coast and in the bay at Santoña make up the most important wetland on Spain's north coast. Spoonbills pass through on migration: up to 60 can be seen at any one time, but presumably many more pass through in the course of a season. There are important numbers of waders in spring and autumn, including up to 700 Curlew and 350 Whimbrel. About 5000 Wigeon feed in the salt-marshes during winter. Santoña is one of the few breeding sites in Spain for Shelduck.

Farther east is the Ría de Guernica, a deep estuary on the Basque coast with salt-marshes and, at the river mouth, a little island. This has a small colony of Shags, and up to 100 Spoonbills and the occasional Osprey pass through the estuary.

The Ría de Guernica is part of a Biosphere Reserve called Urdaibai, which includes the mountains bordering the valley. It is a truly beautiful reserve covering over 22,000 ha. In the mountains there is a good selection of raptors including Short-toed Eagle and Honey Buzzard.

TIMING

The weather in spring can be violent on this Atlantic coast; late August to November is the best period for migrants. Wildfowl arrive in late October and stay until March.

SPECIES

◆ *Resident* Cormorant, Shelduck, Red Kite, Marsh Harrier, Goshawk, Peregrine.
◆ *Breeding season* Shag, Osprey, Black Kite, Honey Buzzard, Short-toed Eagle.
◆ *Passage* Spoonbill, Osprey, waders, Wryneck, Red-backed Shrike.
◆ *Winter* Greylag, Wigeon, Pintail, Common Scoter, Hen Harrier, Grey Plover, windblown divers and auks.

ACCESS

The roads between Ampuero, Treto, Bárcena and Santoña skirt much of the Santoña marshes. The area is best explored on foot, up to two hours before high tide, although care must be taken to avoid being stranded during high spring tides. The Ría de Guernica empties into the Atlantic just east of Bermeo and the road from here to Gernika (Guernica), or from Gernika to Gamecho on the east bank, overlooks the estuary from the hills. There is access from both roads to the shore.

Accommodation is easily found in and around Santoña and Gernika.

LAGUNA DE LAS CAÑAS AND THE LOGROÑO AREA

42°25N 02°23W

On the outskirts of the city of Logroño is a 75-ha irrigation pond with good marshy vegetation and a surprising selection of waterbirds. Indeed, the area contains one of the relatively few heronries in the region and as such is important in a northern context. At least 25 pairs of Purple Heron nest, along with two or three times as many Night Herons. There are also breeding season records of Bittern.

A tiny protected area to the north, Peñalabeja, holds a good collection of birds typical of wooded hills, such as Red Kite, Sparrowhawk, Long-eared Owl and Bonelli's Warbler.

TIMING
There is a good selection of wildfowl on the reservoir during winter, but it is during the breeding season that the site comes into its own.

SPECIES
◆ *Breeding season* Little Grebe, Great Crested Grebe, Purple, Grey and Night Herons, Little Egret, Bittern, Red-crested Pochard, Water Rail, Black-winged Stilt.
◆ *Winter* ducks and grebes, Red Kite.

ACCESS
Access is via tracks leading off the N111 a few kilometres north-east of the city. Peñalabeja can be reached 17 km north of Viana, between the villages of Cabredo and Marañón. Farther north and east, the road between Estella and Alsasua is good for raptors, especially in the area around the villages of Zudaire and Baquedano.

SIERRA DE LA DEMANDA
42°15N 03°00W

La Rioja is a small autonomous Community which could be easily missed on a map, locked as it is between its giant neighbours Castilla y León, Aragón and Navarra. The Sierras that form its short southern border are, however, very much under explored and there is much to offer the birdwatcher – wine-lover or not. The Sierra de la Demanda is shared with Castilla y León, and marks the western end of the Sistema Ibérico Norte, or northern range. The Important Bird Area covers around 1000 km², made up of three protected areas: Demanda national reserve in Castilla y León and Ezcaray and Cameros reserves in La Rioja.

The Sierra is rich in birds of prey, including Golden, Short-toed and Booted Eagles, as well as at least ten pairs of Hen Harrier. There is an isolated population of the threatened Spanish race of Partridge and several species which are restricted in Spain to northern latitudes, such as Treecreeper and Marsh Tit. Much of the natural forest cover is being lost to grazing, or replaced by commercial forestry, but where the original cover of oak and beech remains is the best place to find Woodcock, Honey Buzzard and the very common Tawny Owl. Citril Finches are found in the pine woods.

TIMING
Spring and early summer can be outstanding as the migrants establish their territories and the raptors begin to breed. Golden Eagles, however, will be on eggs from March until May and less in evidence. Autumn brings hoards of migrating Woodpigeons in to the mountain passes.

SPECIES
◆ *Resident* Golden Eagle, Goshawk, Sparrowhawk, Peregrine, Grey Partridge, Woodcock, Eagle Owl, Crag Martin, Blue Rock Thrush, Crested and Marsh Tits, Treecreeper, Cirl and Rock Buntings, Citril Finch, Chough.

Hen Harrier

♦ *Breeding season* White Stork, Black Kite, Short-toed and Booted Eagles, Honey Buzzard, Hen Harrier, Hoopoe, Subalpine and Melodious Warblers, Rock Thrush, Ortolan Bunting.

ACCESS

From the N120 Logroño–Burgos road the C113 runs south from Nájera through the Cameros and Demanda reserves. A range of smaller roads take you into the interior villages. Another road runs south from the N120, starting at Santo Domingo de la Calzada, into the Ezcaray reserve. Remoter stretches of the Sierra, with intact woodland best explored on foot or by four-wheel drive, are reached by taking the road to the Hermitage of San Millán, 8 km beyond the village of San Millán de la Cogolla. This track eventually joins up with a minor road down the other side of the mountains.

UPPER EBRO VALLEY

42°05N 02°45W

South and east of the Sierra de la Demanda are four more IBAs, made up of further sierras of the Sistema Norte. The national reserve of Urbión is the only one of the four with any official protection. Its 1000 km² of pine woods, oak and beech, with mountains rising to 2278 m, enclose some of the most sparsely inhabited parts of Spain. Many villages have been abandoned and cling, eerily silent, to the steep slopes. The grazing pastures around these villages are scrubbing over, and are home to Melodious Warblers, Wrynecks and Green Woodpeckers. The rockier parts are the haunt of Golden Eagles, the woods of Honey Buzzards and, in the east, the *matorral* is home to ten pairs of Hen Harrier.

South and east of the city of Logroño the various tributaries of the Ebro valley have cut deep into the limestone to form precipitous gorges. These *hoces* of the rivers Iregua, Leza and Jubera have important colonies of cliff-nesting birds, such as Griffon Vulture, Peregrine and Eagle Owl. The Cicados valley between Arnedillo and Peña Isasa also holds an important Griffon colony. Once upon a time the wildlife there was even more exciting: at Enciso, there are 130 million year-old dinosaur tracks along the Ruta de los Dinosauros.

The Sierra de Alcarama and the valley of the Río Alhama has over ten pairs of Egyptian Vultures and at least three pairs of Bonelli's Eagles, as well as another Griffon Vulture colony, with some 80 pairs. Peregrine and Eagle Owl are also common.

TIMING

Griffon Vultures frequent the colonies all year round. In October, huge flocks of Woodpigeons, perhaps millions of birds, migrate through the mountain pass (*puerto*) of Santa Inés.

SPECIES

◆ *Resident* Golden and Bonelli's Eagles, Goshawk, Griffon Vulture, Peregrine, Grey Partridge, Eagle Owl, Crag Martin, Blue Rock Thrush, Black Wheatear, Crested and Marsh Tits, Treecreeper, Cirl and Rock Buntings, Chough.

◆ *Breeding season* Black Kite, Short-toed and Booted Eagles, Honey Buzzard, Egyptian Vulture, Hen Harrier, Hoopoe, Subalpine and Melodious Warblers, Rock Thrush, Ortolan Bunting.

◆ *Passage* Woodpigeon.

ACCESS

A picturesque road diverges from the C234 and runs through both Urbión and Demanda, connecting Salas de los Infantes and Abejar. A smaller road runs north from Vinuesa to Puerto de Santa Inés.

RONCESVALLES AREA

43°00N 01°15W

The hills on the border between Navarra and France rise to a little over 2000 m. The great beech forest at Monte de la Cuestión in the Irati valley is the largest in Spain, and some 20 pairs of White-backed Woodpeckers are to be found here, perhaps the best population in the region. They seem to be mainly associated with the more lichen-covered trees. Black Woodpeckers also breed in these woods. There are other important stands of beech in the area, many of which are small nature reserves.

Further north and west are the slightly lower hills of the Gorramendi group, on the French border either side of the N121. There is a more rugged character to the landscape, and Griffon Vulture and other raptors find it to their liking. Of particular note is the occasional presence of Lammergeier, well west of its usual Pyrenean range, along with Red Kite and Egyptian Vulture. White-backed and, this time, Middle Spotted Woodpeckers are characteristic of the beech and oak woods hereabouts.

TIMING

Winters are milder here than in the Pyrenees proper and spring starts earlier. Thus mid-April to June is the best time, but the whole year has much to offer.

SPECIES

◆ *Resident* Goshawk, Sparrowhawk, Griffon Vulture, Lammergeier, Peregrine, Eagle, Long-eared and Tawny Owls, Middle Spotted, White-backed and Black Woodpeckers, Crag Martin, Blue Rock Thrush, Crested Tit, Cirl and Rock Buntings, Chough.

White-backed Woodpecker

◆ *Breeding season* Red Kite, Short-toed Eagle, Honey Buzzard, Egyptian Vulture, Hen Harrier, Hoopoe, Red-backed Shrike, Subalpine and Melodious Warblers, Rock Thrush, Ortolan Bunting.
◆ *Passage* Red and Black Kites, Honey Buzzard.

ACCESS

The Irati forest lies east of Roncesvalles, which is on the C135. A road runs through the woods and hills from south of Burguete to Ochagavía, 30 km to the east. On this road is Arive, from where a smaller road heads north into the Irati forest itself, to Fábrica de Orbaiceta on the slopes of Mendilaz. From Ochagavía a small track winds up to the hamlet of Irati close to the French border.

The small road that runs off right just north of Roncesvalles to the slopes of Orzanzurieta is also good. Off the C135 west of Burguete is Mezquiriz, also a good area for forest birds.

The Gorramendi area is south of the French border post at Dancharinea, on the N121. At Puerto de Otsondo there is a road heading east into the hills. A smaller road crosses the border at Puerto de Izpegui, farther south. There is outstanding scenery here and a good chance of raptors. West of the N121 there are tracks heading into the hills where further tracts of good forest can be explored.

The only hornbeam wood in Iberia is between the villages of Yanci and Aranaz, off the C133; the ultra-humid forests around here are a stronghold of the extraordinary midwife toad, which carries its spawn wrapped around its back legs. Their call is almost indistiguishable from that of the Scops Owl, so take care!

Most of the larger villages provide accommodation.

SIERRAS DE LEYRE, ORBA E ILLÓN

42°48N 01°05W

Descending from the Irati Forest and Roncesvalles are the Irati and Arce valleys, with their spectacular gorges and pine woods. Griffon and Egyptian Vultures nest along their cliffs, along with Alpine Swifts, Blue Rock Thrushes and Choughs. There are a few pairs of Black Woodpeckers in the forests.

South and east of here is the Sierra de Leyre, where the gorges are even more spectacular. Here there are no fewer than 700 pairs of Griffon Vulture, spread among several colonies. At the beautiful and popular Foz de Arbayún a pair of Lammergeiers may often be seen quartering the cliffs from their inaccessible nest site not far away. They are joined by about 150 pairs of Griffon and a host of other raptors including cliff-dwellers like Bonelli's and Golden Eagles and Peregrine. Upstream on the same river, the Salazar, is the Foz de Benasa, with similar birds.

Lumbier is a good base for the area, since it has several hotels, and is itself in the midst of great cliffs which rise to dominate the landscape to the south-east, and is close to the junction of the rivers Irati and Salazar, and their gorges. The Foz de Lumbier and the cliffs (*acantilados*) of la Piedra and San Adrián are, like all the gorges mentioned in this section, protected for their abundant raptor populations, as well as for their otters and other wildlife. Upstream on the Irati is another gorge, the Foz de Ugarrón.

The next valley to the east is that of the Esca, with yet more gorges such as the Foz de Burgui, near the town of that name. Here there are 135 pairs of Griffon, plus Golden Eagle, Peregrine and Chough. On higher ground are Rock Thrushes, less easy to find than the Blue Rock Thrushes of the cliff faces.

TIMING

Resident raptors display from February and start nesting around April, although the Egyptian Vultures do not arrive much before then. The Honey Buzzard is later still, arriving in waves in May. There is year-round interest, with April to July the best period.

SPECIES

◆ *Resident* Golden and Bonelli's Eagles, Goshawk, Griffon Vulture,
   Lammergeier, Peregrine, Eagle Owl, Black Woodpecker, Crag Martin,
   Blue Rock Thrush, Dipper, Crested Tit, Cirl and Rock Buntings, Chough.
◆ *Breeding season* Red and Black Kites, Short-toed Eagle, Honey Buzzard,
   Egyptian Vulture, Hen Harrier, Hoopoe, Alpine Swift, Red-backed Shrike,
   Subalpine and Melodious Warblers, Rock Thrush, Golden Oriole.
◆ *Passage* Red and Black Kites, Honey Buzzard.

ACCESS

The road along the Irati valley between Aoiz and Arive is a rewarding drive, as is the Arce valley road between Aoiz and Burguete.

Foz de Arbayún is north-east of Lumbier, off the road to Navascués. A right turn at Domeño to Usún leads to the river: the best parts are upstream of here.

The C137, which leaves the N240 to run north near Sigués, runs along the Río Esca to Burgui. All along here, and especially around Salvatierra de Esca, is excellent Vulture and raptor country.

The Lumbier area is not far from the river Aragón at Cáseda and Gallipienzo (*see* page 29), and the two areas could easily be combined in a day.

Night Heron

LOWER ARAGÓN VALLEY

42°35N 01°25W

The Aragón river rises on the French border in the region to which it has given its name. Once in Navarra, as it flows from the Yesa reservoir, it carves its way through the Sierra de la Peña. This is a sparsely populated area, with the only evidence of human activity being sheep grazing. Griffon and Egyptian Vultures, Bonelli's and Golden Eagles and Eagle Owls inhabit these cliffs.

There are numerous *sotos*, riverside poplar groves, on both sides of the river near Cáseda and between Carcastillo and Caparroso. Along this stretch there are ten miniscule protected areas, *Enclaves Naturales*, which between them are important for nesting Penduline Tits and Golden Orioles, both species that thrive in poplars, preferring the fluffy seeds for building their nests. Nightingales and Cetti's Warblers are abundant and by far the most obvious inhabitants, however difficult they are to see. Sandbanks along here are likely to have large colonies of Sand Martins and Bee-eaters. An important wetland, the Laguna de Pitillas, is close by. Little Bitterns and Purple Herons breed here, along with a good selection of grebes and ducks.

South-east of here, the Río Arga joins the Aragón. There are further *sotos* on this river, too. One, a 63-ha Natural Reserve, is important for its Night and Purple Herons.

TIMING

The gorges of the Aragón river are good at all times but July to September may be quieter, when the raptors are less dependent on the cliffs for nesting or food. The *sotos* are at their best from April to July. The reedbeds of the Laguna de Pitillas may hold up to 100 Marsh Harriers in winter.

SPECIES
- *Resident* Little Egret, Red-crested Pochard, Golden and Bonelli's Eagles, Goshawk, Sparrowhawk, Griffon Vulture, Marsh Harrier, Peregrine, Water Rail, Eagle and Long-eared Owls, Crag Martin, Blue Rock Thrush, Rock and Cirl Buntings, Chough.
- *Breeding season* Little Bittern, Night and Purple Herons, Red and Black Kites, Short-toed Eagle, Honey Buzzard, Egyptian Vulture, Hen and Montagu's Harriers, Hobby, Scops Owl, Bee-eater, Wryneck, Subalpine and Melodious Warblers, Penduline Tit, Golden Oriole.
- *Autumn and winter* waterfowl, Snipe.

ACCESS
The Sierra de la Peña gorge is reached at Gallipienzo, which is reached by turning south off the N240 at Las Ventas de Judas, about 30 km south-east of Pamplona. In Aibar the Cáseda road leads to a bridge over the river. Before the bridge side roads in the area lead to the poplars.

The *sotos* on the Aragón can be explored from any of numerous farm roads leading from the roads between Carcastillo, Murillo el Fruto, Santacara and Caparroso. The road between Santacara and Pitillas passes close to the Laguna de Pitillas, on the edge of Las Bardenas (below), and on to the N121. The Arga *sotos* are between Funes and Peralta and can be reached from the bridges in those towns.

BARDENAS REALES
42°10N 01°30W

Las Bardenas is one of the most interesting steppe areas of Spain. Most of the area is unprotected, but there are three Natural Reserves, Caídas de la Negra, Vedado de Eguaras and Rincón del Bú, covering about 3000 ha between them.

Black-bellied and Pin-tailed Sandgrouse can often be found flying in small flocks in the evenings, heading for some of the many small lagoons and pools that dot the landscape between October and April.

There are smaller numbers of other steppe species, including Great and Little Bustards and Stone Curlew. The most characteristic small birds are Lesser Short-toed Lark, with around 1000 pairs, and Dupont's Lark.

The cliffs are home to Egyptian Vultures and several colonies of Griffons, as well as Golden Eagles and Eagle Owls. Short-toed Eagles nest in the more wooded parts, such as at Caídas de la Negra.

TIMING
Winter is cold, but usually not as frosty as in other parts of the Ebro valley. By mid-April the warmer weather and summer visitors have arrived.

SPECIES
- *Resident* Peregrine, Great and Little Bustards, Stone Curlew, Pin-tailed and Black-bellied Sandgrouse, Dupont's, Lesser Short-toed, Thekla and Calandra Larks, Black Wheatear, Blue Rock Thrush, Rock Sparrow.
- *Breeding season* White Stork, Egyptian Vulture, Montagu's Harrier, Lesser Kestrel, Bee-eater, Great Spotted Cuckoo, Red-necked Nightjar, Alpine Swift, Tawny Pipit.
- *Winter* Red Kite, Merlin, Woodpigeon.

ACCESS
From the Caparroso–Carcastillo road (*see* page 29), several small roads head
south into Las Bardenas. For example, from Mélida there is a road to the so-
called Castle of Doña Blanca de Navarra, a ruined watchtower, in the heart
of Vedado de Eguaras. This area can also be reached by taking the tracks out
of Valtierra or Arguedas on the N121.

The C125 from Tudela to Ejea de los Caballeros crosses the area, and the
tracks running north from this road between km markers 8 and 9 and
another from kilometre 12 penetrate the Rincón del Bú reserve.

THE WESTERN PYRENEES
42°50N 00°45W

It is convenient to deal with the Pyrenees in three parts, west, central and, in
the next chapter, the Catalan east.

The western portion includes the valleys of the Belagua, Echo, Ansó and
Aragón rivers and adjoining ranges. The habitat ranges from the highest cols
on the French border to alpine meadows and valley pastures. In all the valleys
Lammergeiers can be found, currently enjoying a recovery in their population.
Smaller target species include the much more difficult Wallcreeper and the
two special woodpeckers: White-backed and Black. Red-backed Shrikes are
common at lower altitudes, especially around the farmsteads north of the N240.

The Echo valley has proved good for Wallcreepers, especially around the
area known as Boca del Infierno. The cliffs around this area are also good for
Lammergeiers, which often sail back and forth along the sheer face,
sometimes in the company of the more plentiful Griffon Vulture. The quarry
north of Villanúa on the road to Somport is another traditional Wallcreeper
site. The border area at Somport is good for Rock Thrush, Alpine Chough
and Alpine Accentor, as well as marmot and chamois. Lammergeiers can
often be seen soaring between Spain and France here. White-backed
Woodpeckers are frequently recorded in the Belagua valley at Belagua.

TIMING
The whole Pyrenean range is spectacular in late Spring and Summer (late
May–July), for birds, flowers and butterflies. Alpine birds can be encountered
almost anywhere at lower altitudes in winter.

SPECIES
◆ *Resident* Red Kite, Golden Eagle, Goshawk, Griffon Vulture,
   Lammergeier, Peregrine, Capercaillie, Ptarmigan, Rock Dove, Eagle Owl,
   White-backed and Black Woodpeckers, Crag Martin, Blue Rock Thrush,
   Dartford Warbler, Alpine Accentor, Crested Tit, Cirl and Rock Buntings,
   Citril Finch, Rock Sparrow, Chough, Alpine Chough.
◆ *Breeding season* Black Kite, Short-toed and Booted Eagles, Honey
   Buzzard, Egyptian Vulture, Montagu's Harrier, Alpine Swift, Hoopoe,
   Water Pipit, Red-backed Shrike, Subalpine and Melodious Warblers, Ring
   Ouzel, Rock Thrush, Wallcreeper, Ortolan Bunting.
◆ *Passage* Red and Black Kites, Honey Buzzard.

ACCESS
Coming off the main N240 Pamplona–Jaca road, all the valleys mentioned
have good, if slow, roads running south-north along them to high altitude.

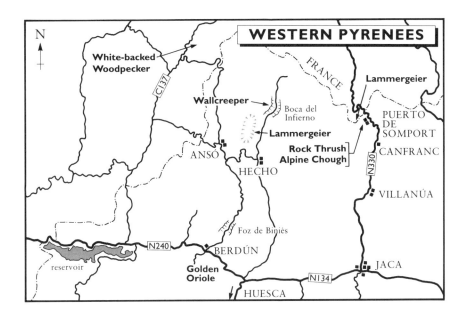

The Villanúa quarry is along this road, 2.1 km past the Hotel Reno on the right hand side heading north. Good general birdwatching spots include the Echo between Boca del Infierno and La Mina, the Biniés gorge, north of Berdún and the Arbayún gorge, east of Lumbier. There is accommodation at Berdún in the Ansó valley, Jaca, and at the ski resort of Candanchú, near Somport.

Sierra de San Juan de la Peña

42°30N 00°45W

This part of the pre-Pyrenean range supports a remarkable diversity of birds of prey including Lammergeier, Egyptian and Griffon Vultures, Short-toed and Bonelli's Eagles and Peregrine. About 300 ha is declared a Natural Monument, but the Important Bird Area, an unofficial designation based on its true worth, covers some 17,000 ha. The area is best known for its monasteries. To the east, near Jaca, lies the smaller Peña Oroel range.

The scrub-covered slopes are a favourite haunt of Black-eared Wheatear, Blue Rock Thrush and Cirl and Rock Buntings. The more wooded slopes are reliable for Black and Middle Spotted Woodpeckers, Crested Tit and Crossbill.

TIMING

May and June are the best months when, along with the birds, orchids such as elderflower and early purple can be enjoyed.

SPECIES

◆ Resident Red Kite, Golden and Bonelli's Eagles, Griffon Vulture, Peregrine, Eagle Owl, Black and Middle Spotted Woodpeckers, Crag Martin, Blue Rock Thrush, Crested Tit, Cirl and Rock Buntings, Crossbill.

◆ *Breeding season* Black Kite, Short-toed Eagle, Honey Buzzard, Lesser Kestrel, Hoopoe, Red-backed Shrike, Melodious Warbler, Ortolan Bunting.

◆ *Winter* Alpine Accentor, Wallcreeper.

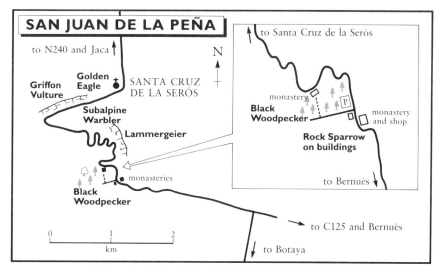

ACCESS

The monastery is signposted off the N240, west of Jaca. The road climbs up through the picturesque village of Santa Cruz de los Serós. Peña Oroel is reached from the small road which runs east off the C125, 3 km south of Jaca.

RIGLOS

42°25N 00°40W

The impressive sandstone cockscomb ridge of Riglos dominates the landscape for miles around.

The Sierra de Santo Domingo, of which this is part, is otherwise less well known. This is a pity because these hills are very good for raptors, with 20 pairs of Red Kites, ten pairs of Egyptian Vultures, five of Golden Eagles and regular sightings of Bonelli's Eagles and Lammergeiers. At Riglos itself, Black Wheatear is a feature, usually quite close to the village and relatively tame. Alpine Swifts chase along the cliff face, and Griffon Vultures and Blue Rock Thrushes breed.

There are several reservoirs in the area which are worth checking for ducks and grebes and, in spring and autumn, migrant waders. Embalse de la Peña has a fringe of reeds where Great Reed Warbler is common. In summer, Hobbies often hawk over the water.

TIMING

Black Wheatears and some of the raptors are present all year. From April to September the hills are alive with small birds and summer raptors.

SPECIES

◆ *Resident* Red Kite, Golden and Bonelli's Eagles, Griffon Vulture, Peregrine, Eagle Owl, Crag Martin, Blue Rock Thrush, Cirl and Rock Buntings.

◆ *Breeding season* Short-toed and Booted Eagles, Honey Buzzard, Egyptian Vulture, Lesser Kestrel, Hobby, Hoopoe, Alpine Swift, Tawny Pipit, Red-backed Shrike, Subalpine and Melodious Warblers, Ortolan Bunting.

◆ *Winter* Alpine Accentor, Wallcreeper.

ACCESS

The main N240 Pamplona–Huesca road crosses the Sierra and passes close to Riglos. The C125 south from Jaca also passes into the Sierra, joining the N240 at Santa Maria. There is a huge crag just south of Pueblo Nuevo de Salinas that is good for vultures, Red Kite and Golden Eagle. Riglos itself is about 11 km farther south, past the Embalse de la Peña. A left turn past Murillo de Gállego, then left again, leads to the village.

SIERRA DE GUARA
42°20N 00°10W

A scenically impressive regional park of over 80,000 ha at the southern edge of the Pyrenees, north-east of the city of Huesca, this is the biggest of the pre-Pyrenean ranges and consists of a limestone massif with numerous deep gorges. The Park includes the *sierras* of Gabardiella, Guara, Arangol, Balces and Sevil, with Tozal de Guara, at 2077 m, its highest peak.

There are five pairs of Lammergeier, ten of Egyptian Vulture and over 200 pairs of Griffon. Red Kites, Honey Buzzards and Peregrines are fairly common and there are at least five pairs each of Short-toed and Golden Eagles.

To the north of the park is another Important Bird Area, the unprotected, and almost uninhabited, Oturia-Canciás range, whose 20,000 ha hold a few more pairs of Lammergeiers and Golden Eagles.

TIMING

Birds of prey are in evidence all year, and winters are generally less susceptible to weather problems than in the Pyrenees proper. Spring, however, comes late and the woods do not liven up until May.

SPECIES

◆ *Resident* Golden Eagle, Griffon Vulture, Peregrine, Eagle Owl, Crag Martin, Blue Rock Thrush, Cirl and Rock Buntings.

◆ *Breeding season* Red Kite, Honey Buzzard, Short-toed and Booted Eagles, Egyptian Vulture, Hobby, Hoopoe, Alpine Swift, Tawny Pipit, Red-backed Shrike, Subalpine and Melodious Warblers, Ortolan Bunting.

ACCESS

There is a network of small roads leading north from the N240 Huesca–Barbastro road. Many of them lead to hermitages which are interesting in their own right as well as good points of access into the wilder parts of Guara. Three are particularly noteworthy: those of San Martín, San Cosme and la Virgen de Araro. The Oturia–Canciás range can be reached off the picturesque Boltaña–Biescas road, the N260. Numerous small roads and forest tracks penetrate the area.

CENTRAL PYRENEES
42°40N 00°00

The central Pyrenees include the area between the Aragón valley in the west and the Esera valley in the east. This covers the Ordesa National Park and four Important Bird Areas, and is especially important for Lammergeier and other raptors. The pine forests are a stronghold of the Pyrenean race of Capercaillie and the high tops are good for Ptarmigan. It is also in the higher parts of this central sector that the Snow Finch is easiest to find.

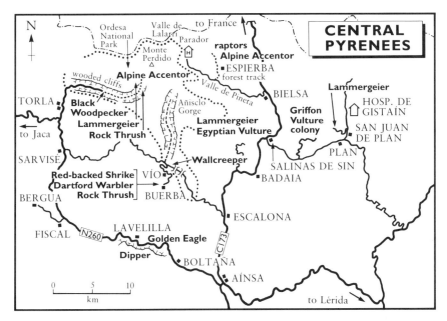

The Ordesa National Park is a series of valleys, the most famous of which is the Ara valley which is bound by two great walls of limestone which tower above their cloaking forests: beech on the lower parts, then pine, giving way to bare rock. Here chamois and ibex are at their most abundant. The 3353 m-high Monte Perdido towers over more huge cliffs, vast glacial cirques and alpine meadows. The Park information centre will suggest a range of possible hikes, from gentle strolls to major expeditions. It is possible to walk into France, and to stop at one of a range of refuges on the way. This route to Gavarnie may be the best way of seeing Snow Finch but it is very much for the mountain enthusiast, and only if fully equipped with the right maps, food, clothes and information. Otherwise, the shorter hikes within the park may well produce Golden and Bonelli's Eagles, Black Woodpecker, Rock Thrush, Crested Tit and Citril Finch. The Añisclo gorge is a good site for Wallcreeper.

Perhaps the most important Lammergeier population is to be found in the Gistaín-Cotiella valleys east of Bielsa. Lammergeiers can often be seen at the rubbish tip outside San Juan Juan de Plan, on the road to Gistaín. The forests here are also important for Capercaillie and Black Woodpecker.

TIMING AND BIRDS
As for the western Pyrenees plus Snow Finch.
ACCESS
The Ordesa National Park is most usually reached via Torla, where there are several hotels. Access to its Añisclo, Escuaín, and Pineta valleys are via side roads off the C173. The Añisclo gorge is reached along a well-marked road leading from Escalona to Ereta de Bies and the Ermita de San Urbez, at one end of the gorge. The *Parador* de Monte Perdido is in the Pineta Valley and is a good base for walking the area. The Gistaín valley is reached via a road which branches east off the C173 south of Bielsa, towards Plan.

POSETS–LA MADALETA–ENTECADA

42°40N 00°30E

This high mountain area borders Catalunya and is one of the remoter parts of the Pyrenees. It includes a large proportion of land over 3000 m and several high peaks, of which Aneto, at 3404 m, is the highest in the Pyrenees. There are woods and forests of Scots pine, beech and silver fir. The remarkable forests of Vallibierna and Artiga de Lin are a stronghold of brown bear.

The Benasque valley is the best-known and most accessible part of the area, and as it climbs ever higher, a typical selection of mountain specialities can be found, such as Golden Eagles, of which about five pairs nest in the valley. Lammergeiers quarter the hillsides and Black Woodpeckers are common in the pine forests. Above the treeline are Ptarmigan.

The eastern border of this region is formed by the N230 Lleida–France road. South of the Viella tunnel the road is bordered to the west by the peak of Vallibierna and its forest, with Capercaillie and Black Woodpecker. East of the road is a restricted area called Baish Arán, a refuge for brown bear.

TIMING

June and August are notoriously stormy months, so birdwatching is best in May and early July.

SPECIES

◆ Resident Golden Eagle, Griffon Vulture, Lammergeier, Peregrine, Capercaillie, Ptarmigan, Partridge, Rock Dove, Eagle and Tengmalm's Owls, White-backed and Black Woodpeckers, Crag Martin, Blue Rock Thrush, Alpine Accentor, Crested Tit, Wallcreeper, Rock Bunting, Citril and Snow Finches, Rock Sparrow, Chough, Alpine Chough.

◆ *Breeding season* Black Kite, Short-toed Eagle, Honey Buzzard, Hoopoe, Water Pipit, Red-backed Shrike, Ring Ouzel, Rock Thrush, Ortolan Bunting.

◆ *Passage* Red and Black Kites, Honey Buzzard.

ACCESS

The Benasque valley is reached from the C260 road by taking the C139 valley road. There are numerous forest tracks leading up the mountains from any of the villages along this road. The road from just north of Benasque through Cerler leads to Llano del Ampriu, from where a short walk to the peak of El Gallinero should reveal all the alpine species. There are hikes up to the French border for which information and maps can be obtained in Benasque.

Ptarmigan

WETLANDS AND SIERRAS AROUND HUESCA

42°05N 00°39W

Due west of Huesca is the Embalse de la Sotonera, near Tormos. The chief importance of this reservoir IBA lies in its strategic position on the migration route of Cranes. In spring it is among the last stop-over points before the birds have to negotiate the Pyrenees on their way north. They will have spent the winter feeding in the *dehesas* of Extremadura and in February they leave for the lagoons of the north-east. Gallocanta (page 40) is the best-known site on this flight path, but thousands pass through the Sotonera Reservoir, with maximum counts reaching 7200 in the first half of March. The Embalse de Sotonera is off the N240 near Huesca. A southward turn 13 km north of Huesca at Esquedas leads to Montmesa. The Cranes tend to congregate in the marshy areas west of the village. The cereal-growing area south of the reservoir, to the north of the village of Gurrea de Gállego, is worth exploring for Great and Little Bustards and sandgrouse.

The northward spread of Black-shouldered Kites has now reached this area, and there are reports of two pairs in a small area almost immediately west of the reservoir. The triangle of roads between Valpamas, on the N125, Piedratajada and Puendeluna, on the west bank of therío Gállego, encircle the area.

LOS MONEGROS

41°25N 00°15W

Los Monegros are large expanses of plains, in some areas almost devoid of vegetation, with several deep gullies and cereal fields. Dotted about are seasonal lagoons or *saladas*, which in winter attract wildfowl but which by summer are nothing more than pans of salt.

Los Monegros extends over more than 70,000 ha stretching east of Zaragoza, almost as far as the city of Lleida (page 47). The whole area is important for steppe birds. The Great Bustard was once a denizen of much of the Aragonese steppe, but is now restricted in this region to Los Monegros, and its population has reached critical levels: about 30 birds. Part of the reason for this is the massive transformation of some parts of Los Monegros under irrigation schemes of the 1940s, some of which were so badly planned that they led to wholesale desertion of the land by hundreds of farming families. There are new irrigation schemes on the drawing board which pose considerable threat to the remaining area. However, there is also a new plan to create a National Park, which may help.

Other species typical of this habitat type are well represented. Pin-tailed and Black-bellied Sandgrouse, Dupont's Lark and Lesser Short-toed Lark are all common. Montagu's Harriers quarter the wheat fields in summer and some of the villages still have small colonies of the endangered Lesser Kestrel. There are numerous seasonal lagoons between the Ebro and the NII which hold wildfowl in winter and are good for passage Dotterel in April.

TIMING

The area is most rewarding from October to early June. Outside this period the birds are there, but heat haze and crop height is an obstacle. By contrast, January can be bitterly cold.

SPECIES
- *Resident* Peregrine, Great and Little Bustards, Stone Curlew, Pin-tailed and Black-bellied Sandgrouse, Dupont's, Lesser Short-toed, Thekla and Calandra Larks, Black Wheatear, Blue Rock Thrush, Rock Sparrow.
- *Breeding season* White Stork, Egyptian Vulture, Montagu's Harrier, Lesser Kestrel, Bee-eater, Great Spotted Cuckoo, Red-necked Nightjar, Tawny Pipit, Spectacled Warbler.
- *Winter* Red-crested Pochard, Golden Eagle, Merlin.
- *Passage* Dotterel.

ACCESS
Much of the area is almost uninhabited, but is crossed by good roads. The area between Candasnos, 51 km west of Lleida on the NII, and Ontiñena, 20 km to the north is good for birds. Some 9 km along this road there is a right turn to Ballobar; 4.2 km further along a track, which is mostly sound, leads into the best area. Another track crosses this one after 3.6 km. A right turn here leads to an area of salt steppe, which often holds water. The seasonal ponds in this area are a good place to wait for sandgrouse in the early mornings.

Bujaraloz lies some 19 km west of Candasnos. Between here and Sástago to the south, and Castejón to the north, is the core of the Los Monegros area. The road heading south from Bujaraloz (the C230) branches right towards Alborge, on the Ebro, after a kilometre. The numerous tracks off left and right from this road are usually fruitful, especially in the area marked by a ruined jailhouse, overlooking a large salty lagoon. North of Bujaraloz the C230 crosses some spectacular landscape and the road off left to Monegrillo also has useful tracks leading from it.

THE EBRO AT ZARAGOZA
41°30N 00°45W

Zaragoza is one of the largest cities in Spain and as such is a regional centre of some importance, boasting a well-connected international airport. Several Important Bird Areas exist nearby, including Los Monegros and Belchite (below). The Ebro runs through the city, before creating a 25-km-long IBA beginning 12 km downstream at Pastriz.

Between here and Pina de Ebro are a series of *galachos*, an Aragonese word meaning oxbow lakes, which are important for their breeding herons. Of particular note are the two or three pairs of Bitterns, a species nearing extinction in Spain. There are also around five pairs of Little Bittern, 40 pairs of Night Heron and several pairs of Little Egret and Purple Heron. In all, 200 species have been recorded on the 140-ha reserve of Galacho de La Alfranca, which forms a small part of the IBA.

Now unconnected with the river, the *galachos* are fed entirely from underground supplies, which are in demand for irrigation in the surrounding farms.

Much of the area has been planted with poplar in recent years, attracting Penduline Tits and Golden Orioles. The strategic location of these *sotos* along one of the great watercourses of the Iberian peninsula gives them a particular importance for migrating and wintering passerines. During spring and autumn almost any warbler can turn up, along with flycatchers and often extraordinary gatherings of species such as Nightingale, Woodchat Shrike and Wryneck.

TIMING

March to May and again in September and October can be outstanding for falls of small migrants, roosting swallows and other birds that the *sotos* attract.

SPECIES

◆ *Resident* Little Grebe, Great Crested Grebe, Bittern, Little Egret, Water Rail, Marsh Harrier.

◆ *Breeding season* Little Bittern, Night and Purple Herons, Black Kite, Scops Owl, Bee-eater, Wryneck, Penduline Tit, Golden Oriole, migrants.

ACCESS

There is a small nature reserve near Pastriz, reached via a local road off the NII or through the suburb of Santa Isabel. From here, a local road leads to the Galacho de Alfranca reserve. There is a further 25 km of good bird-watching downstream although access is difficult. There are local roads from Pina del Ebro and, on the right bank, El Burgo de Ebro which are worth trying.

BELCHITE AND THE ZARAGOZA STEPPES

41°20N 00°45W

The steppes south of Zaragoza constitute one of the best-preserved areas of its kind in the Ebro valley, although recently substantial tracts have been ploughed with grant aid from the European Community. Nevertheless, it is one of the most important areas in Spain for Black-bellied Sandgrouse, with a staggering 800–1000 pairs. There are almost as many Pin-tailed. Great Bustards are now reduced to a dozen or so wanderers, but there are small numbers of Little Bustards in the Alfamén plains, west of Muel.

With 800 pairs of Dupont's Lark and up to 2000 pairs of Lesser Short-toed, the 40,000-ha expanse of steppe north-east of Belchite is the most important area in the north of Spain for these species. Immediately to the west is an area of low hills and plains along the lower Huerva valley. This is an important area for birds of prey, including Golden and Short-toed Eagle. In winter, Golden Eagles wander over to Belchite.

The Belchite steppes were the focus in 1992 of a Steppes Campaign carried out by SEO, the RSPB and Vogelbescherming, the Dutch BirdLife partner. As a result, the EU provided funds to create a nature reserve at El Planerón.

TIMING

Up to 200 Dotterels pass through the area in mid-April. In June and July beware possible confusion between Dupont's Lark and juvenile Tawny Pipit.

SPECIES

◆ *Resident* Golden Eagle, Great and Little Bustards, Stone Curlew, Pin-tailed and Black-bellied Sandgrouse, Eagle Owl, Dupont's, Lesser Short-toed, Thekla and Calandra Larks, Black Wheatear, Blue Rock Thrush.

◆ *Breeding season* White Stork, Black Kite, Short-toed Eagle, Egyptian Vulture, Montagu's Harrier, Lesser Kestrel, Bee-eater, Red-necked Nightjar, Tawny Pipit.

◆ *Winter* Peregrine, Merlin.

◆ *Passage* Dotterel.

ACCESS

The SEO reserve at El Planerón lies on the road between Belchite and Quinto, 6.2 km beyond Codo and is clearly marked. The track leads to a small

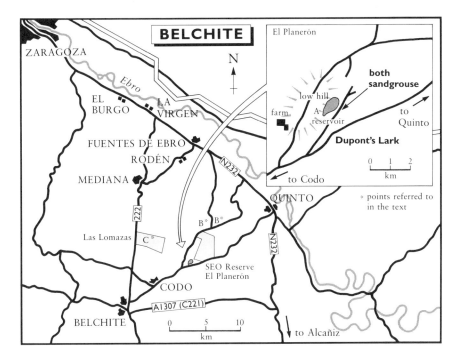

reservoir (map point A) where sandgrouse come to drink in mid-morning. A few hundred metres before this signposted track is a parallel track which overlooks the reservoir from a higher vantage point and runs on into further good areas of steppe (point B). There is an information centre on the outskirts of Belchite village. The nearby Las Lomazas reserve (point C) requires a permit which is obtained by writing to the Dept. Agricultura, Vasquez de Mella 10, 50071 Zaragoza, allowing a good month.

ALCAÑIZ
41°03N 00°16W

This historic town makes a good base in order to explore several areas without uprooting for a few days: Belchite, Los Monegros and the Ríos Martín and Guadalope (below) are within reasonable driving distance.

Close to Alcañiz on the N232 are some important seasonal lagoons surrounded by salty steppe habitat where Little Bustards, Dupont's and Lesser Short-toed Larks are found, and where Cranes pass through in November and February. Coming from the town, a track leads off left to the main *salada* a little beyond the turn to Teruel. Farther along the N232 is a reservoir which is worth a scan for the occasional uncommon duck or diver.

Caspe is 25 km north of Alcañiz. West of here, along the C221 is a series of small lagoons where Purple Herons and Little Bitterns breed and which have a good selection of waders and wildfowl on migration and in winter respectively. The first of these is reached by taking the left turn at Chiprana to the station. The second is at km post 113 where there is another left turn.

Ríos Guadalope and Martín

40°45N 00°40W

In the north and east of the sparsely populated Teruel province, the rivers Martín and Guadalope run through the rugged foothills of the *Sistema Iberico*, limestone country with cliffs and gorges, pinewoods and oak scrub.

The cliffs along the course of the surprisingly modest Río Martín, near Híjar, house a colony of over 170 pairs of Griffon Vultures, as well as Egyptian Vultures, Golden and Bonelli's Eagles and Eagle Owls. There are a further 100 pairs of Griffons downstream in the nearby Sierra de Arcos.

The road between Híjar, which is 29 km north-west of Alcañiz on the N232, and Ariño, 25 km to the south via Albalate del Arzobispo, runs parallel to the river through the Sierra de Arcos. Several of the imposing massifs which tower over the road hold colonies of vultures, and the updraughts attract these and the occasional Bonelli's Eagle.

The Río Guadalope, a few kilometres to the south, is scenically more spectacular, with similar species, including a large colony of Choughs. Small bird interest includes Blue Rock Thrush, Black Wheatear and Dipper.

From Alcañiz the N420 leads to Calanda where a local road runs to Mas de las Matas, 16 km to the south, and thence, along the Guadalope valley to Castellote. Just before this village there is a vulture colony by the road, where it crosses a small river. From Castellote the Las Cuevas road skirts a reservoir. The cliffs, gorges and rock stacks in and alongside the reservoir are spectacular, and can be good for large raptors. A left turn after 9 km leads to the abandoned village of Santolea, beyond which are some high cliffs where Bonelli's Eagles, Griffon and Egyptian Vultures nest.

Gallocanta

40°46N 01°30W

Half-way between Madrid and Zaragoza lies the site of the greatest concentration of Common Cranes in western Europe. The Laguna de Gallocanta is the largest natural lagoon in the Iberian peninsula, although its water levels vary with the season and according to the considerable annual fluctuations in rainfall. The Cranes' route takes them over the Pyrenees, over the steppes of Zaragoza and on to Gallocanta. It is essentially a migration resting and feeding area, but an increasing number of birds stay the winter. The best way to appreciate them is to wait until evening, when huge numbers fly in from their feeding grounds. The spring migration is more concentrated in both space and time than the autumn, so that the spectacle is greatest then: recent counts have been of up to 50,000 birds, and 20,000 is typical.

This amazing sight is not, however, the only source of the lagoon's natural wealth and importance. Up to three-quarters of the West Palaearctic population of Red-crested Pochard winter here at times: 8000 is a normal January count, but 35,000 have been recorded here. Other mid-winter statistics confirm that this is a wetland of great importance: 3,000 Gadwalls, 20–80,000 Pochards and 12–40,000 Coots, for example. In the breeding season the lagoon is not without interest, with Black-winged Stilts, Whiskered and Gull-billed Terns breeding.

The drier parts of the depression have Pin-tailed and Black-bellied Sandgrouse and Stone Curlew all year round. South-east of Gallocanta is an

area of high *páramo*, which also has these species as well as Little Bustards and a very high concentration of Dupont's Larks.

TIMING
The autumn passage of Crane usually takes place between the end of October and early December, with a peak in mid-November. The spring return is at its peak in late February. Winters are bitterly cold.

SPECIES
- *Resident* Marsh Harrier, Little Bustard, Stone Curlew, Pin-tailed and Black-bellied Sandgrouse, Dupont's, Lesser Short-toed, and Thekla Larks.
- *Spring* White Stork, Black Kite, Short-toed Eagle, Montagu's Harrier, Lesser Kestrel, Black-winged Stilt, Pratincole, migrant waders, Gull-billed and Whiskered Terns, Bee-eater, Red-necked Nightjar, Tawny Pipit.
- *Passage* Common Crane, migrant waders.
- *Winter* wildfowl, Red Kite, Hen Harrier, Peregrine, Merlin, Calandra Lark.

ACCESS
The Laguna de Gallocanta is about 100 km south-west of Zaragoza beyond Daroca, which is on the N330. From Daroca take the C211 towards Molina

41

de Aragón. After 19 km there is a turn along the C4241 to the lake. Good views can be obtained from Gallocanta village. From here there are tracks leading to some hides. There is a minor road, linking Gallocanta with the villages of Berrueco, Tornos, Bello and Las Cuerlas, encircling the lagoon. The southern and eastern sides are usually most rewarding for watching the Cranes. This area is becoming increasingly popular at weekends, and there is some risk of disturbance to the Cranes, so a mid-week visit is preferable. There is accommodation in Daroca.

To the south-east, the Paramera de Blancas is between the villages of Blancas and Torralba de los Sisones (literally Torralba of the Little Bustards!). This village is 5 km south east of Bello (*see* above); 7 km farther is Villalba de los Morales from where a rural road crosses the *páramo* to Blancas.

MONTES UNIVERSALES AND LLANOS DE POZONDÓN
40°25N 01°40W

The Sierra de Albarracín, part of the area known as Montes Universales, lies to the west of Teruel capital. The mountains have extensive oak forests with a corresponding range of typical birds, such as Bonelli's Warbler and Pied Flycatcher. The area is important for birds of prey, including ten pairs of Golden Eagle and 20 pairs of Bonelli's.

A short distance to the north-east of the Montes Universales is a small area of high *páramo*, the Llanos de Pozondón, which lies at around 1400 m above sea level and is covered with *Erinacea* scrub and sheep. There are 100 or so pairs of Dupont's Lark and small numbers of Black-bellied Sandgrouse nesting.

TIMING
Snow is frequent between November and April; spring and autumn may be wet.

SPECIES
◆ *Resident* Goshawk, Buzzard, Bonelli's and Golden Eagles, Griffon Vulture, Peregrine, Eagle and Tawny Owls, Great Grey Shrike, Blue Rock Thrush, Black Redstart, Crested Tit, Rock Bunting, Rock Sparrow, Raven.
◆ *Breeding season* Black Kite, Short-toed and Booted Eagles, Honey Buzzard, Egyptian Vulture, Hoopoe, Red-rumped Swallow, Woodchat Shrike, Bonelli's Warbler, Rock Thrush, Black-eared Wheatear.

ACCESS
Albarracín is a small Moorish fortified town in the mountains, 32 km west of the provincial capital town of Teruel. The road from Albarracín on to Orihuela is highly rewarding for birds, and time should be allowed for frequent stops at likely-looking places.

The Montes Universales National Reserve is adjacent to the Serranía de Cuenca to the east, but the two are connected only by small local roads, which can be confusing. A road runs south to Guadalaviar, 26 km away. From here the road continues west for 16 km to Herreria de los Chorros, which is 5 km south of Tragacete in the Serranía de Cuenca.

Pozondón is 19 km east of Orihuela on the Santa Eulalia road. The *llanos* are between Pozondón and Almohaja. A 5-km track runs north between the two villages and can be comfortably walked.

EASTERN SPAIN

EASTERN SPAIN

N

FRANCE
ANDORRA

AIGUAMOLLS
DE L'EMPORDÀ

AIGÜES TORTES AND
THE CATALAN PYRENEES

THE CATALAN
PRE-PYRENEES

SERRA DE MONTSEC

CAP DE
CREUS

CATALUNYA

ARAGÓN

LLEIDA
LLEIDA STEPPES

BARCELONA
LLOBREGAT DELTA

SERRAS DE TARRAGONA

TARRAGONA

ELS PORTS DE BESEIT

EBRO DELTA

PRAT DE CABANES–TORREBLANCA

CASTELLÓ DE LA PLANA

CASTILLA-LA MANCHA

VALÈNCIA

CASTELLÓ AREA

VALÈNCIA

ALBUFERA DE VALÈNCIA

Mediterranean Sea

BENIDORM AREA

EMBALSE DEL HONDO

ALICANTE
SALINAS DE SANTA POLA

MURCIA

MURCIA

SALINAS DE TORREVIEJA

SIERRAS AND VALLE
DEL GUADALENTIN

MAR MENOR
AND
CARTAGENA

0   50   100
km

From the snowy alpine landscapes of the Catalan Pyrenees to the hot and arid coastal hills of Murcia, the three eastern regions of Spain cover an immense variety of birdwatching possibilities. For the most part, however, their fame lies in their long association with cheap package travel. As a general rule the anarchic coastal development of the 1960s and 1970s has not left its mark inland, and there remains considerable rural charm and natural interest that millions of holidaymakers systematically ignore.

Away from the Pyrenees and the narrow coastal plain the eastern regions are hilly without being mountainous. Bonelli's Eagle enjoys a European stronghold here, although it has declined in recent years.

There are dozens of wetlands along the east coast and the Ebro Delta and the Albufera de València are the second and third in importance in the Iberian peninsula. Other notable wetlands include Aiguamolls on the French border and the saltpans of southern València. Regional specialities include

Moustached Warbler, which is relatively common in many of the wetlands, and Audouin's Gull, which is frequent on the coast.

Flights, either charter or scheduled, are available into Girona, Barcelona, València and Alicante. The Catalan Pyrenees are easily reached by road from France. The Catalan language is predominant in Catalunya as is a closely related dialect in northern València. Most towns of any size have two versions of their name, and in general, I have used local names.

BIRDWATCHING SITES

AIGÜES TORTES AND THE CATALAN PYRENEES

42°40N 01°30E

Rising to 2951 m, the Pyrenees in this easternmost sector contain some of the best-preserved areas in the entire range. The Aigües Tortes National Park was created as long ago as 1955 in order to maintain some of the best Pyrenean wildlife habitat in Spain. Despite this, in 1991 the boundaries were reduced slightly to make way for a ski run, provoking an outcry in Catalunya and beyond. There are at least three pairs of Lammergeier and an extraordinary range and density of other raptors, including ten pairs of Short-toed Eagle and 18 pairs of Golden Eagle.

The National Park includes the high-altitude lake known as the Estany de Sant Maurici. Although this is in itself of limited interest for birds, it is scenically very striking. It is a good place to see and photograph Citril Finch, which have learnt to feed on the crumbs left behind by the large numbers of visitors who arrive on summer weekends. The woods on the way up to the *estany* are some of the best in Spain for Black Woodpecker and, nearer the tree-line, Tengmalm's Owl. Several species rare in Spain can be found here, such as Marsh Tit, Yellowhammer and Bullfinch. Red-backed Shrikes breed in the scrubby areas close to the main road in the western part of the park.

Tengmalm's Owl is one of the specialities of the area north of the Viella tunnel (*see* also page 35), although it is strictly nocturnal and calls mainly during the late winter months, when access is difficult.

Immediately to the east of Aigües Tortes, and stretching to the border with Andorra, is the Monteixo–L'Orri–Tornafort range with similar species.

TIMING

As for other Pyrenean areas. Some of the trails are well known and wardened, making this is an area where winter hiking is less risky than elsewhere in the Pyrenees.

Snow Finch

SPECIES
◆ *Resident* Goshawk, Golden Eagle, Griffon Vulture, Lammergeier, Peregrine, Capercaillie, Grey Partridge, Ptarmigan, Tengmalm's and Eagle Owls, Black Woodpecker, Crag Martin, Blue Rock Thrush, Black Redstart, Wallcreeper, Dipper, Alpine Accentor, Crested Tit, Rock Bunting, Snow and Citril Finches, Crossbill, Rock Sparrow, Chough, Alpine Chough.
◆ *Breeding season* Black Kite, Short-toed Eagle, Honey Buzzard, Hoopoe, Red-backed Shrike, Bonelli's Warbler, Ring Ouzel, Rock Thrush.

ACCESS
There are two routes into the Aigües Tortes National Park. From the Aran valley to the west *(see* page 35), a road leaves the N230 3 km north of El Pont de Suert to Boí, where there is an information centre and signs into the park. From the east, the Estany de Sant Maurici is reached via Espot, which is off the C147. There is an information centre at Espot and it is an 8-km walk or (in summer) drive from here to the lake through excellent woods. Accommodation is available in Espot and Boí, and there are refuges in the park. Map booklets produced by *Editorial Alpina* are available in both villages, and walkers are advised to buy the two that cover Sant Maurici and Montardo.

The mountains north of Aigües Tortes, on the border with France, are traversed by the C142 which runs east off the N230 from Viella to numerous villages where simple hikes can be made into the valleys. At Salardú there is a forest road which leads to a hiking trail along the Río Guarda de Rudo and on, after a good hour, to some of the mountain lakes. Farther along this road is the mountain pass at Bonaigua, which is worth a stop to scan for eagles and Alpine Chough. The forest on the other side of the pass is one of the largest and best preserved in the area. Alternatively, 10 km north of Viella is a track to the hermitage of Artiga de Lin where some more outstanding forest can be explored. The Monteixo–L'Orri–Tornafort range is reached by taking the road that leads off the C147 at Llavorsi to Alins and on to Areu. There is plenty of choice in accommodation along the C142 and C147 roads.

THE CATALAN PRE-PYRENEES
42°20N 01°40E
In the hills which lie south of the Catalan Pyrenees are limestone rocks and cliffs and deep gorges where Catalunya's largest Griffon Vulture colonies breed and where Lammergeiers and Peregrines can be seen playing the updraughts.

At the heart of the area is the Natural Park comprising the Cadí-Moixeró range, which is as high in places as the Pyrenees proper. This is some 41,000 ha of rocky hills with large tracts of pine forest. It is important not only for birds, but as a refuge for a high population of chamois, pine martens and other mammals. Reptiles and amphibians are also well represented with western whip snake, green lizard (which is absent from most of the Iberian Peninsula) and the endemic Pyrenean brook salamander. Its considerable bird interest includes most of the Pyrenean raptors, including a pair or two of Lammergeiers, Tengmalm's Owl, Black Woodpecker and Red-backed Shrike.

To the west are several lower ranges such as the Serra de Sant Gervás and the Serra de Boumort. These areas are good for the three vultures and cliff-dwellers such as Eagle Owl and Chough.

TIMING
As for the Pyrenean sites, but access is easier in winter. Winter may see the arrival of high mountain birds such as Wallcreeper, Alpine Accentor and Snow Finch.

SPECIES
◆ *Resident* Goshawk, Golden and Bonelli's Eagles, Griffon Vulture, Lammergeier, Peregrine, Capercaillie, Grey Partridge, Ptarmigan, Tengmalm's and Eagle Owls, Rock Dove, Black Woodpecker, Water Pipit, Crag Martin, Blue Rock Thrush, Black Redstart, Dipper, Crested Tit, Rock Bunting, Citril Finch, Crossbill, Rock Sparrow, Chough, Raven.
◆ *Breeding season* Black Kite, Short-toed Eagle, Honey Buzzard, Alpine Swift, Hoopoe, Red-backed Shrike, Subalpine, Bonelli's and Melodious Warblers, Rock Thrush.
◆ *Winter* Wallcreeper, Alpine Accentor, Snow Finch.

ACCESS
The C1411 passes through the Cadí range, unfortunately through a tunnel. South of the range, at Bagà, there is an information centre. The southern end of the Natural Park can be explored by taking the minor road from Bagà village to Coll de Pall, 20 km to the east. From the *coll* a walk across to the west for a kilometre or so should reveal most of the typical high meadow species.

The northern slopes are approached from Bellver de Cerdanya, which is north of the tunnel on the southern edge of the Cerdanya game reserve. Some 8 km to the west, at Martinet, a road heads south towards Montellà, forking after a couple of kilometres. The right turn towards Villec is largely unpaved, leading beyond Villec to Estana. From here there are trails which lead through box scrub, woods and up to the higher passes and meadows. Both Bagà and Bellver have plenty of accommodation. The scenic road that links Berga, on the C1411, with the C1313 to the west, runs along the southern edge of the IBA.

The Serra de Boumort is reached via minor roads from La Pobla de Segur, which is well to the west on the C147, 73 km north of Balaguer. From La Pobla a road crosses the area running east through El Pont de Claverol and Hortoneda de la Conca to the C1313 at Organya.

The Serra de Sant Gervàs is west of the C144. From Senterada, 10 km north of La Pobla, there is a minor road which penetrates the *serra* to the Hermitage (*ermita*) of Sant Gervàs.

Serra de Montsec

42°05N 00°55E

The Serra de Montsec lies immediately south of the Serra de Sant Gervàs. It has a particularly good population of Egyptian Vultures and a few pairs of Bonelli's Eagles, along with Golden and Short-toed. Several interesting bodies of water harbour a good selection of waterbirds. The Sant Lorenç reservoir, has breeding Purple Herons and Little Bitterns, along with typical reedbed warblers such as Great Reed and Savi's. The cliffs near this reservoir are where the Bonelli's Eagles breed, and sometimes have Wallcreepers in winter.

The area is north of Balaguer, which is on the C1313, 26 km north of Lleida (see below). From Balaguer there is a local road, the C147, which leads to Camarassa. After 13 km, just before Camarassa, a left turn leads to Sant Lorenç and the reservoir. The road between Balaguer and La Pobla de Segur via Ager and Tremp can be highly productive. At Ager a forest road leads north into the serra where a good selection of raptors can be seen against a spectacular scenic backdrop. A long circular route of about 125 km involves turning onto the C1412 at Tremp to Coll de Comiols and Artesa de Segre, thence back to Balaguer. This takes in the Terradets (or Cellers) reservoir, where a good selection of waterbirds breeds and winters, as well as a spectacular gorge. Balaguer offers a range of accommodation in one of Catalunya's more interesting medieval towns.

Lleida Steppes

41°30N 00°40E

The Catalan city of Lleida (Lérida) is on the eastern edge of the great steppe area of Aragón known as Los Monegros (page 36). There are remnant steppes to the west and to the south of the city, with Catalunya's most important grassland bird populations. These include around 60 Little Bustards, 200 Pin-tailed Sandgrouse and small numbers of Black-bellied in the plains to the south. Here there is an interesting mix of habitats, with undulating grass and cereal plains alternating with scrubby areas and salt steppes.

This is the western edge of the Lesser Grey Shrike's European range, and there are about ten pairs in the scrub and orchards to the south. The Dupont's Lark finds its only Catalan breeding ground here, in the thyme scrub – timoneda – of a small reserve created recently near Alfés. Nearby, there is a Protected Landscape Area, at Utxesa, consisting of a reservoir with good emergent vegetation owing to its relatively constant water levels. It was created specifically to protect species rare in west Catalunya: Purple Heron and Little Bittern, typical reedbed warblers such as Great Reed and Savi's, and wintering and migrating waterfowl.

TIMING

From July to November the cereal fields are relatively uninteresting and it is necessary to seek out the fallows or the barren salt steppes.

SPECIES

◆ *Resident* Peregrine, Little Bustard, Stone Curlew, Pin-tailed and Black-bellied Sandgrouse, Dupont's, Lesser Short-toed, Thekla and Calandra Larks, Penduline Tit, Black Wheatear, Blue Rock Thrush, Rock Sparrow.

Lesser Grey Shrike

◆ *Breeding season* Purple Heron, Little Bittern, White Stork, Egyptian Vulture, Montagu's Harrier, Lesser Kestrel, Quail, Bee-eater, Roller, Great Spotted Cuckoo, Red-necked Nightjar, Tawny Pipit, Black-eared Wheatear, Great Reed, Subalpine and Savi's Warblers, Lesser Grey Shrike, Golden Oriole.

◆ *Winter* waterfowl, Merlin, Wallcreeper (on Lleida Old Cathedral!).

ACCESS

The A2 highway runs south of Lleida and forms the northern border of the Cogull-Alfés IBA. From junction 6 take the Lleida spur as far as the N230. Follow this south for 2 km to Albatàrrec from where a road goes to Alfés. Minor roads and tracks between here, El Cogul, Aspa and Granyena de las Garrigues afford good access to the range of habitats. The section of road between Aspa and Artesa de Lleida to the north is also worth exploring. The Utxesa reservoir is west of here, reached via Sarroca de Lleida or Torres de Segre west of the N230.

The recently destroyed steppe IBA west of Lleida is no longer worth visiting. To the north the C148 between Alfarràs and Balaguer and between Balaguer and Bellcaire d'Urgell may yield Little Bustard in spring.

AIGUAMOLLS DE L'EMPORDÁ

42°20N 03°10E

Since 1983 Aiguamolls de l'Empordá, tucked into the extreme north-east corner of Spain, has been a Natural Park, designated by the Catalan Parliament not a moment too soon. For 2000 years the area had been known to the many civilizations which inhabited it as a business centre surrounded by swamp. Indeed the name Empordá derives from the ancient Greek for trading station. Once an extensive area of fresh and salt marsh, the wetland had dwindled to its present less than 1000 ha under the advance of sunflower, maize and barley cultivation.

The Natural Park comprises three reserve areas, broadly divided into salt-marsh, fresh water and river woodland. In the last few years there have been some welcome signs of management success. Bitterns have returned to breed, Marsh Harriers have increased from one to ten pairs and Purple Gallinules have been reintroduced. The area is also important as one of only two places in Spain where the Lesser Grey Shrike breeds, with up to 17 pairs at Aiguamolls and others beyond the park. A total of 324 species is recorded.

The fresh-water reserve (Parc Natural 1) is best explored from Castelló d'Empúries, 4 km north of El Cortalet. Beyond this village a bridge crosses La Mugeta lagoon where Little Bitterns breed and Penduline Tits can be found. The Castelló to Palau-Saverdera road crosses an area known as Tres Ponts, which is the best area for Bitterns, and has Rollers and Lesser Grey Shrikes as well. Beyond the last of the three bridges is a sign on a power pylon pointing to the Vilahut lagoon. In winter this lagoon holds a good variety of wintering waterfowl, whereas in the breeding season Purple Herons and Little Bitterns are in evidence. This is the stronghold for Purple Gallinules, and in early May is usually visited by the occasional Red-footed Falcon.

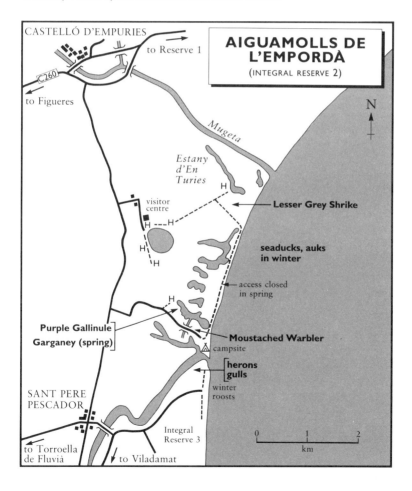

The salt-marsh reserve (Parc Natural 2) can be appreciated by taking a trail from the information centre at El Cortalet. A fresh-water lagoon has been created here, with two hides overlooking it. A raised hide, often a good place to watch Rollers, is another 250 m further on. The salt-marsh can be viewed from a lookout point a short distance on. In winter, there may be up to 20,000 ducks as well as Flamingos and Hen Harriers in this area. A bridge across the Corredor Canal is a good spot for watching Moustached Warblers and Penduline Tits. Abandoned rice paddies farther along the trail are good for herons, waders (especially in late spring and autumn) and, with luck, Bittern. Also in Parc 2 is a new trail at the Estany d'En Turies. There are three hides on the trail which are good for the elusive reed-dwelling species such as Little Bittern and Purple Gallinule.

TIMING
Outstanding all year, but May, with both passage birds and active breeders around, is perhaps the most rewarding month.
SPECIES
♦ *Resident* Yelkouan Shearwater, Little and Cattle Egrets, Bittern, Marsh Harrier, Purple Gallinule, Stone Curlew, Hoopoe, Cetti's, Moustached and Fan-tailed Warblers, Penduline Tit.
♦ *Breeding season* Cory's Shearwater, Little Bittern, Night, Squacco and Purple Herons, Garganey, Black Kite, Short-toed Eagle, Eleanora's Falcon, Black-winged Stilt, Kentish Plover, Whiskered Tern, Great Spotted Cuckoo, Nightjar, Bee-eater, Roller, Lesser Grey Shrike, Subalpine, Savi's, Great Reed, Melodious Warblers, Golden Oriole.
♦ *Passage* Glossy Ibis, Honey Buzzard, Osprey, Eleanora's Falcon, waders, Black Tern, Wryneck, Red-throated Pipit, warblers, chats.
♦ *Winter* Black-throated Diver, Gannet, wildfowl, Hen Harrier.
ACCESS
Aiguamolls is 75 km south of Perpignan in France and 15 km from Figueres. The reserve is just south of Castelló d'Empúries, which is on the C260 Figueres–Roses road. There is an information centre in El Cortalet (tel. 972 454222 or 250322), which is open from 9.30 a.m. to 7 p.m. in summer, closing an hour earlier beween 1 October and 31 March. Binoculars can be hired, and guided walks are available. There is accommodation in Figueres, Castelló d'Empúries and the other villages in the area.

CAP DE CREUS
42°00N 03°30E
The rocky coast immediately south of the French border is geologically the eastern extreme of the Pyrenees, although the flora and fauna are unmistakably Mediterranean. The *garrigue* – open dry scrub of lentisc, rosemary and lavender – is home to a healthy population of Spectacled Warblers. There are small pine woods and patches of cork and holm oak. These are important for Orphean Warblers and for spring and autumn falls of migrants.

Cap de Creus itself is a prime sea-watching location. Yelkouan and Cory's Shearwaters pass by in summer, especially around dusk and early morning, or during onshore winds. The cliffs are home to Blue Rock Thrushes and Black Wheatears and the odd pair of Bonelli's Eagles.

TIMING

After the first severe weather of winter in the Pyrenees, there is a good chance of seeing Alpine Accentor and Wallcreeper at lower altitudes on Sant Salvador and Cap de Creus respectively.

SPECIES

◆ *Resident* Cory's and Yelkouan Shearwaters, Bonelli's Eagle, Peregrine, Thekla Lark, Crag Martin, Black Wheatear, Blue Rock Thrush, Dartford Warbler, Firecrest, Rock and Cirl Buntings.

◆ *Breeding season* Alpine and Pallid Swifts, Tawny Pipit, Lesser Grey Shrike, Black-eared Wheatear, Rock Thrush, Spectacled, Subalpine and Orphean Warblers, Ortolan Bunting.

◆ *Winter* Gannet, Golden Eagle, Great Skua, Wallcreeper, Alpine Accentor.

ACCESS

Cap de Creus is east of Figueres, which is 24 km south of the French border on the A7, or 32 km north of Girona on the same highway. Between Cadaqués and Cap de Creus, at the end of a minor road to the north, the landscape is of olives, almonds and rocky scrub, and occasional stops are worthwhile. There is ample accommodation in Port de la Selva, Cadaqués and Roses. Aiguamolls de l'Empordá (above) is a few kilometres to the south.

LLOBREGAT DELTA

41°17N 02°04E

Within a few kilometres of the centre of Barcelona is a wetland oasis of immense potential as sanctuary from the city's energetic pace. The Riu Llobregat reaches the sea on the southern fringe of the city and forms a delta which, despite enormous pressure, still harbours abundant bird interest.

Twenty-five pairs of Little Bittern breed in the reedbeds, along with Spotted and, possibly, Little Crakes. Breeding waders include Black-winged Stilts and Kentish Plovers. The area is important as a staging post for migrants of all kinds, including up to 200 Audouin's Gulls and 2000 Black Terns. A staggering 12,000 Mediterranean Gulls were counted in the winter of 1990/91 and Moustached Warbler is at least a winter visitor which may breed in the future.

That, and everything else, depends on how this site, arguably the most sought-after development plot in Spain, is treated in the future. Barcelona's air and sea ports are in this area and both have extension plans. Private initiatives include another golf course: pressure on local politicians to ignore the natural richness of the area, not to mention its official Natural Park status, is huge.

TIMING

Late March to June is ideal for breeding and migrating birds, and migrants appear again from late August to early November.

SPECIES

◆ *Resident* Little Egret, Marsh Harrier, Kentish Plover, Whiskered Tern, Monk Parakeet (feral), Hoopoe, Cetti's and Fan-tailed Warblers, Penduline Tit.

◆ *Breeding season* Little Bittern, Night and Purple Herons, Black-winged Stilt, Audouin's Gull, Great Spotted Cuckoo, Short-toed Lark, Great Reed Warbler, Golden Oriole.

◆ *Passage* waders, Black Tern, Pallid and Alpine Swifts, Wryneck, Water Pipit.

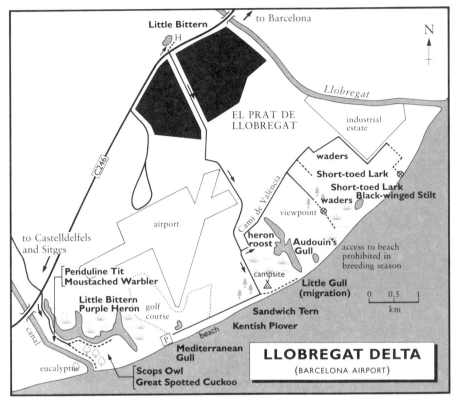

◆ *Winter* Gannet, Cattle Egret, wildfowl including Ferruginous Duck,
Merlin, Mediterranean and Little Gulls, Caspian and Sandwich Terns,
Water Pipit, Bluethroat, Moustached Warbler.

ACCESS

From Barcelona the airport road leads towards El Prat de Llobregat, where, in
the Casa de Cultura in Plaza Pau Casals there is an exhibition on the delta.

There are three walking/driving nature trails or *itinerarios faunisticos* (*see*
map) which cover the range of habitats and species to be found in the delta.
These are: the Central Delta, taking in the Bassa de Prat lagoon, El Prat
beach, Ricarda and La Podrida lagoons; the Remolar–Filipines Nature
Reserve; and the Les Sorres–Murta Lagoon area.

Sundays and public holidays are best avoided, especially in the beach area.
There are military and private areas in the delta, and these must be respected
if public support for the area is to be maintained.

SERRAS DE TARRAGONA

41°20N 00°50E

The low mountains of the Catalan coastal range include the *serras* of
Montsant, Cardó, Tivissa, Montagut and Montmell, which surround the city
of Tarragona, as well as the Natural Park of Sant Llorenç del Munt, which is
to the north-east, behind Barcelona. They are strongholds of the Bonelli's,
Golden and Short-toed Eagles, Eagle Owl and Peregrine.

Black Wheatears and Dartford Warblers are typical among the smaller birds, and Red-necked Nightjars are relatively common, especially in the *serras* around Tivissa.

TIMING
Winters are mild, and rainfall is concentrated in spring and autumn.
SPECIES
- *Resident* Golden and Bonelli's Eagles, Peregrine, Eagle Owl, Thekla Lark, Crag Martin, Dipper, Black Wheatear, Blue Rock Thrush, Dartford Warbler, Firecrest, Rock and Cirl Buntings.
- *Breeding season* Short-toed Eagle, Red-necked Nightjar, Alpine and Pallid Swifts, Tawny Pipit, Black-eared Wheatear, Subalpine and Orphean Warblers, Ortolan Bunting.
- *Winter* Wallcreeper.

ACCESS
The Serra de Montsant can be appreciated from the spectacular C242 road which runs from the N420, 20 km west of Tarragona, to l'Espluga de Francolí on the N240. Interesting diversions from the C242 include the Poblet Monastery, near L'Espluga. There are good walks in the area, enabling the cliffs and outcrops to be thoroughly explored, such as behind the village of La Morera de Montsant, or at the Siurana river and reservoir, east of Cornudella. The road between Poblet and Prades runs through some of the best-preserved oak forest on the region, and forest tracks provide good access.

For the Parc Natural de Sant Llorenç there is an information centre in Coll d'Estenalles (tel. 93 8317300) on the Terrassa–Talamanca road. Terrassa is 21 km inland from Barcelona on the A18 highway.

EBRO DELTA
40°43N 00°44E
At its mouth the Ebro has formed sand bars and spits, shingle beaches and salt-marsh which, over the centuries, have built up to create Spain's second most important wetland. Some 7800 ha have been incorporated into a Natural Park, but the total wetland area is over four times larger. Like most Mediterranean wetlands, the delta has a long history of human occupation and exploitation. Traditional activities include reed-cutting, hunting, fishing and grazing.

The delta has been one of the centres of Spain's rice-growing industry since Valencian growers introduced the crop a hundred years ago. Some 15,000 ha of paddies contribute to habitat diversity, by artificially providing fresh water during the summer. Squacco Herons in particular, but herons and ducks generally, find the paddies very much to their liking. The management of their water levels is the dominant factor in the control of water levels.

Around 100,000 ducks spend the winter in the lagoons and flooded rice paddies, while the breeding population of gulls, terns and waders is internationally important. Over 4000 pairs of Audouin's Gull form the world's largest colony of this globally threatened species. Unexpectedly in 1993 the colony rose to an astonishing 9300 pairs, while none at all bred in Italy. Other statistics are almost as impressive: 1–2000 pairs each of Black-winged Stilt and Kentish Plover; 650 pairs of Little Tern; 1500 pairs of

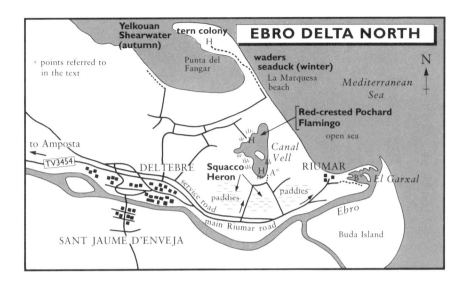

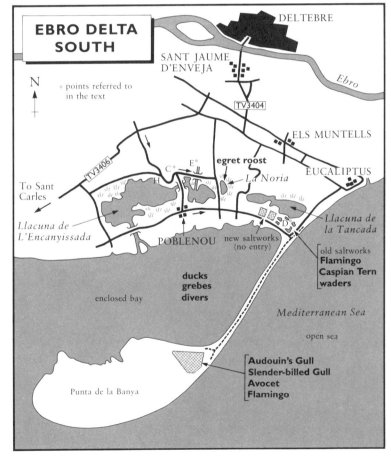

Whiskered Tern; 350 pairs of Squacco Heron, 450 pairs of Purple Heron as well as lesser numbers of Pratincoles, Gull-billed Terns and Avocets. Over 1300 pairs of Red-crested Pochard make this one of the most important places in the world for this attractive duck.

In 1992 Flamingos bred in the delta for the first time in three centuries, but sadly all 2000 pairs failed, due to disturbance by fire-fighting aircraft on a practice run. A couple of hundred pairs were more successful in 1993, and around 2000 winter in the park every year. Among the smaller birds, the Moustached Warbler is important, restricted to a relatively few wetlands in the western Mediterranean. Penduline and Bearded Tits are frequent, neither species being particularly common in Spain.

The northernmost part of the delta comprises the sand spit and dunes of Punta del Fangar, where in spring and summer there is a large tern colony, nesting alongside Kentish Plovers and the odd Oystercatcher. The largest lagoon on the north side is the Canal Vell, which is particularly important when the paddyfields are dry, in late winter and early spring. At the mouth of the Ebro on the north bank is the area known as El Garxal, a lagoon which is important for wildfowl, terns and Little Egrets in spring. Red-crested Pochard gather here, and Audouin's and Slender-billed Gulls are relatively easy to see.

The southern portion of the delta is dominated by the Encanyissada and Tancada lagoons and the wide, sweeping sand spit of Punta de la Banya. At the eastern end of l'Encanyissada is the little reedy lagoon known as La Noria, which has an impressive mixed heronry and roost: the arrival of hundreds of birds from all over the delta as dusk sets in is very impressive. There is also the chance of Glossy Ibis, a non-breeding visitor.

The Punta de la Banya is the best area in the delta for breeding gulls and terns, with Audouin's, Slender-billed and usually Mediterranean Gulls, Little, Sandwich, Common and, occasionally Caspian and Lesser Crested Terns. Private saltworks, where Audouin's Gulls, Flamingos and Avocets congregate, can be watched from a nearby hide. Waders are abundant during migration.

TIMING
From late January to March the paddyfields are mostly dry, and interest is therefore concentrated in the natural lagoons and saltworks. There is considerable pressure on the beaches in summer and at weekends.

SPECIES
- *Resident* Black-necked Grebe, Little and Cattle Egrets, Bittern, Flamingo, Red-crested Pochard, Marsh Harrier, Avocet, Kentish Plover, Slender-billed Gull, Sandwich and Whiskered Terns, Hoopoe, Lesser Short-toed Lark, Cetti's, Moustached and Fan-tailed Warblers, Bearded and Penduline Tits.
- *Breeding season* Little Bittern, Night, Squacco and Purple Herons, Garganey, Black Kite, Black-winged Stilt, Pratincole, Audouin's Gull, Sandwich, Lesser Crested, Little and Black Terns, Bee-eater, Short-toed Lark, Woodchat Shrike, Savi's, Great Reed and Melodious Warblers, Golden Oriole.
- *Passage* waders, Sandwich and Black Terns, Pallid and Alpine Swifts, Wryneck, Water and Red-throated Pipits.
- *Winter* Great White Egret, wildfowl, Hen Harrier, Peregrine, Merlin, Mediterranean Gull, Caspian and Sandwich Terns, Crag Martin, Water Pipit, Bluethroat.

ACCESS

For the northern delta, take the Tortosa exit off the A7 and head for Deltebre. The Deltebre information centre ('Ecomuseu') is off the road leading from the town centre towards Jesus i Maria.

The starting point for excursions into the northern delta is the road running along the main irrigation channel which bypasses Deltebre, leading to Riumar. Canal Vell is reached by turning left 4 km beyond Deltebre. The paddyfield area starts immediately and Squacco Herons are often seen at the roadsides. The road bears sharp right at a restaurant (map point A). There is an elevated hide – *mirador* – which is reached by taking a track from the restaurant car park for 300 m. A nominal charge is made. There is another hide on the opposite side of the lagoon, reached via the Deltebre-La Marquesa road.

About 9 km from Deltebre on the Riumar road a left turn at the fork leads to El Garxal (point B), reached by taking two successive right forks at Riumar and bearing left along good sandy tracks past the red-and-white telecom mast.

The Fangar point is reached by following signs to La Marquesa beach. Once on the Fangar point, stick to the tracks behind the dunes and you should not get bogged down, but avoid the area during storms, when the point may flood. There is an elevated hide overlooking the tern nesting beach, which is otherwise off limits.

A car ferry plies across the river between Deltebre and Sant Jaume d'Enveja. For the southern sector, start at the 'Casa de Fusta' information centre (point C: closed Mondays) at L'Encanyissada lagoon, where there is an observation tower. This is reached by taking the Sant Jaume d'Enveija road from Amposta and following signs to the *Refugi-Museu*, or by taking the ferry to Sant Jaume and heading towards Sant Carles. From the centre a road heads east, and a right turn at the sluice takes you over a bridge which affords a good view of the lagoon on either side of the road. The village at the end of this road is Poblenou. A left turn here leads to a road running parallel to the coast and on to some excellent old saltpans (point D). Alternatively, turn left at the sluice where another bridge (point E) overlooks the reedbeds and is a good place for wintering Bluethroat. This road leads on to the La Noria heronry, where a right turn leads back to the coast road.

The saltpans are on the left of the road towards the beach and are worth as much time as you can allow. A left turn at the next junction leads past the Tancada lagoon, a right to Punta de la Banya. The saltworks at the end of the point are accessible if there are no roadworks, by taking the sand track on the landward edge of the dunes.

A range of hotels are available at L'Aldea, Amposta, Deltebre, Sant Carles de la Ràpita and Sant Jaume. There are camp sites at Riumar and L'Apolla.

ELS PORTS DE BESEIT

40°50N 00°15E

The mountain ranges running roughly parallel to the coast of southern Catalunya and northern València make an interesting detour from the coastal resorts or the Ebro Delta. Immediately behind Tortosa and the Ebro Delta are the Ports de Beseit, a rocky National Reserve covering about 30,000 ha. The reserve was created in 1966 to protect the Spanish ibex, which was close to extinction. There are now 6000 in the reserve and signs of overpopulation.

There are extensive stands of pine and several good oak woods. The mountains are generally rocky limestone with cliffs and gullies that harbour Griffon Vultures, Golden and Bonelli's Eagles, Peregrines and Choughs.

From Tortosa, the northern part of the area can be explored by taking the N230 north as far as Xerta and turning off to Paüls dels Ports. About 1.5 km before this village, by the road on the right, is a gully which can be explored on foot. The local road from Tortosa south to La Sènia (*see* below) skirts the south-east flank of the Beseit hills and runs on to the Montes de Benifassar (below).

PRAT DE CABANES–TORREBLANCA

40°14N 00°12E

There are several small, reasonably well-preserved coastal marshes in València, and Prat de Cabanes, north of Castelló, is particularly unpolluted considering the huge pressures on this coast. Protected under València's Natural Landscape law, this shallow, mostly seasonal lagoon is 9 km long and covers nearly 900 ha.

Around 100 pairs of Pratincoles and 11 pairs of Montagu's Harriers are particularly noteworthy, but the 40 or so pairs each of Little Bitterns and Black-winged Stilts add considerably to the reserve's interest. There are around 400 pairs of Moustached Warblers, making Prat de Cabanes one of the most reliable areas for this Mediterranean speciality.

The northern end of the marsh contains some semi-permanent lagoons, where there is a nature trail. The wetland is separated from the sea by a pebbly spit, occasionally giving way to sand. There are salt-marshes, reedbeds and, at the southern end, stands of maritime juniper, which can be good for migrant passerines in spring and autumn. There are several species of fish found only in the coastal marshes of southern Catalunya and València. They are well represented here but are threatened in other wetlands by pollution.

TIMING

Prat de Cabanes is flooded only in winter, although the lagoons in the north contain water for longer periods. Late April combines both the unpredictability of migration with an abundance of breeding birds.

SPECIES

- *Resident* Little Egret, Red-crested Pochard, Marsh Harrier, Kentish Plover, Cetti's and Moustached Warblers.
- *Breeding season* Little Bittern, Purple Heron, Montagu's Harrier, Baillon's Crake, Black-winged Stilt, Avocet, Pratincole, Audouin's Gull, Little and Sandwich Terns, Short-toed Lark, Woodchat Shrike, Nightingale, Great Reed Warbler.
- *Passage* Black-necked Grebe, Glossy Ibis, waders, warblers, flycatchers.
- *Winter* grebes, wildfowl, Audouin's and Mediterranean Gulls, Bluethroat.

ACCESS

From Torreblanca on the N340 the road to Torrenostra on the coast passes a right turn after 2 km. This leads to a peat drying area, the start of the trail which explains both the nature and the history of the old peat diggings that formed the lagoons. Accommodation can be found in Torreblanca and throughout the area.

There is a visitor centre at the southern end of the reserve, reached by taking the coast road from the N340 just south of Ribera de Cabanes. There are further access points off the main road. These are located in some published material by reference to km marker posts, but these are being altered as stretches of the road are successively upgraded. Make for Torrenostra from Torreblanca if in doubt.

CASTELLÓ AREA
40°00N 00°00

The provincial capital of Castelló (or Castellón) de la Plana is an interesting base for the many coastal wetlands and hills which lie between Prat de Cabanes and València city. To the north, the Marjal de Oropesa is a few kilometres south of Prat de Cabanes and is easily reached from the town of the same name. There are a few pairs of Little Bitterns here, and Night Herons and Squacco Herons are regular. The lighthouse to the south is worth trying for passing Cory's Shearwaters.

The mouth of the Río Millars (Mijares), just south of Castelló, is good for passage waders, terns, gulls and Flamingos, and has a breeding population of Black-winged Stilts and Moustached Warblers. The road north-east out of Burriana on the right bank affords access.

The Almenara lagoons, north of Sagunt, are reached from the coast road east from Almenara and south from Casa-Blanca. This is classified as an Important Bird Area largely because of the 700 or so Red-crested Pochards that winter there. In spring and summer, some 65 pairs of Black-winged Stilt and 20 pairs of Little Bittern breed, and Purple Herons and Pratincoles are regular.

The Marjal de El Moro is a small marsh with abundant vegetation near Puçol, 23 km north of València. It has between 15 and 25 pairs of Little Bitterns nesting along with 100 pairs of Black-winged Stilt and about 20 pairs of Pratincole. An occasional pair of Marbled Teal takes the Valèncian total to around 20 pairs, making the region the second in importance after Andalucía for this globally threatened species. The coast road from Puçol to Playa de Mar and the road south from El Grao de Sagunt border the area.

All along this stretch of coast are rewarding sea-watching points, where both Cory's and Yelkouan Shearwaters can be seen, often in huge numbers, passing along the coast. Peñiscola, Benicàssim and Borriana are known watch-points. Inland from Benicàssim a local road leads up into the Serra de les Santes where there is a spectacular protected area, the Desert of Palms, where Bonelli's Eagles, Peregrines, Eagle Owls and Goshawks breed.

ALBUFERA DE VALÈNCIA
39°20N 00°15E

The Albufera de València was once one of the largest areas of marsh and open water in Spain but land reclamation, urban development, industrial pollution and tourism have taken their toll.

Its declaration, in 1986, as a Natural Park comprising the 2800-ha lagoon and some 18,000 ha of marsh and dunes may save the remaining wildlife habitat, as there is now a management plan which seeks to address the worst of the problems. This is, however, currently under-funded.

L'Albufera is the third most important site in Spain for wintering wildfowl and is of considerable importance for breeding waterbirds, especially herons. In 1993, after several years of increased regularity as a migrant and winter visitor, two pairs of Glossy Ibis bred in L'Albufera, the first breeding record in Spain for decades. However, as with all great wetlands, the presence of rarities is only part of the story. 260 species have been recorded, of which 80 breed. 120 pairs of Little Bittern, 150 pairs of Night Heron, 1500 pairs each of Cattle and Little Egrets, 105 pairs of Squacco Heron and 40 pairs of Purple Heron attest to l'Abufera's importance, as do its wintering wildfowl, including 10–30,000 Shovelers and an amazing 6–12,000 Red-crested Pochards. There are also around 30 breeding pairs of this attractive duck.

Immediately south of the city is the mouth of the river Turia, which is worth stopping at, especially in winter when a large roost of Little Gulls occurs.

TIMING
The cycle of water management in the rice paddies affects the area considerably. Late winter, therefore, sees interest concentrated in the Albufera itself.

SPECIES
◆ *Resident* Little and Cattle Egrets, Glossy Ibis, Flamingo, Red-crested Pochard, Marsh Harrier, Avocet, Kentish Plover, Audouin's Gull, Whiskered Tern, Kingfisher, Hoopoe, Lesser Short-toed Lark, Cetti's and Moustached Warblers, Bearded Tit.

◆ *Breeding season* Little Bittern, Night, Squacco and Purple Herons, Black-winged Stilt, Pratincole, Audouin's Gull, Sandwich and Little Terns, Bee-eater, Short-toed Lark, Woodchat Shrike, Nightingale, Savi's and Great Reed Warblers, Golden Oriole.

◆ *Passage* Black-necked Grebe, Garganey, Booted Eagle, Little and Temminck's Stints, Curlew Sandpiper, Dunlin, Ruff, Spotted Redshank, Greenshank, Green and Common Sandpipers, Audouin's Gull, Sandwich, Whiskered and Black Terns, Nightjar, Pallid and Alpine Swifts, Wryneck, Water Pipit, Redstart, Black Redstart, Melodious Warbler, Pied Flycatcher.

◆ *Winter* Yelkouan Shearwater, Black-necked Grebe, Marbled Teal, Ferruginous Duck, wildfowl, Mediterranean and Little Gulls, Caspian and Sandwich Terns, Crag Martin, Water Pipit, Bluethroat, Penduline Tit.

ACCESS

Flights to València city and Alicante to the south are readily available from many European countries. The busy coast road runs via El Saler along the eastern boundary of the Albufera proper. There is a lay-by (map point A) at a jetty 3.1 km south of the junction with the highway which gives a good view. The road to El Palmar has more vantage possibilities. From this village it is possible to walk or drive among the rice paddies fringing the Albufera (map point B). Between Perelló and Sueca there are usually large concentrations of wintering waterfowl before the paddies are drained in late winter.

The Spanish Ornithological Society runs an ornithological station (Av. Los Pinares, 106; 46012 València; tel. 96 1610847) which can be consulted for the latest information on the area.

BENIDORM AREA

39°50N 00°20W

Marjal de Pego-Oliva is a fairly well-preserved seasonal marsh covering around 1400 ha near Oliva. Over 80 pairs of Little Bittern, 20 pairs of Purple Heron and 30 pairs of Whiskered Tern nest there, along with Penduline Tits and Moustached Warblers. There is a healthy winter roost of herons and waterbirds. The N332 passes the area 7.5 km south of Oliva, which is in turn 73 km south of València. The C3318 to Pego leaves this road and, after crossing over the A7 autoroute, crosses the marsh.

The C3318 north of Benidorm is a good route into the Sierra de Espadan, where Bonelli's Eagles are reasonably common. The nearby Saladar de Calpe is a Natural Park. This small wetland is a regular haunt of loafing Audouin's Gulls, and has Black-winged Stilts and Kentish Plover breeding. From July to October, and to a lesser extent through the winter, there is a good selection of waders. The Peñón itself has a colony of Pallid Swifts nesting on the cliffs and a good selection of wild flowers.

EMBALSE DEL HONDO

38°20N 00°42W

The southernmost part of Alicante province is blessed with some of the most interesting wetlands in south-east Spain. This and the next three sites combine to create an area of outstanding interest, well worth a few days' exploration.

Embalse del Hondo (or, in Valèncian, El Fondó) is a pair of irrigation reservoirs. They are surrounded by natural vegetation and some remaining natural lagoons. It was declared a Natural Landscape Area in 1988, largely because of its importance for breeding herons, with 105 pairs of Little Bittern, 40 pairs each of Night and Purple Herons, a few pairs of Squacco Heron, 250 of Little Egret and 350 of Cattle Egret.

Spain's two globally threatened ducks, Marbled Teal and White-headed Duck, both breed in small numbers, along with Red-crested Pochard and a Spanish rarity, the Shelduck. In total, 180 species are listed for the reserve.

TIMING
Of year-round interest.

SPECIES
- *Resident* Little and Cattle Egrets, Flamingo (occasional), Marbled Teal, White-headed Duck, Red-crested Pochard, Marsh Harrier, Avocet, Kentish Plover, Whiskered Tern, Kingfisher, Hoopoe, Cetti's and Moustached Warblers, Bearded Tit.
- *Breeding season* Little Bittern, Squacco and Purple Herons, Garganey, Black-winged Stilt, Pratincole, Whiskered Tern, Bee-eater, Savi's and Great Reed Warblers, Golden Oriole.
- *Passage* Black-necked Grebe, Night Heron, Booted Eagle, waders, Black Tern, passerines.
- *Winter* Black-necked Grebe, wildfowl, Osprey, Merlin, Water Pipit, Bluethroat, Penduline Tit.

ACCESS
El Hondo is 33 km north of Murcia city, a few kilometres south-west of Elx (Elche) and north-east of Catral. From Elx, take the N340 to just past Crevillente, then the C3321 towards Dolores. Immediately after the railway crossing a left turn in El Realengo leads to the reservoirs. There are tarmacked roads along the western edge of the area and running between the two reservoirs which are worth exploring, with frequent stops.

SALINAS DE SANTA POLA
38°13N 00°35W

On the coast due east of El Hondo is the small resort of Santa Pola which is a good base for a few days' exploration of the area. Immediately south of the town are some extensive saltworks covering 2500 ha, designated as a Natural Landscape Area.

In winter, a few hundred Flamingos can be seen, although they are commoner at the end of summer, when up to 2500 may congregate. Santa Pola is part of a chain of salty wetlands linking the Camargue with the Ebro Delta, Fuente de Piedra and Doñana. The other denizen *par excellence* of these hypersaline habitats is the Avocet, of which there are about 450 pairs.

Marbled Teal breeds here, one of the first places to be colonized from Andalucía in the recent welcome expansion of this species. Other interesting breeding birds include Little and Whiskered Terns and the ubiquitous inhabitant of Mediterranean saltpans, the Kentish Plover.

TIMING
The saltworks are at their best in spring. Flamingos, Audouin's Gulls and migrant waders in late August get the autumn off to a good start.

Kentish Plover

SPECIES
- *Resident* Little Egret, Flamingo, Red-crested Pochard, Marsh Harrier, Avocet, Kentish Plover, Slender-billed Gull (rare breeder), Sandwich Tern, Hoopoe, Lesser Short-toed Lark, Cetti's Warbler.
- *Breeding season* Little Bittern, Night and Purple Herons, Marbled Teal, Black-winged Stilt, Pratincole, Audouin's Gull, Little and Whiskered Terns, Bee-eater.
- *Passage* Black-necked Grebe, Garganey, Osprey, Booted Eagle, waders, Audouin's Gull, Black Tern, Wryneck, Water Pipit.
- *Winter* Black-necked Grebe, Spoonbill, wildfowl, Osprey, Mediterranean and Little Gulls, Crag Martin, Water Pipit, Bluethroat.

ACCESS

Santa Pola is 21 km south of Alicante on the N332 which goes on past the town across the salinas and allows good views over much of the area. This is generally adequate, but the saltworks themselves can be visited with permission of the companies concerned. It is worth seeking this 'on spec' at the various gates, although to be certain of permission, it is necessary to contact the Environment Agency in València (tel. 96 3866359).

SALINAS DE TORREVIEJA

38°03N 00°40W

Thirty km south along the coast from Santa Pola is Torrevieja, where there are two interconnected wetlands. One, the Laguna de La Mata, is used to regulate the water levels in the other, a saltworks complex almost identical to the one at Santa Pola. A similar range of birds is found there, although the Torrevieja complex is just within the range of the Rufous Bushchat, which in València is restricted to the far south.

The larger expanse of these southerly wetlands means that greater numbers of birds are found there, and there are one or two species worthy of special mention. Up to 3500 Black-necked Grebes winter there, their numbers depending on water levels here and at rival sites. The same is true of Red-crested Pochard, of which 2–3000 normally winter.

The N332 runs to the east of the lagoons, and the C3321 Torrevieja–Benijófar runs between the two sites, giving good views over the Torrevieja salinas. There is a good dirt track running along the southern edge of La Mata lagoon, for closer access.

SIERRAS AND VALLE DEL GUADALENTÍN

37°45N 01°25W

The uplands of Murcia province comprise a diverse range of habitats. Many of the hills are wooded, with pine and oak predominant. Golden and Bonelli's Eagles are present at fairly high density in the Sierra Espuña, one of only two protected areas in the province, and in the Sierra de Ricote near Archena. Griffon Vultures, Short-toed Eagles, Peregrines and Chough are also common throughout the area, and there is a healthy population of Eagle Owls. The Sierra Espuña Natural Park starts just west of Alhama de Murcia which is on the N340. From there the C3315 to Mula runs west and north. About 2.5 km out of town a left turn leads into the park and onto the slopes of Morrón (1441 m) and Espuña (1585 m) before descending towards Totana.

Between Lorca and Murcia the A7 runs along the valley of the Guadalentín river. There are wide plains on either side of the river, much of which comprise *salares*, areas of abundant halophytic vegetation. There are several pairs of Montagu's Harriers and Little Bustards in the area between Totana and Alhama. Lesser Short-toed Larks are common and at dusk small groups of Black-bellied Sandgrouse may be seen in flight. The *salares* are 7.5 km south-east of Alhama de Murcia on the Cartagena road where there is a right turn towards Mazarrón. The road divides again several times in the heart of the area.

MAR MENOR AND CARTAGENA

37°45N 00°45W

The 'Lesser Sea' north-east of Cartagena in Murcia is a unique hypersaline lagoon covering over 16,000 ha. It is connected to the sea only by a handful of inlets which breach a spit of land some 25 km long. In several places there are saltpans surrounded by reeds, salt-marshes and sandy areas.

The birdlife is similar to the other wetlands along this stretch of coast, and there are particularly important colonies of Little Tern (300 pairs), Avocet and Kentish Plover. Flamingos and Black-necked Grebe are abundant in winter, and Red-breasted Mergansers are commoner here than anywhere else in Spain, with up to 400 recorded. Audouin's Gulls are frequent visitors.

A road runs along the coastal strip northwards from Cabo de Palos, affording good views of the lagoon, although sprawling apartment blocks have spoilt much of this seaward stretch. The landward fringe has a road running round it. The best area is at the northern end, where the saltpans south-east of San Pedro de Pinatar are well worth exploring for a couple of hours.

The nearby Sierra de Escalona is worth checking *en route*. There is an important winter concentration of young Bonelli's and Golden Eagles, with around 50 Bonelli's counted in 1991.

Cartagena is worth more than a passing mention in its own right. Founded in the third century BC by the Carthaginians, it was the principal port along this coast until Drake's attack on the town in 1588. There are many monuments to its long history, most notably the Torre Ciega, a Roman tower and sepulchre which has been declared a national monument.

Trumpeter Finches are found in the low coastal *sierras* south-east of the city, between the Escombreras headland and the Playa del Gorguel, along with Bonelli's Eagles, Peregrines and Blue Rock Thrush.

CENTRAL SPAIN

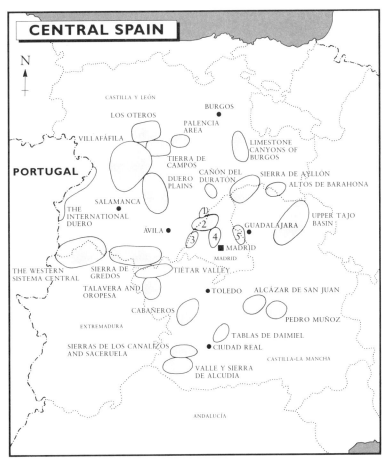

1 *Segovia*, 2 *Sierra de Guadarrama*, 3 *Sierra de Malagón and El Escorial*,
4 *El Pardo*, 5 *Jarama-Lozoya*

This chapter looks at the autonomous regions of Castilla y León, with its endorreic plains heaving with Great Bustards and its wild canyons; Madrid province, mountainous and surprisingly rich in wildlife, and Castilla La Mancha, with its wetlands and *dehesas*. It is a huge and diverse area.

The plains of Castilla y León are one of the world strongholds of grassland species such as the two Bustards, the sandgrouse and Stone Curlew. There are big, historic cities such as Salamanca, Valladolid, León and Burgos and thousands of tiny villages. Dotted about the treeless landscape are traditional brick dovecots. Squabs were once an important source of meat. Linking the grassy plains with the mountains of the Sistema Central are *cañadas*, traditional droving roads hundreds of kilometres long. Castilla–La Mancha takes its name from the Moorish *Al Mansha*, the dry country. There were important grasslands here, too, but they are mostly now intensively farmed under sunflowers and vines. There are hundreds of lagoons and marshes which between them hold hundreds of thousands of wildfowl, herons and waders at various times of the year.

Madrid is the natural entry point for visitors to central Spain, since it is literally in the geographic centre of the country (the exact centre is marked by a stone in Puerta del Sol). There are other international airports just outside the area, in València, Sevilla and Zaragoza.

BIRDWATCHING SITES

TIERRA DE CAMPOS

42°00N 05°00W

The vast plains of Castilla y León owe their ornithological importance to the generations-old tradition of low-intensity cropping and grazing. This is a sparsely populated area characterized by vast and dramatic skies and open, gently undulating landscapes. Barley, wheat and oats rotate with grass, lucerne and fallows to generate a modest income: fertilizers, pesticides and irrigation water are used in moderation if at all. This is, of course, changing. Much of the Tierra de Campos and the similar plains of Villafáfila (*see* page 66) are being converted to corn and sugar beet as irrigation networks spread across the landscape under generous grants and subsidies from the EU.

This could be bad news for one of Europe's most spectacular and threatened birds. In the 3000 km² of Tierra de Campos there are about 2500 Great Bustards. Spain and Portugal are now the stronghold for this magnificent bird, with around three-quarters of the world population between them.

In 1993, however, a new agricultural support scheme explicitly linked to the Great Bustard was announced. EU support is to be made available to farmers living in an area of Castilla y León the size of East Anglia. The intention is to encourage them to maintain bustard-friendly farming methods.

TIMING

Between August and March the Great and Little Bustards form flocks, which can be found relatively easily once harvest is over.

SPECIES

◆ *Resident* Great Bustard, Stone Curlew, Black-bellied Sandgrouse, Calandra Lark, Great Grey Shrike.

◆ *Breeding season* White Stork, Night Heron, Black Kite, Montagu's Harrier, Lesser Kestrel, Little Bustard, Red-necked Nightjar, Bee-eater, Roller, Hoopoe, Tawny Pipit, Spectacled Warbler.

◆ *Winter* Red Kite, Grey Heron, wildfowl, Hen Harrier, Peregrine, Merlin, Common Crane, Golden Plover, Lapwing.

ACCESS

The western portion of the Tierra de Campos is contiguous with Villafáfila and can be explored from the roads that run between Villalpando, Medina, Villalón, Castromocho and Palencia. A good area to sample is about 30 km north-west of Palencia, between Frechilla and Guaza de Campos, a few kilometres to the west.

The area immediately south-east of Fuentes de Nava, which is west of Palencia, is the site of a 5000-ha lagoon, now drained. A remnant wetland was re-established a few years ago. The road to Mazariegos on the N610 crosses the area, which is good for waterbirds, post-breeding concentrations of White Storks, and passage Spoonbills.

PALENCIA AREA

42°00N 04°30W

At the eastern edge of the Tierra de Campos is Palencia. The city lies close to the confluence of two rivers, the Carrión and the Pisuerga. There are important riverine woodlands with a good selection of birds including two of the most important Night Heron colonies in Spain. These are in Husillos, on the Carrión river, 9 km north of Palencia off the C615; and on the Pisuerga at Dueñas, 16 km south of the city, off the N620 Valladolid road.

South-west of the city is an area of *páramo*, high plains covered in thyme and French lavender scrub, with woods of holm oak. This is typical Dupont's Lark habitat, with at least ten pairs, and similar numbers of Little Bustard and Stone Curlew. The wooded areas are good for Orphean Warbler. The best areas are west of Dueñas, best explored by taking the road between there and Santa Cecilia del Alcor, and walking out into interesting-looking areas.

LOS OTEROS

42°15N 05°25W

To the north of the Tierra de Campos is a somewhat more densely populated plain, Los Oteros, which lies east of the river Esla, south of León city. Great and Little Bustards, Pin-tailed Sandgrouse and Montagu's Harriers are common.

All the villages of the area have the words '*de los Oteros*' in their names, so you will know when you have arrived! The N601 south of León forms the eastern edge of the area. From Santas Martas, 25 km south of the city, the road continues for a further 8 km before a turn right takes you towards Valencia de San Juan. This road is the southern edge, and north from this road there are smaller roads and tracks, such as the left turns out of Matadeón and Quintanilla. These lead in turn to a veritable network of roads and tracks which makes exploration of the plains relatively straightforward.

VILLAFÁFILA

41°50N 05°40W

The plains of the Villafáfila area are typical of the North Meseta, a semi-arid, treeless plain, sunbaked in summer, bitterly cold in winter. Dotted about are brackish lagoons which dry out in summer to leave shallow, salt-crusted depressions.

Over 120 species have been recorded here, and the area is one of the most important places in the world for Great Bustard, with 1500–1800 recorded as

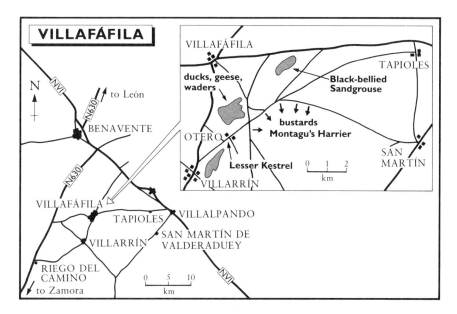

breeding and wintering. Other typical steppe birds include Little Bustard, Black-bellied Sandgrouse and Stone Curlew. In winter, there are important concentrations of Lapwings, Golden Plovers, pipits and larks.

The lagoons hold important winter populations of Greylag, with up to 15,000 recorded. The number of geese depends largely on the condition of the lagoons compared with that of others in the region. Typically, 5000 would be counted in January. Spoonbills and Cranes put in regular appearances on migration. In late summer Black Storks may concentrate if conditions are right. Along the shores of the dammed river Esla to the west is Spain's only regular site for wintering Bean Geese, although numbers have decreased in recent years.

TIMING
The cold winter weather starts in November, and coincides with the arrival of wildfowl and flocks of plovers and larks. These disperse in early March, as the bustards start to take up their territories.

SPECIES
- *Resident* Buzzard, Great and Little Bustards, Stone Curlew, Black-bellied Sandgrouse, Calandra Lark.
- *Breeding season* White and Black Storks, Black Kite, Montagu's Harrier, Lesser Kestrel, Black-winged Stilt, migrant waders, Red-necked Nightjar, Bee-eater, Roller, Hoopoe, Tawny Pipit, Spectacled Warbler.
- *Passage* Spoonbill, Crane.
- *Winter* Bean and Greylag Geese, wildfowl, Red Kite, Hen Harrier, Peregrine, Merlin, Common Crane, Golden Plover, Lapwing.

ACCESS
The core of this superb area is centred around the village of Villafáfila, which is reached by turning east off the N630, 14 km south of Benavente. The three main lagoons are east and south of the village. Laguna de Barillos is about

6 km east of Villafáfila, just south of the Villalpando (*see* page 66) road. A track left off this road, 3.5 km out of Villafáfila leads to Laguna Grande and on, via Otero de Sariegos, to Laguna de Salinas near the village of Villarrín.

The plains around these villages are outstanding for bustards and other steppe birds. Any of the small roads and tracks running though the vast area bounded by the NVI, N630 and N122 would be productive. The best areas to concentrate on are Villafáfila itself; roads off the NVI between Villalpando and Villardefrades or between Mota del Marqués and Tordesillas; the area around Gallegos del Pan, 10 km north of the N122, via a turning to Coreses 12 km east of Zamora; and the area around Peleas de Abajo, turning left about 14 km along the N630.

Accommodation can be found in Benavente and Villalpando.

DUERO PLAINS

41°00N 05°05W

Immediately farther south in the North Meseta plain are two more grassland IBAs in the area around Madrigal de las Altas Torres. The great river Duero marks the northern border of this area, between Toro in the west and Tordesillas in the east. The stretch between Castronuño and Pollos is a small IBA where a heronry has been established, comprising 140 pairs of Grey Heron and about half as many Night Herons.

The plains themselves are yet another important stronghold for the Great Bustard and other species typical of the dry cereals and rough grazing which characterizes so much of the region.

TIMING

For the plains, see Villafáfila. In the heronries, the Grey Herons and Little Egrets get started in February, the Night Heron in spring. There is usually something to see until August, if only juveniles sitting around waiting to be fed.

SPECIES

◆ *Resident* Red Kite, Buzzard, Great and Little Bustards, Stone Curlew, Pin-tailed and Black-bellied Sandgrouse, Calandra Lark.

◆ *Breeding season* White Stork, Night and Grey Herons, Little Egret, Black Kite, Montagu's Harrier, Lesser Kestrel, Black-winged Stilt, Red-necked Nightjar, Bee-eater, Roller, Hoopoe, Tawny Pipit, Spectacled Warbler.

◆ *Passage* Spoonbill, waders, Black Stork.

◆ *Winter* Bean and Greylag Geese, wildfowl, Hen Harrier, Peregrine, Merlin, Common Crane, Golden Plover, Lapwing.

ACCESS

The Duero can be reached by taking the Pollos turning off the N620, 9 km west of the centre of Tordesillas. Between here and Castronuño there are several tracks leading to the willows and poplars at the waters edge. Between Castronuño and Villafranca de Duero the road offers the chance to find Stone Curlew and, in summer, Pin-tailed Sandgrouse.

Madrigal de las Altas Torres is on the C610, 26 km south of Medina. It can also be reached from Alaejos and Castrejón via local roads across the plain. From Madrigal to Peñaranda de Bracamonte, 28 km farther along the C610, is an outstanding area criss-crossed by small roads and estate tracks.

Calandra Lark

THE INTERNATIONAL DUERO

41°00N 06°20W

The border between Portugal and the Spanish provinces of Zamora and Salamanca runs down the centre of the Duero, or, as it is called in Portugal, the Douro. The two countries share some 80,000 ha of granite cliffs, evergreen oak scrub and agricultural land containing some of their best raptor populations. For the Portuguese part, *see* page 166.

The Spanish sector comprises the left bank of the river from the Embalse de Villalcampo, to the junction with the Río Águeda. The Zamora part supports a higher density of Bonelli's Eagles, Peregrines and Eagle Owls, while Egyptian and Griffon Vultures are more common in Salamanca province. Black Storks nest throughout the area as do Golden Eagles.

TIMING
Of interest all year round. Black Storks arrive in mid-April or earlier, White Storks and Alpine Swifts having arrived a month before. By late summer Black Storks start to congregate at the reservoirs.

SPECIES
- *Resident* Grey Heron, Red Kite, Buzzard, Griffon Vulture, Goshawk, Sparrowhawk, Peregrine, Eagle Owl, Hoopoe, Thekla Lark, Great Grey Shrike, Dipper, Blue Rock Thrush, Black Wheatear, Dartford Warbler, Azure-winged Magpie, Chough, Rock Sparrow, Rock Bunting.
- *Breeding season* White and Black Storks, Black Kite, Booted and Short-toed Eagles, Egyptian Vulture, Lesser Kestrel, Red-necked Nightjar, Bee-eater, Spectacled and Subalpine Warblers, Black-eared Wheatear

ACCESS
The road between Fermoselle and Trabanca, the C525, and the roads from Fermoselle to the river at the Bemposta reservoir or Pinilla de Fermoselle to the north are good. It is worth trying the road which links Zamora with the Portuguese town of Miranda do Douro and the various smaller roads leading off this one within the last 10 km or so to the border.

In the southern sector, try the road from Hinojosa to Salto de Saucelle and on to Saucelle, Vilvestre, Aldeadávila and Salto de Aldeadávila and Pereña.

Golden Eagle

LIMESTONE CANYONS OF BURGOS

41°40N 03°07W

The area bounded by the NI Burgos–Aranda del Duero highway to the west and the Sierra de la Demanda to the east contains a diverse range of habitats divided between three Important Bird Areas. The predominant landscape features are the limestone canyons carved by rivers such as the Lobos, the Arlanza and the Mataviejas.

The gorges are home to a healthy population of typical cliff-nesters such as Griffon and Egyptian Vultures, Peregrine, Eagle Owl and Bonelli's Eagle. There is a natural park, the Cañon del Río Lobos, which is visited at weekends by huge numbers of people. A more peaceful alternative is the nearby Peñas de Cervera range.

South of this area are the plains of Caleruega, where there remains a small population of Great Bustards, Black-bellied Sandgrouse and Dupont's Larks.

TIMING
Temperatures are less extreme than in either the *páramos* of Castilla y León or the Sistema Iberico Norte nearby. Therefore good, comfortable bird-watching can be expected throughout the year.

SPECIES
- *Resident* Golden Eagle, Buzzard, Griffon Vulture, Great Bustard, Stone Curlew, Black-bellied Sandgrouse, Eagle Owl, Hoopoe, Short-toed, Dupont's and Calandra Larks, Great Grey Shrike, Dartford Warbler, Chough, Azure-winged Magpie, Rock Sparrow.
- *Breeding season* White Stork, Black Kite, Booted and Short-toed Eagles, Montagu's Harrier, Egyptian Vulture, Hobby, Lesser Kestrel, Bee-eater, Tawny Pipit, Black-eared Wheatear.

ACCESS
The Peñas de Cervera are crossed by several highly scenic roads, such as the C110, off the N234. Covarrubias is at the centre of the area, and the road east from here back onto the N234 at Hortigüela follows the Arlanza river. The road south from Covarrubias is also excellent, and leads to Caleruega where small roads radiate south into the plains.

THE WESTERN SISTEMA CENTRAL

40°30N 06°10W

The Sistema Central is a massive range of rugged mountains running half-way across Spain. This western end comprises the Sierra de Gata and the Peña de Francia and continues into Portugal as the Serra da Malcata (page 167).

The *sierras* here are neither as high nor as rugged as Gredos or Guadarrama, rising to 1367 m. They are, however, more remote and are sparsely populated. In the Sierra de Gata, 90 per cent of the land is forested, either by natural oak and chestnut or, for the most part, pine plantations. To the north-east, the Peña de Francia has rather more natural forest.

Lynx are present throughout the area, but since they are very difficult to see, birds of prey are the main attraction here. There are 30–40 pairs of Black Vultures. The majority nest in the Peña de Francia, but they forage widely throughout the whole range. There are healthy populations of Griffon Vultures, Spanish Imperial Eagles, Booted Eagles and Black Storks.

South of the Sierra de Gata is a reservoir, the Embalse de Borbollón. An island in the middle has a heronry with around 1200 pairs of Cattle Egrets and small numbers of Night Herons, Little Egrets and Grey Herons. Cranes winter in the *dehesa* which surrounds the lake, and there is a good breeding population of Black Kites, and Black-shouldered Kites. This area also contains some cereal land with a good selection of typical species. Another reservoir, the Embalse de Gabriel y Galán, is surrounded by *dehesa* with Black Storks nesting and Cranes in winter.

TIMING

Temperatures range between freezing in January and 40 °C in July. In late summer Black Storks congregate in groups at the reservoirs. Cranes arrive in November and stay until late February.

SPECIES

♦ *Resident* Little and Cattle Egrets, Red and Black-shouldered Kites, Goshawk, Buzzard, Bonelli's, Golden and Spanish Imperial Eagles, Griffon and Black Vultures, Peregrine, Great Bustard, Stone Curlew, Black-bellied Sandgrouse, Eagle Owl, Blue Rock Thrush, Crested Tit, Rock Bunting, Rock Sparrow, Chough, Raven, Azure-winged Magpie.

♦ *Breeding season* White and Black Storks, Night Heron, Black Kite, Short-toed and Booted Eagles, Honey Buzzard, Egyptian Vulture, Montagu's Harrier, Hobby, Great Spotted Cuckoo, Hoopoe, Red-rumped Swallow, Woodchat Shrike, Melodious and Bonelli's Warblers, Black-eared Wheatear.

♦ *Winter* Common Crane, Golden Plover.

ACCESS

The Peña de Francia can be reached in various ways. One should aim for the village of La Alberca (which has been designated a National Monument for its beauty and unique architecture) and the Las Batuecas National Reserve. A scenic road runs through both places from the C515 Ciudad Rodrigo–Bejár road at El Cabaco to Las Mestas, 27 km to the south.

The Sierra de Gata and the Borbollón reservoir can be reached from the C526 which runs between Coria and Ciudad Rodrigo. About 1 km south of Moraleja, a road runs north-east towards the reservoir and on to San Juan on the C513. From here a road winds up to the village of Gata.

SIERRA DE GREDOS

40°16N 05°00W

The Sierra de Gredos, running from Plasencia in Extremadura to Ovila in Castilla y León, contains the highest and remotest parts of the Sistema Central, with peaks reaching up to 2592 m. Snow lies in the gullies all year round, and the white-topped peaks dominate the flatter Tiétar valley to the south, forming a spectacular backdrop to the *dehesas* of Monteagudo (*see* page 83).

The slopes of Gredos are cloaked in forests of Pyrenean oak and pine, some natural, some planted. Citril Finches are common, and usually tame, in the pinewoods. The higher regions are covered in alpine grassland and bare rock. Alpine Accentors are plentiful above the tree-line. Lower slopes are haunted by Black Vultures, Spanish Imperial Eagles and Black Storks. The best population of Bluethroat in Spain is found on the fragrant, broom-covered slopes of Gredos' southern face, and Rock Thrush is fairly easy.

There is a National Hunting Reserve (*Coto Nacional*) in the heart of the range, set up in 1905 by Alfonso XIII to save the endemic Spanish ibex from extinction. As a result, this is the best area in Spain to see this impressive beast. There are also plentiful wild boar, wildcat and a few remaining wolves. Gredos is botanically very rich, with several species and subspecies which are endemic or practically so.

TIMING

Winter is relatively mild on the southern slopes, but at higher altitudes and on the northern side can be cold, foggy and often snowy. Late April to July are ideal times to see Gredos at its best, preferably not at weekends. Weekdays tend to be busy only in August.

Ortolan Bunting

SPECIES
- *Resident* Red Kite, Goshawk, Buzzard, Bonelli's, Golden and Spanish Imperial Eagles, Griffon and Black Vultures, Peregrine, Rock Dove, Eagle and Long-eared Owls, Great Grey Shrike, Alpine Accentor, Blue Rock Thrush, Black Redstart, Crested Tit, Rock Bunting, Rock Sparrow, Chough, Raven, Azure-winged Magpie.
- *Breeding season* White and Black Storks, Black Kite, Short-toed and Booted Eagles, Honey Buzzard, Egyptian Vulture, Great Spotted Cuckoo, Hoopoe, Red-rumped Swallow, Water Pipit, Woodchat Shrike, Melodious, Bonelli's and Orphean Warblers, Rock Thrush, Black-eared Wheatear, Redstart, Bluethroat, Ortolan Bunting.
- *Passage* storks and raptors.

ACCESS
El Barco de Ávila, 77 km south-east of Ávila is a good starting point. From here the C500 is a picturesque road running east for 32 km to Hoyos del Espino. From here a local road heads south into the Coto Nacional de Gredos to the Refugio del Club Alpino. The C500 continues through Hoyos del Espino to the C502 Ávila–Talavera road. This is an alternative approach either to the *Coto Nacional* or over the massif, via Puerto del Pico. Off the C502 there are roads leading to the mountain villages such as El Arenal, or San Esteban del Valle. The C502 continues into the Tiétar valley.

The southern boundary of the IBA is at Arenas de San Pedro, on the C501. From here a small road leads to Guisando and on towards the peak of La Mira (2343 m). A marked trail leads from El Raso, which is off the C501 (turn north 5 km west of Candeleda), into the *Coto Nacional* below the 2592-m peak of Almanzor.

Accommodation is plentiful, with a *Parador* in Navarredonda to the east of Hoyos del Espino, and small hotels in most other villages in the area.

SIERRA DE AYLLÓN
41°15N 03°20W
The Sierra de Ayllón is at the eastern end of the Sistema Central and is an almost unpopulated area of rugged mountains covered in *Cistus* scrub. There are important stands of beech forest, oak woods and plantations of pine. There are several medieval castles in the area. East of Ayllón is an area of foothills set in a rugged landscape with many small gorges and numerous villages.

Golden Eagles are relatively common in the *sierra* proper, and the area is generally very good for birds of prey. The area to the east of Ayllón is important for Griffon Vultures, with over 100 pairs.

TIMING
The high tops can be among the coldest places in Spain during the winter, but lower slopes are relatively mild. Some of the forest tracks are impassable at this time.

SPECIES
- *Resident* Red Kite, Goshawk, Buzzard, Bonelli's and Golden Eagles, Griffon Vulture, Peregrine, Capercaillie, Eagle and Long-eared Owls, Great Grey Shrike, Blue Rock Thrush, Black Wheatear, Crested Tit, Rock Bunting, Rock Sparrow, Chough.

◆ *Breeding season* White and Black Storks, Black Kite, Short-toed and Booted Eagles, Honey Buzzard, Egyptian Vulture, Hoopoe, Red-rumped Swallow, Water Pipit, Woodchat Shrike, Melodious and Bonelli's Warblers, Rock Thrush, Black-eared Wheatear, Redstart, Bluethroat, Ortolan Bunting.

◆ *Winter* Black Vulture, Spanish Imperial Eagle.

ACCESS

The Madrid section of the Sierra de Ayllón is a National Reserve which can be reached from the south via Lozoyuela on the A1 (*see* also page 80). From here, or from Buitrago to the north, roads run north-east to Montejo de la Sierra. Roads north of here lead to various villages in the foothills. From the north, there are two forest roads into the reserve from Cantalojas, which is 6 km west of Galve de Sorbe. The beechwood of Tejera Negra is between Cantalojas and Riofrío de Riaza on one of the routes out of Cantalojas (take the right fork).

The area east of Ayllón is an IBA with the village (and castle) of Caracena at its centre. The rivers Tiermes and Caracena have interesting gorges. A route linking Ayllón, Liceras, Montejo de Tiermes, Hoz de Arriba and Hoz de Abajo on minor roads should reveal a good selection of raptors and cliff-nesting birds. The nearby ruins of the pre-Roman settlement of Termanica have an easily viewed Griffon Vulture colony by the car park. This site is about 6 km east of Montejo de Tiermes. The immediate surroundings are dominated by a rocky ridge where Golden Eagles and Egyptian Vultures may also be found.

ALTOS DE BARAHONA

41°20N 02°30W

Immediately east of the Sierra de Ayllón is a high, stony, limestone plateau, the *altos*, which surrounds the small town of Barahona. There are some small cliffs along the many small rivers which cross the 50,000–ha area, but the majority is under dry cereal cultivation or sheep-grazed scrub.

Dupont's Lark is *the* bird of these *altos*: with 2000–3000 pairs it is probably the best area in Spain, and therefore Europe, for this elusive species. Other birds include a small population of Little Bustards and Black-bellied Sandgrouse, plenty of Stone Curlews and good numbers of raptors.

Barahona is 25 km south of Almazán on the C101. The N111 crosses the eastern part of the area between 18 and 38 km south of Almazán. Just south of Puerto de Radona turn westwards to Barahona and beyond to Rello traversing most of the IBA. Smaller roads and tracks off this road lead into the best scrub areas, although it is inadvisable to drive off the roads both for the car's and the birds' sakes.

SEGOVIA

40°58N 04°08W

The ancient city of Segovia is an ideal base for a few days' birdwatching. Its famous Roman aqueduct, one of the biggest and best preserved of the ancient world, has thousands of Swifts' and several Black Redstarts' nests in it. The city is classified as an Important Bird Area on account of its high White Stork population, which is augmented every evening by a roost that forms on the cathedral. In July and August this is an especially good spectacle as adults and newly fledged young vie for space on the pinnacles. The overspill is absorbed by the nearby Alcázar, a fairytale castle all turrets and spires – and storks. The best places from which to watch this are the pavement bars in the main square. Some 20 pairs of Chough also nest on the cathedral, along with Rock Sparrows. Most evenings a Peregrine tries its luck at the Chough roost. The countryside around Segovia is a stronghold of Black and Red Kites.

There are some low hills and cliffs to the north of the city which can be explored by taking the Espirdo road off the N110.

TIMING
The storks are present from January to August and, in smaller numbers, throughout the year.

SPECIES
◆ *Resident* Red Kite, Spanish Imperial and Golden Eagles, Goshawk, Griffon and Black Vultures, Eagle Owl, Woodlark, Great Grey Shrike, Black Redstart, Rock Sparrow, Chough, Raven.
◆ *Breeding season* White Stork, Black Kite, Honey Buzzard, Short-toed and Booted Eagles, Egyptian Vulture, Lesser Kestrel, Scops Owl, Hoopoe, Red-rumped Swallow, Woodchat Shrike, Melodious and Bonelli's Warblers, Rock Thrush.
◆ *Passage* Black Stork, raptors.
◆ *Winter* Peregrine, Stock Dove.

ACCESS
Segovia can be used as a base for exploring the Sierra Guadarrama, El Escorial and Duratón. The city is at the intersection of the N601 Madrid–Valladolid road with the N110 Ávila–Aranda del Duero road. There are numerous hotels and *hostales*, and several famous restaurants.

Cañón del Duratón

41°20N 03°50W
This spectacular gorge has recently been declared a natural park, partly to protect the 250 pairs of Griffon Vultures from rock-climbers. Some 5000 ha of rocky steppe, cliffs and pine woods are now included in the protected area. 13 species of raptor and five species of owl are recorded as nesting in the park. The rocky steppe *en route* from Sepúlveda is good for Thekla and Short-toed Larks, as well as the elusive Dupont's Lark. At the gorge, in addition to the Griffons, there are Peregrines, Egyptian Vultures, Crag Martins and, from mid-April, Booted Eagles. At nightfall the deep call of the Eagle Owl can be heard. During the day, and with a lot of luck, a careful scan of the cliffs with a telescope might reveal a roosting bird. Hobbies breed in the pine woods in the south-west of the park, along with Short-toed Eagles.

Nearby is Pedraza, a beautiful hill-top village with a magnificent seventeenth-century square. A castle overlooks a deep ravine. Here there are nesting Blue Rock Thrushes, Rock Sparrows and Choughs. In the ravine Red-rumped Swallows, Red Kites and Griffon Vultures can be seen, and Golden Orioles and Cetti's and Melodious Warblers heard.

TIMING
Griffons nest from December to July; Dupont's Larks sing mainly in February and March. There can be snow in winter and searing heat in July and August.

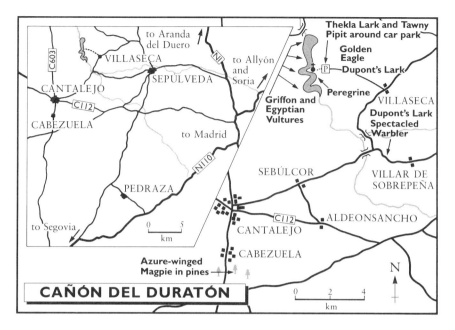

CAÑÓN DEL DURATÓN

SPECIES
- *Resident* Great Crested Grebe, Cormorant, Grey Heron, Red Kite, Buzzard, Griffon and Black Vultures, Peregrine, Stone Curlew, Eagle Owl, Hoopoe, Short-toed, Dupont's, Calandra and Thekla Larks, Grey Wagtail, Great Grey Shrike, Dartford Warbler, Chough, Rock Sparrow.
- *Breeding season* White Stork, Black Kite, Booted and Short-toed Eagles, Montagu's Harrier, Egyptian Vulture, Hobby, Lesser Kestrel, Bee-eater, Tawny Pipit, Spectacled Warbler, Black-eared Wheatear, Golden Oriole.
- *Winter* Hen Harrier, wildfowl, Common Crane.

ACCESS
From the attractive old town of Sepúlveda, take a minor road which heads west to the gorge via Vilar de Sobrepeña. This road runs through excellent *páramos*, low scrub, where Spectacled and Dartford Warblers breed, along with Dupont's Larks. Turn right farther along this road to Villaseca and follow signs for the Ermita de San Frutos. This ruined monastery is at the edge of the gorge along a fairly rough but passable track out of the village.

Accommodation is plentiful in Segovia, Aranda del Duero and Pedraza.

SIERRA DE GUADARRAMA
40°50N 04°00W
There can be few European capitals whose boundaries are marked by the foothills of a mountain range of great ornithological importance. The snow-capped Sierra de Guadarrama can be seen from many of Madrid's taller buildings and the smell of cistus occasionally wafts down from the hills into the city itself. This makes the Sierrra de Guadarrama by far the most popular haunt for Madrileño day-trippers, so the hills are best avoided at weekends.

It is well worth the effort. The Sierra Guadarrama is a Black Vulture stronghold, and other raptors abound. Griffon Vultures, Goshawks and Golden Eagles can often be seen from the main roads either side of the mountain passes. The hills behind village of Manzanares el Real are a good spot for Griffon Vultures and Eagle Owls, and Azure-winged Magpies have spread here recently. Manzanares itself has a good population of White Storks from February to July, and the large reservoir across the road is good for ducks, migrating waders and the occasional Black Stork. In the fields at the north-east corner of the lake, where the Chozas river enters, small groups of Little Bustards can be seen in late summer.

The Puerto de la Morcuera is a mountain pass where the hillsides are broom-covered and highly scented in summer. Water Pipits, Ortolan Buntings, Rock Buntings and, usually, Bluethroats breed here. North of the pass, the road passes through some delightful countryside in the Rascafría valley. There are grassy meadows which are full of orchids – at least six species – and Quail. Honey Buzzard nest in the oakwoods.

TIMING
Winter is cold, foggy and often snowy: this is a good time to find the large eagles. There are signs on all the main roads out of Madrid to indicate whether or not the various passes are open. Late April to July are ideal to see Guadarrama at its best. Peonies, hoop-petticoat narcissi and various orchids add to the pleasure. Weekends should be avoided if at all possible.

SPECIES
◆ *Resident* Red Kite, Goshawk, Buzzard, Bonelli's, Golden and Spanish Imperial Eagles, Griffon and Black Vultures, Peregrine, Rock Dove, Eagle and Long-eared Owls, Great Grey Shrike, Blue Rock Thrush, Black Redstart, Crested Tit, Rock Bunting, Rock Sparrow, Chough, Raven.

◆ *Breeding season* White and Black Storks, Black Kite, Short-toed and Booted Eagles, Honey Buzzard, Egyptian Vulture, Hoopoe, Red-rumped Swallow, Water Pipit, Woodchat Shrike, Melodious and Bonelli's Warblers, Rock Thrush, Black-eared Wheatear, Redstart, Bluethroat, Ortolan Bunting.

ACCESS
Manzanares el Real is reached quickly from Madrid on either of two highways: to Colmenar Viejo or Collado-Villalba. The road from Manzanares to Rascafría climbs up and over Puerto de la Morcuera.

The highest pass over the *sierra* is on the road to Segovia (page 74), at Puerto de Navacerrada, which is a ski resort and is entirely different in character from Puerto de la Morcuera. A small road leads off opposite the main junction a couple of hundred m up to a toboggan run where, if there are not too many people about, Citril Finches, Crested Tits and Pied Flycatchers can be found. From here the road to Rascafría is very worthwhile. A stop at any of the frequent lay-bys should yield Black Vultures overhead and Rock Buntings around about.

The palace gardens at San Ildefonso and the woods at nearby Valsaín are worth checking for Honey Buzzards, Black Vultures, Booted, Golden and Spanish Imperial Eagles overhead. Pied Flycatchers, Short-toed Treecreepers, Goldcrests, Firecrests and red squirrels are common in the gardens.

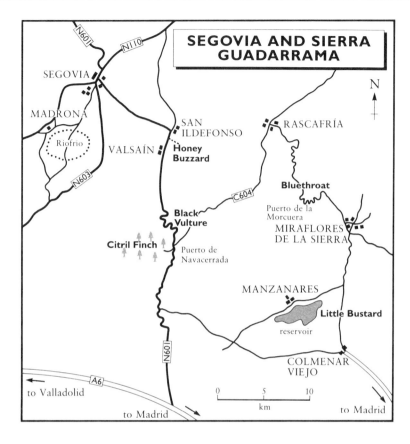

SIERRA DE MALAGÓN AND EL ESCORIAL

40°30N 04°10W

This part of the Sistema Central range is one of the more familiar mountain areas around Madrid, if only because some of the busiest highways in the country cross it. At El Escorial there is a royal palace, traditional last resting place of the Spanish monarchy, and something of a tourist trap. There is extensive holm oak *dehesa*, pine forest, river valleys and high tops.

To the east, Puerto de Guadarrama is, as its name suggests, the beginning of the Guadarrama range proper but there are good reasons to explore the Sierra de Malagón as well, not least the high concentration of Spanish Imperial Eagles, with some ten pairs.

Access is straightforward over much of the area. From junction 2 of the A6 toll road the road to El Escorial can be scanned for raptors. A road to the right runs through the Valle de los Caídos, or valley of the fallen. This park was established by Franco to commemorate the dead of the civil war. At the entrance gate, a ticket (free) must be obtained. It is in theory forbidden to stop along the 5-km road, but this would be difficult to enforce. In any case, it runs largely through dense pine forest of a type which can explored more easily outside the park. If the park is closed (and, indeed, if not) stop before the gate and explore on foot. Spanish Imperial Eagles sometimes haunt the area around the entrance. The road leads to a great stone cross, visible for miles around, and a monastery. There are cafés and toilets here. Stop in the car park and scan from the steps of the cross. Spanish Imperial, Booted and occasional Bonelli's Eagles can be watched from here. Firecrests breed in the monastery gardens.

The C505 road from El Escorial to El Encinar de los Reyes and on to Madrid runs through *dehesas* and by a large reservoir. Black Storks and raptors can be seen from this road.

El Pardo

40°35N 03°45W

For centuries this vast park was the private preserve of the kings of Spain, then that of Franco. It is remarkable in that it starts, literally, in metropolitan Madrid and stretches north, an unbroken *dehesa*, for something like 20 km. As a haunt of Spanish Imperial Eagles and Black Vultures it brings these threatened species within sight of a modern city. Much of it has *de facto* protection, as some 15,000 ha remain the property of the royal family. Road access is limited to a relatively small area. Some 125 species of birds, 19 of reptiles and 35 of mammals have been recorded.

A reservoir dominates the centre of the park, is important for wintering Coots, wildfowl and roosting Cranes. Black Storks congregate here after breeding and Ospreys pass over it on spring and autumn migration.

TIMING

There is practically year-round interest. Weekends should be avoided.

Cirl Bunting

SPECIES

◆ *Resident* Red Kite, Buzzard, Spanish Imperial Eagle, Griffon and Black Vultures, Eagle and Long-eared Owls, Hoopoe, Woodlark, Great Grey Shrike, Dartford Warbler, Firecrest, Crested Tit, Cirl Bunting, Azure-winged Magpie.

◆ *Breeding season* White Stork, Black Kite, Short-toed and Booted Eagles, Honey Buzzard, Egyptian Vulture, Scops Owl, Red-necked Nightjar, Bee-eater, Woodchat Shrike, Melodious and Bonelli's Warblers, Black-eared Wheatear, Golden Oriole.

◆ *Passage* Black Stork, Osprey.

◆ *Winter* Great Crested Grebe, Cormorant, Grey Heron, wildfowl, Peregrine, Common Crane.

ACCESS

Road access is limited but there are footpaths leading off from the various stopping places. The C601 runs off the main NVI a kilometre or so north of Moncloa district and its triumphal arch. From here a right turn leads to La Quinta, where a restaurant can be found and access gained to the woods. Otherwise, farther up the C601 is El Pardo township, beyond which is El Cristo and the reservoir. It is possible to walk around here, too, and to gain good views over much of the park from this elevated vantage point.

JARAMA–LOZOYA
40°15N 03°30W

This interesting and varied area earns its place in a birdwatching itinerary not least because it is a only a few minutes' drive from Madrid's international airport at Barajas. Great and Little Bustards breed and winter in the fields east of the C103 at Valdetorres de Jarama. From the international terminal, take the A2 motorway east towards Alcalá de Henares, taking the exit east of the airport. Head north on the C103 to Valdetorres. Take any of the wide, smooth tracks off the road and stop and scan every 100 m. Black-bellied Sandgrouse, Red Kites and Calandra Larks are also common, Montagu's Harriers breed and Hen Harriers winter.

Some 15 km to the north of Valdetorres is Torrelaguna. The back road from here to Lozoyuela, farther north, is very scenic, winding up *cistus*-covered hills where Booted Eagles, Woodchat Shrikes and Black-eared Wheatears are common in spring and summer. This is a delightful, slow way into the Sierra Guadarrama. A few kilometres north-west of Torrelaguna are the twin villages of Patones de Abajo and Patones de Arriba. The latter is supposedly deserted, but in fact is popular at weekends with Madrid day-trippers. The rocky valley leading up to this pretty hamlet has nesting Black Wheatears, Blue Rock Thrushes, Crag Martins and Melodious Warblers.

UPPER TAJO BASIN
40°48N 02°15W

As the Tagus, or Tajo, leaves the Serranía de Cuenca it forms an almost continuous limestone canyon, some 80 km long. The newly created Alto Tajo Natural Park seeks to protect a very important population of birds of prey, including over 100 pairs of Griffon Vultures, a dozen pairs of Egyptian Vultures, as well as several pairs each of Bonelli's Eagles, Peregrines and Eagle Owls.

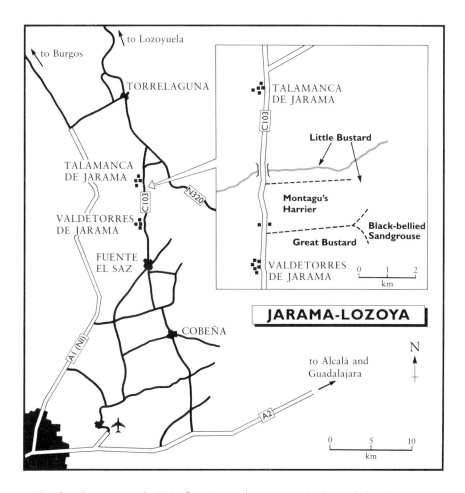

Farther downstream the Tajo flows into a large reservoir, the Embalse de Entrepeñas, while its nearby tributary, the Guadiela, forms the Embalse de Buendía. The latter is of great importance as an overnight roost for Cranes, since it is directly *en route* between Gallocanta (page 40) and the *dehesas* of Extremadura. This part of the river basin is also good for raptors, including seven pairs of Golden Eagles.

To the north of the area, around Maranchón, there is an area of *páramo*, with Little Bustards, Black-bellied Sandgrouse and Dupont's Larks.

TIMING
The Cranes pass through primarily in February and late October/ November.
SPECIES
◆ *Resident* Golden and Bonelli's Eagles, Buzzard, Griffon Vulture, Eagle Owl, Hoopoe, Great Grey Shrike, Dartford Warbler.
◆ *Breeding season* Black Kite, Booted and Short-toed Eagles, Egyptian Vulture, Bee-eater, Tawny Pipit, Black-eared Wheatear.
◆ *Autumn and winter* wildfowl, Common Crane.

Short-toed Eagle

ACCESS

The Alto Tajo Natural Park can be explored via a small road which for 20 km runs parallel to the river between Peñalén and Casas del Campillo. The C202 south of Molina leads to Peñalén via Caserio de Terzaguilla and Poveda. From Casas del Campillo another route returns to Molina, initially following the Río Gallo from its junction with the Tajo.

The Entrepeñas and Buendía reservoirs are either side of the N320, 50 km east of Guadalajara. The road from Sacedón south to the dam, fourteen km away, is a worthwhile diversion. The Parameras de Maranchón surround the town of that name on the N211, 42 km north-west of Molina. Between there and Layna to the north is a particularly good area.

TALAVERA AND OROPESA

39°48N 04°20W

The NV highway from Madrid to Badajoz and Portugal runs past (or until recently, through) these two towns: Talavera with its famous pottery, Oropesa the ancient hilltop town with its fifteenth-century castle, now a *Parador*. They are in Castilla-La Mancha but give a foretaste of Extremadura a few kilometres farther west.

Lesser Kestrels are often to be seen hawking in small flocks in the plains along the highway, White Storks are common in the villages of the area and the first extensive areas of *dehesa* appear. A detour off the main road and into the cereal and grassland plains should reveal Great and Little Bustards and, in spring and summer, Montagu's Harrier.

Downstream of Talavera the Tajo is again dammed and the resulting Embalse de Azután holds, like the reservoir 50 km upstream at Castrejón, a heronry. This time there are fewer Night Herons (80 pairs) but many more Cattle Egrets: over 2000 pairs.

TIMING
The heronry is busy all year round, with either breeding or roosting birds in residence.
SPECIES
◆ *Resident* Cattle Egret, White Stork, Black-shouldered Kite, Buzzard, Great and Little Bustards, Stone Curlew, Calandra Lark, Penduline Tit, Azure-winged Magpie, Spanish Sparrow.
◆ *Breeding season* Night Heron, Black Kite, Montagu's Harrier, Lesser Kestrel, Bee-eater, Roller, Hoopoe.
◆ *Winter* Osprey, Red Kite, wildfowl, Lapwing, Golden Plover.
ACCESS
There are some islands in the reservoir, where herons roost and breed, including one close to the old bridge in Talavera de la Reina. The reservoir is best watched by leaving Talavera south on the N502 and turning right after 10 km to Las Herencias. If permission is sought at the private estate 'Villa Aurora', it is possible to walk from the street named *calle* La Estación to the reservoir opposite the heronry.

Roads running north of Oropesa to Corchuela or Las Ventas de San Julian afford a view of the plains, before heading into the *dehesas* of Monteagudo and the Tiétar valley (below). A smaller road south-east out of Oropesa to Calera y Chozas cuts through both *dehesa* and grassland.

TIÉTAR VALLEY
40°10N 05°00W
The centre of the Tiétar valley is one of the least densely populated and best preserved parts of Spain. It comprises some 90,000 ha of *dehesa*, grassland and scrub, the best of which is accessible only in four-wheel drive vehicles.

In winter the *dehesas* hold good numbers of Cranes, which come to feed on the acorns. There is a good population of Spanish Imperial Eagles, whose aerial courtship display can be seen from January to March. Black-shouldered Kites nest and from April onwards, three pairs of Black Storks breed in the valley itself. Dartford Warblers are common in the cistus scrub. The valley holds a good population of otters and is a stronghold of lynx and wildcat.

There are plans for a huge reservoir in the area: as yet this magnificent area has no official protection.

TIMING
November to February is a good time for raptors and Cranes, then the breeding birds take over until mid-summer when things quieten down somewhat.
SPECIES
◆ *Resident*: Red and Black-shouldered Kites, Goshawk, Spanish Imperial Eagle, Griffon and Black Vultures, Little Bustard, Stone Curlew, Eagle and Long-eared Owls, Hoopoe, Crag Martin, Dartford Warbler, Firecrest, Crested Tit, Cirl Bunting, Azure-winged Magpie.

◆ *Breeding season* White and Black Storks, Black Kite, Short-toed and Booted Eagles, Honey Buzzard, Egyptian Vulture, Montagu's Harrier, Hobby, Quail, Scops Owl, Red-necked Nightjar, Bee-eater, Roller, Woodchat Shrike, Melodious, Spectacled, Orphean and Bonelli's Warblers, Black-eared Wheatear, Golden Oriole.

◆ *Passage* Spoonbill, storks and raptors, Osprey, passerines.

◆ *Winter* Great Crested Grebe, Cormorant, Grey Heron, wildfowl, Hen Harrier, Peregrine, Common Crane.

ACCESS

From Candeleda, on the C501, the Oropesa road crosses the river, an excellent general vantage point. Estate roads between here and Ventas de San Julian provide access to the *dehesas*. Normally there is no objection but remember to close gates and respect the rights of the landowners. The road from Oropesa to Las Ventas de San Julián runs through some of the best Black-shouldered Kite country.

Candeleda, the main town in the area, has a high population of urban Crag Martins and plenty of accommodation.

ALCÁZAR DE SAN JUAN

39°30N 03°10W

In *La Mancha Húmeda* is one of the characteristic landscapes of the dry plains of the South Meseta: complexes of seasonal lagoons of varying sizes, fed by a combination of rivers, springs and rainfall. Most have no outlet except evaporation and in summer they leave flat, salt-crusted pans of dry mud. Few of these lagoons are more than a dozen hectares in extent but collectively they are a wetland area of immense importance.

To the north and west of Alcázar de San Juan the lagoons are set in an area of intensive cultivation, and the excessive abstraction of groundwater for irrigation is a serious threat to the wetland. The characteristic birds of this habitat are Gull-billed Terns, Pratincoles and Red-crested Pochard, all of which breed in good numbers. The surrounding fields remain good for steppe birds such as bustards, Pin-tailed Sandgrouse and Stone Curlew.

TIMING

Between late June and October there is little or no water, but outside these periods the area can be outstanding.

SPECIES

◆ *Resident* Black-necked Grebe, Little and Cattle Egrets, Red-crested Pochard, Marsh Harrier, Great and Little Bustards, Stone Curlew, Kentish Plover, Pin-tailed Sandgrouse, Hoopoe, Fan-tailed Warbler, Bearded Tit.

◆ *Breeding season* Night and Purple Herons, Garganey, Black Kite, Lesser Kestrel, Spotted Crake, Avocet, Black-winged Stilt, Pratincole, Gull-billed and Whiskered Terns, Great Spotted Cuckoo, Bee-eater, Short-toed Lark.

◆ *Passage* Osprey, waders, Black Tern.

◆ *Winter* wildfowl, Crane, Hen Harrier, Peregrine, Merlin, Penduline Tit.

ACCESS

The general area is 50–60 km north of Daimiel town on the N420, or 120 km south of Madrid on the NIV. From Alcázar de San Juan or Madridejos the C400 takes you to Villafranca de los Caballeros. On the way a right turn along a farm track by two white farmhouses leads to a large lagoon with an island on which Avocets and Gull-billed Terns nest. From Villafranca the local road to Quero, to the north-west, or another to Villacañas, runs alongside several lagoons.

One of the best areas in Castilla-La Mancha for Great Bustard, and an important place for Little Bustard, Pin-tailed Sandgrouse and typical plains birds such as Stone Curlew and Calandra Lark lies, in the area around Tembleque, south of the historic city of Aranjuez. Take the road from La Guardia to Lillo, thence to Tembleque. From here tracks radiate west into the plains.

PEDRO MUÑOZ

39°25N 02°45W

Nearby to the east is a similar area between Pedro Muñoz and Las Pedroñeras. The species composition of the two areas is similar, but in spring the number of breeding Black-necked Grebes here is striking: at 150 pairs this may be the largest colony in Europe. The most important lagoons are the Laguna de Manjavacas, where around 200 pairs of Gull-billed Terns breed, and the Laguna de Pedro Muñoz. In some years migration can be especially good, with Temminck's Stints, Ospreys and Red-Throated Pipits seen almost daily in late March and April, and frequent records of rarities. Lagoons that hold water in summer, such as (usually) Manjavacas, can attract important concentrations of Black-necked Grebes and Gull-billed Terns in July.

Pedro Muñoz is 23 km east of Alcázar on the N420. Immediately outside the town, on the El Toboso road, is a good lagoon with a hide. About 11 km farther, there is a right turn to Las Mesas. This road runs alongside Laguna de Manjavacas and several smaller lagoons.

The small lagoon outside Miguel Esteban is a SEO reserve, and has had breeding White-headed Ducks in recent years. This is reached just before the village, with access tracks on the left if coming from El Toboso.

The lagoon between Montalbo (on the NIII 30 km east of Tarancón) and El Hito a few kilometres to the west, can hold up to 10,000 Cranes in the

evenings in early and late winter, but these numbers are exceptional and highly influenced by rainfall, and a few hundred is more usual.

Many of the lagoons referred to in this section have hides, which are always locked. They can be used by prior arrangement by writing to the Cabañeros HQ (*see* below), but in most cases the lagoons can be viewed from public roads as well.

Accommodation is available in Mota del Cuervo, Alcázar and Daimiel.

CABAÑEROS
39°25N 04°20W

The Montes de Toledo are a densely vegetated, and virtually uninhabited, mountain range covering some 200,000 ha. There are extensive *dehesas* of evergreen oak, dense areas of cistus scrub and woods of several oak species and strawberry tree. A very wild place, with good populations of lynx, otter, roe deer and ichneumon. The *montes* are huge estates used for extensive livestock raising, traditional forestry and hunting.

The story of one such estate, Cabañeros, has passed into the legend of Spain's young conservation movement. Earmarked for years as a future bombing range, an unprecedented campaign culminated recently in its declaration as a National Park. Now the challenge is on to manage the area after years of neglect, for the benefit of its hundred pairs of Black Vultures, Spain's second largest colony. Throughout the *montes* there are also healthy populations of Black-shouldered Kites, Black Storks, White Storks, Booted, Short-toed, Spanish Imperial and Golden Eagles and Eagle Owls.

TIMING
Imperial Eagles are very noticeable when they display, during February and March. Late April to June is the best time for breeding birds, while winter is good for Cranes and the resident raptors.

SPECIES
◆ *Resident* Red and Black-shouldered Kites, Goshawk, Buzzard, Golden and Spanish Imperial Eagles, Griffon and Black Vultures, Great and Little Bustards, Eagle and Long-eared Owls, Hoopoe, Woodlark, Great Grey Shrike, Blue Rock Thrush, Dartford Warbler, Firecrest, Crested Tit, Cirl Bunting, Azure-winged Magpie.
◆ *Breeding season* White and Black Storks, Black Kite, Short-toed and Booted Eagles, Honey Buzzard, Egyptian Vulture, Montagu's Harrier, Hobby, Scops Owl, Bee-eater, Roller, Woodchat Shrike, Melodious, Spectacled and Bonelli's Warblers, Rufous Bushchat, Black-eared Wheatear, Golden Oriole.
◆ *Winter* Great Crested Grebe, Cormorant, Grey Heron, wildfowl, Hen Harrier, Peregrine, Merlin, Common Crane.

ACCESS
The information centre is at Pueblo Nuevo del Bullaque, off the C403 about 36 km south of Las Ventas. The park entrance itself is halfway along a local road linking the information centre with Santa Quiteria. Guided walks are offered by prior arrangement: independent birdwatching is limited to the (very good) areas outside the park and along the roads. The Park headquarters address is Alarcos 21, 13001 Ciudad Real.

Bearded Tit

Tablas de Daimiel

39°00N 03°45W

Tablas de Daimiel was first designated as a protected area in 1966, becoming a National Park in 1973. However, over the last 30 years *La Mancha Húmeda* has lost some 30,000 ha of water, due mainly to the unplanned and indiscriminate pumping of groundwater for irrigation. There have been subtle habitat changes, with the extensive sedge beds having been invaded by reeds, which are less dependent on regular flooding. Now the lost water is partly replaced by the diversion of a river into the park, and restrictions on irrigation may be compensated with European Union funds.

At its best, Las Tablas de Daimiel is a wetland of outstanding importance as a breeding ground for Little Bitterns, Purple Herons and Red-crested Pochard, and as a wintering ground for tens of thousands of ducks and large flocks of Cranes in winter. In the fields around the park there are still scattered populations of Little Bustards, Stone Curlews and Pin-tailed Sandgrouse.

TIMING

In spring and summer, it is advisable to check beforehand what the water levels are like; in winter this should be less of a problem, but be prepared for freezing temperatures.

SPECIES

◆ *Resident* Black-necked Grebe, Red-crested Pochard, Marsh Harrier, Little Bustard, Stone Curlew, Pin-tailed Sandgrouse, Hoopoe, Fan-tailed and Cetti's Warblers, Bearded and Penduline Tits.

◆ *Breeding season* Little Bittern, Night and Purple Herons, Little Egret, White Stork, Garganey, Black Kite, Short-toed and Booted Eagles, Montagu's Harrier, Lesser Kestrel, Black-winged Stilt, Pratincole, Whiskered Tern, Great Spotted Cuckoo, Scops Owl, Bee-eater, Roller, Wryneck, Short-toed Lark, Red-rumped Swallow, Tawny Pipit, Woodchat Shrike, Savi's, Great Reed and Melodious Warblers, Golden Oriole.

◆ *Passage* waders, Black Tern, Wryneck, Bluethroat, Black-eared Wheatear, warblers and flycatchers.

◆ *Winter* wildfowl, Hen Harrier, Peregrine, Short-eared Owl, Water Pipit.

ACCESS

Daimiel is at the intersection of the N420 and the N430, 29 km north-east of Ciudad Real. The National Park is signposted off the N430. There is an information centre (tel. 926 852058), trails and hides, including an impressive multi-storey tower hide in the National Park. The park closes on Mondays and late visitors may be turned away on busy weekends. There is good, inexpensive accommodation in Daimiel town.

LOS CANALIZOS AND SACERUELA

38°50N 04°30W

A wide plain with small mountains rising to 884 m and abundant *dehesa*, to the south of the Montes de Toledo and immediately north of the next site. The area is sparsely populated and therefore still harbours a few lynx. Bird interest includes about 20 pairs of Black Vultures and three pairs each of Golden and Spanish Imperial Eagles.

Small estate roads and tracks penetrate the area from the encircling roads which link (anticlockwise) Almadén, Abenója, Luciana, Puebla de Don Rodrigo (the last two on the N430), Agudo and on down the N502 back to Almadén. Most of the estate roads seem to lead to Saceruela at the hub of the area.

VALLE Y SIERRA DE ALCUDIA

38°40N 04°30W

A wide, grassy valley surrounded by hills, to the north of the Sierra Madrona. The N420 crosses the area and a road turns off westwards towards some lead mines at Bienvenida. This is a useful detour *en route* between Tablas de Daimiel and the Sierra Morena. From this road a careful scan should reveal winter flocks of Little Bustards, Crane and Golden Plovers. Both sandgrouse are present. In spring and summer they, along with some 100 pairs of Little Bustards, stay to breed and are joined by several pairs of Montagu's Harriers. The N420 then runs into extensive oak scrub and dehesa with Black-shouldered Kites, Black Vultures and Spanish Imperial Eagles. Various forest tracks and minor roads penetrate the woods either side of Puerto de Niefla.

SOUTHERN SPAIN AND GIBRALTAR

SOUTHERN SPAIN
WITH GIBRALTAR

PORTUGAL

EXTREMADURA

TALAVÁN
EMBALSE DE ALCÁNTARA
MONFRAGÜE
CÁCERES TO THE PORTUGUESE BORDER
SIERRAS DE LAS VILLUERCAS
CÁCERES
THE INTERNATIONAL TAJO
CÁCERES-TRUJILLO PLAINS
TRUJILLO AREA
CÁCERES TO MÉRIDA
SIERRA DE SAN PEDRO
BADAJOZ
LA SERENA
BADAJOZ BORDERLANDS
SOUTHERN BADAJOZ
JERÉZ DE LOS CABALLEROS
SIERRA MORENA (EAST)
SIERRA DE CAZORLA
SIERRA MORENA (WEST)
ANDALUCÍA
CÓRDOBA
SOUTH CÓRDOBA WETLANDS
SOUTH-EASTERN STEPPES
AYAMONTE AND PIEDRAS MARSHES
HUELVA MARSHES
SEVILLA
UTRERA, LAS CABEZAS AND ESPERA LAGOONS
FUENTE DE PIEDRA
GRANADA
SIERRA NEVADA
SIERRA ALHAMILLA-CAMPO DE NIJAR
DOÑANA
RONDA AND GRAZALEMA
GUADALQUIVIR LEFT BANK
CABO DE GATA
BAHÍA DE CÁDIZ
MÁLAGA
ROQUETAS DE MAR
LAGOONS OF CADIZ AND JERÉZ
LOS ALCORNOCALES
Atlantic Ocean
TARIFA AND LA JANDA
GIBRALTAR
Mediterranean Sea

N

The *dehesas* of Extremadura have been likened to African savannah. These are open tracts of woodland, usually of either holm or cork oak. They are managed traditionally for their cork, charcoal, forage, firewood and shelter. Between the trees a crop of barley may be grown every few years, rotating with fallow and grazing. Even the acorns are put to good use, as pig forage and in making the traditional *licor de bellota*. The vast *dehesas* are of exceptional importance for birds and other wildlife.

Andalucía is the hot, bright, lively southern extreme of Europe. There are the high *sierras* of Cazorla and Nevada, and wetlands. The Guadalquivir marshes (Coto Doñana) rank as one of the great bird areas of Europe, but the other coastal marshes and the dozens of scattered lagoons of Andalucía add considerably to this ornithological richness.

There are daily flights into southern Spain from most European capitals. Seville, Almería and Málaga are the main entry points, with hundreds of charter and package deals available for Málaga. Gibraltar is well connected to London and is an alternative approach to the south, as is Faro on the Algarve.

BIRDWATCHING SITES

MONFRAGÜE

39°40N 05°45W

If you wanted to design a natural park which combined the best of Extremadura's habitats, contained plenty of its typical plants and animals and was readily accessible, you could not improve on the Natural Park of Monfragüe. Here is some of the best *dehesa* in Spain, some truly natural Mediterranean scrub, rocky hills and woods.

It may be the best area in the world for the globally threatened Black Vulture, with nearly 150 pairs. There is also a big colony of Griffon Vultures and several pairs of Egyptian. One of the big attractions is Peñafalcón, a great rock rising out of the Torrejón reservoir. You can park opposite and watch a

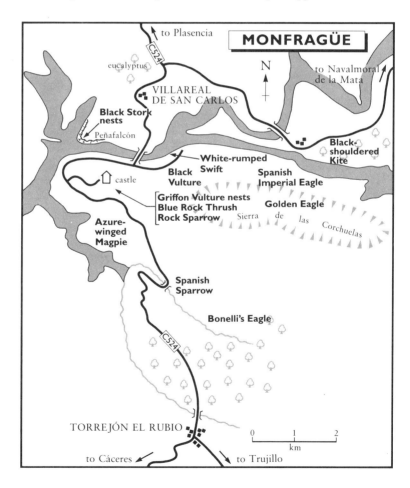

SOUTHERN SPAIN AND GIBRALTAR

colony of Griffons coming and going, Peregrines, Choughs, Blue Rock
Thrushes, Rock Buntings and Rock Sparrows. Perhaps the prize bird here is
the Black Stork, which nests on the rock across the river, low enough for the
chicks to be seen from the road. Less easily seen, but present in good numbers
in the *dehesa*, is the Black-shouldered Kite, while some eight pairs of Spanish
Imperial Eagles make this one of the world strongholds of the species. The
raptor list does not end there, and Golden, Bonelli's and, especially, Booted
Eagles can be found.

In recent years, a small population of White-rumped Swifts, a species
which has spread to Spain from tropical Africa since the mid-1960s, has
colonized in the area around Puente del Cardenal.

TIMING
Monfragüe is interesting all year round, but Extremaduran temperatures can
soar to 45 °C in July and August, even in these hills. Black Storks arrive in
March and congregate in post-breeding flocks in July and August before
leaving for the south.

SPECIES
◆ *Resident* Red and Black-shouldered Kites, Goshawk, Buzzard, Spanish
  Imperial, Golden and Bonelli's Eagles, Griffon and Black Vultures,
  Peregrine, Rock Dove, Eagle and Long-eared Owls, Hoopoe, Woodlark,
  Thekla Lark, Great Grey Shrike, Blue Rock Thrush, Black Wheatear,
  Sardinian and Dartford Warblers, Firecrest, Crested Tit, Spanish and Rock
  Sparrows, Rock and Cirl Buntings, Azure-winged Magpie.
◆ *Breeding season* White and Black Storks, Black Kite, Short-toed and
  Booted Eagles, Honey Buzzard, Egyptian Vulture, Montagu's Harrier,
  Hobby, Scops Owl, Bee-eater, Roller, White-rumped Swift, Red-rumped
  Swallow, Woodchat Shrike, Orphean, Spectacled and Bonelli's Warblers,
  Rufous Bushchat, Black-eared Wheatear, Golden Oriole.
◆ *Winter* Great Crested Grebe, Cormorant, Grey Heron, wildfowl, Hen
  Harrier, Common Crane, Alpine Accentor.

ACCESS
Both the castle and Peñafalcón are just off the C524 Plasencia–Trujillo road.
In Villareal de San Carlos there is an information centre and bar. Just north
of the village a road runs east to join with the C511. This can be rewarding,
too. Accommodation can be found nearby in Torrejón el Rubio. However,
since both Trujillo and Plasencia are beautiful old towns, with plenty of bird
interest in themselves, it is worth using either as a base.

EMBALSE DE ALCÁNTARA
39°45N 06°30W
Just upstream of the Portuguese border, the river Tajo meets a dam at the
historic town of Alcántara and rises up its steep banks to flood one of the
largest reservoirs in Europe. Alcántara itself is an elegant town, with many
superb buildings perched over the Tajo. It has a thriving population of White
Storks, with over 20 nests on the church alone. Lesser Kestrels inhabit many
of the buildings.

Much of the surrounding habitat is *dehesa*, with Black-shouldered Kites,
Black Kites, Booted Eagles, Black Vultures and Spanish Imperial Eagles. The

cliffs at the edges of the reservoir hold important populations of Black Storks, Egyptian Vultures, Griffon Vultures and Peregrines. In the grasslands interspersed among the *dehesa* landscape Little Bustards may be found.

TIMING
White Storks are back at Alcántara by New Year, followed in February by Lesser Kestrels, as the Cranes begin to leave.
SPECIES
♦ *Resident* Red and Black-shouldered Kites, Goshawk, Buzzard, Spanish Imperial Eagle, Griffon and Black Vultures, Peregrine, Eagle and Long-eared Owls, Hoopoe, Woodlark, Great Grey Shrike, Blue Rock Thrush, Sardinian and Dartford Warblers, Firecrest, Crested Tit, Spanish and Rock Sparrows, Rock and Cirl Buntings, Azure-winged Magpie.
♦ *Breeding season* White and Black Storks, Black Kite, Short-toed and Booted Eagles, Honey Buzzard, Egyptian Vulture, Montagu's Harrier, Hobby, Scops Owl, Bee-eater, Roller, Red-rumped Swallow, Woodchat Shrike, Spectacled and Bonelli's Warblers, Black-eared Wheatear.
♦ *Winter* Great Crested Grebe, Cormorant, Grey Heron, wildfowl, Golden and Bonelli's Eagles, Hen Harrier, Common Crane.
ACCESS
Alcántara is 48 km north-west of Cáceres and 75 km east of Castelo Branco in Portugal. The area immediately south-east of the town, on the side road between Villa del Rey and Mata de Alcántara, is outstanding, as is the road from Cáceres. From Alcántara north to Coria the road passes through almost uninhabited grasslands and *dehesa*. The C526 to Coria from Cáceres via the N630 is particularly good. About 8 km south of Coria a road leads west to Ceclavín and on to the reservoir opposite Alcántara. Roads and tracks leading right from this road run towards the Alagón arm of the reservoir. North of Coria on the C526 is the Sierra de Gata (page 71).

TALAVÁN
39°40N 06°20W
South and east of the Alcántara reservoir is an interesting plains area to the north of Cáceres, with cereals and *dehesas*. By driving the roads between Monroy, Santiago del Campo, Hinojal and, especially, Talaván, Great and Little Bustards, Black-bellied and Pin-tailed Sandgrouse can be seen all year round. There are tracks off these roads into the estates and it is advisable to ask permission to drive them. In winter, Cranes feed in the *dehesas* north of Monroy, where in spring there are Black-shouldered Kites. A good spot for this species is north of Monroy. It is reached by turning right at the T-junction onto the Cáceres–Monfragüe road. After 2.7 km a track on the right leads into a cultivated area where the kites can sometimes be seen. The small reservoir south of Talaván is worth exploring on foot.

SIERRAS DE LAS VILLUERCAS
39°40N 05°25W
The picturesque and historic town of Guadalupe is set in mountainous country between the Montes de Toledo to the east and Trujillo to the west. The hills around the town are folded into narrow, parallel ranges with steep

Orphean Warbler (male)

valleys. Lynx still roam the dense scrub and oak woods that cloak their slopes, and wildcat and otter further attest to their wildness. There is thus a characteristic selection of birds of prey, with Spanish Imperial Eagles and Black-shouldered Kites particularly noteworthy. Black Storks are also relatively common.

TIMING
Spanish Imperial Eagles are most noticeable in February and March when they are displaying, before the summer raptors arrive: Black Kite in March, Short-toed and Booted Eagles in April and Honey Buzzards in late April and May.

SPECIES
- *Resident* Cattle and Little Egrets, Red and Black-shouldered Kites, Goshawk, Buzzard, Spanish Imperial, Golden and Bonelli's Eagles, Griffon and Black Vultures, Peregrine, Eagle and Long-eared Owls, Hoopoe, Woodlark, Great Grey Shrike, Dipper, Blue Rock Thrush, Sardinian and Dartford Warblers, Firecrest, Crested Tit, Spanish and Rock Sparrows, Rock and Cirl Buntings, Azure-winged Magpie.
- *Breeding season* White and Black Storks, Black Kite, Short-toed and Booted Eagles, Honey Buzzard, Egyptian Vulture, Hobby, Scops Owl, Red-necked Nightjar, Great Spotted Cuckoo, Bee-eater, Roller, Orphean and Bonelli's Warblers, Black-eared Wheatear, Golden Oriole.
- *Winter* Common Crane.

ACCESS
The area is crossed by two main roads, the C401 from the Castilla–La Mancha boundary through Guadalupe to Zorita (below); and the NV Navalmoral–Trujillo road. The best roads for exploring the area unite these two main east–west routes: from Guadalupe north to Castañar and Navalmoral; from Cañamero or Logrosán north to the Puerto de Miravete and so on. This last site, on the main NV, is an excellent migration watchpoint. A road west from Berzocana to Madroñera and Trujillo passes through unbroken *dehesa*.

TRUJILLO AREA
39°30N 05°50W

Trujillo is a beautiful, walled, hilltop town with plenty of accommodation and good food. The main square is the best place in Spain, perhaps the world, for watching Lesser Kestrels. In April and May it is not unusual to see a hundred or more wheeling about over the town. The world population of Lesser Kestrel has plummeted. In Spain, there remain around 5000 pairs, a catastrophic decline from some 100,000 birds at the end of the 1960s.

The Lesser Kestrels feed over the plains around the town where there is a very healthy population of Montagu's Harriers and both bustards. The C524 towards Monfragüe and Plasencia passes through superb *dehesa* with several pairs of Black Storks in summer and feeding Cranes in winter. The busy NV north of Trujillo, and the local road to Torrecillas, pass through good raptor habitat, and the reservoirs west of Torrecillas are worth exploring for Black Storks. Close to Trujillo, there is a right turn towards Belén, from which a track crosses the plains. Frequent scanning should enable bustards and sandgrouse to be seen. ADENEX has an information centre in Belén.

The C524 south-east from Trujillo has a high density of birds of prey, especially the stretch from Zorita to Madrigalejo. Short-toed Eagles are particularly common. Great and Little Bustards, Pin-tailed and Black-bellied Sandgrouse can be seen from this stretch, just south of Zorita, where also Pratincoles breed and Cranes winter.

CÁCERES–TRUJILLO PLAINS
39°25N 06°10W

The wide, undulating grazing plains of Cáceres province may appear empty and monotonous as you drive along the fast N521 road from Trujillo. In fact, they rank among the most important bird areas of Spain. Some 25,000 ha of grassland, cereals and garrigue (lavender scrub) are home to around 1000 Great Bustards and maybe twice as many Little Bustards.

There are important numbers of other grassland species, too. In summer over 100 pairs of Stone Curlew and at least 50 each of the two sandgrouse share the plains with the two big insectivores: Lesser Kestrels, on their feeding forays from the colonies in Cáceres and Trujillo, and Rollers. Small groups of Cranes can be seen from November to February.

TIMING
In winter, the birds will be in flocks. In spring it is a matter of scanning with a telescope for fluffy bundles of white feathers – displaying male Great Bustards, or listening for the 'raspberry' call of the Little Bustards.

SPECIES
- *Resident* Red Kite, Buzzard, Great and Little Bustards, Stone Curlew, Pin-tailed and Black-bellied Sandgrouse, Dupont's and Calandra Larks, Great Grey Shrike, Azure-winged Magpie.
- *Breeding season* White Stork, Black Kite, Montagu's Harrier, Lesser Kestrel, Red-necked Nightjar, Bee-eater, Roller, Hoopoe, Tawny Pipit, Spectacled Warbler.
- *Winter* Cormorant, Grey Heron, wildfowl, Hen Harrier, Griffon and Black Vultures, Peregrine, Merlin, Common Crane, Golden Plover, Lapwing.

ACCESS
A short road turns north off the N521 about 7 km east of Cáceres leading to a reservoir. This road often turns up Great Bustards, Calandra Larks and Spanish Sparrows. The C912 towards Monfragüe leads, after 10 km, to a right turn to Casa de Figueroba. This road crosses excellent bustard habitat.

CÁCERES TO MÉRIDA
39°20N 06°20W
Between Cáceres and Mérida lies a 68-km stretch of busy road, the N630 which crosses some outstanding *dehesa* where Black Storks and Black-shouldered Kites breed and Cranes winter. Around 20 km south of Cáceres is the Río Salor plain, which stretches to the Sierra de San Pedro (page 96). There are good numbers of Great and Little Bustards, Pin-tailed Sandgrouse and Montagu's Harriers here.

A few kilometres south-east of Cáceres is the Sierra de Fuentes, where Booted and Short-toed Eagles can be found in summer. In the Sierra de Montánchez, east of the main highway, there is a good selection of raptors and, in the village of Arroyomolinos, several nests of White-rumped Swifts.

Mérida's fame rests largely in its impressive Roman remains, including a well-preserved amphitheatre. The Guadiana river in Mérida has a roost of Cattle Egrets, and there are usually Golden Orioles singing from the nearby poplars. Near the village of Trujillanos is the Cornalvo Natural Park. This is some 11,000 ha of *dehesa* around a small Roman reservoir. Two pairs of Black Storks breed, and there are up to 20 in the post-breeding period. Black-shouldered Kites and Honey Buzzards are relatively common and there is a very dense population of Montagu's Harriers to the south.

TIMING
There is no shortage of interest in all months of the year, although April–June are the best months overall.
SPECIES
◆ *Resident* Cattle and Little Egrets, Grey Heron, Red and Black-shouldered Kites, Goshawk, Buzzard, Spanish Imperial Eagle, Griffon and Black Vultures, Great and Little Bustards, Eagle and Long-eared Owls, Hoopoe, Woodlark, Great Grey Shrike, Sardinian and Dartford Warblers, Firecrest, Crested and Penduline Tits, Cirl Bunting, Azure-winged Magpie.
◆ *Breeding season* White and Black Storks, Night Heron, Black Kite, Short-toed and Booted Eagles, Honey Buzzard, Egyptian Vulture, Montagu's Harrier, Hobby, Scops Owl, Bee-eater, Roller, Woodchat Shrike, Great Reed, Melodious, Spectacled and Bonelli's Warblers, Black-eared Wheatear, Golden Oriole.
◆ *Winter* Hen Harrier, Peregrine, Common Crane.
ACCESS
The track heading west from Valdesalor to the railway line and the road west from Aldea del Cano afford good opportunities to explore the Río Salor plains. A minor road running north-east from Aldea crosses a well-preserved region on the south bank of the Salor reservoir with a healthy population of Pratincoles, Little Bustards and Black-bellied Sandgrouse. The Cornalvo Natural Park is 16 km east of Mérida.

CÁCERES TO THE PORTUGUESE BORDER
39°40N 06°50W

West of Cáceres is an interesting area, with the villages of Malpartida and Arroyo de la Luz at its centre. A small reservoir north of Arroyo de la Luz has a large (2000 pairs) Cattle Egret colony and a good population of Red-necked Nightjars around about. This is reached by taking the C523 north of the village and turning right along a track after 2.5 km. There are several hundred Little Bustards and Stone Curlews in the area and 50 or so pairs each of the two sandgrouse. There is an interesting colony of White Storks on rocks at the Barruecos lagoons south of Malpartida.

Around the village of Brozas, is a wide plain of some 85,000 ha with grasslands, cereal cultivation and extensive *dehesas*. It is an exceptionally important area for steppe birds, including around 50 pairs of Montagu's Harriers, a thousand Great Bustards, 1000 pairs of Stone Curlew and 500 pairs each of the two sandgrouse. There is also a heronry, with 85 pairs of Grey Herons, and Black Storks and raptors breed in the *dehesas*. Cranes spend the winter under the oaks. This area, which is immediately south of the Alcántara reservoir (*see* page 91), is crossed by the C523, which passes by some of the winter lagoons. The roads and tracks running south into the plains from Brozas are best. Brozas itself has an important population of White Storks (44 pairs in 1989), and one of the largest known Lesser Kestrel colonies, with over 70 pairs.

SIERRA DE SAN PEDRO
39°20N 06°45W

The Sierra de San Pedro, stretches from south of Cáceres to the Serra de São Mamede in Portugal (page 171). The area contains some of the best Mediterranean forest, with woods and *dehesas* of holm and cork oak, scrublands of *Cistus*, French lavender and strawberry tree and grasslands. The presence of Spanish lynx in one of its world strongholds owes much to the sparseness of the human population.

There are dozens of pairs of Black-shouldered Kites, at least 100 pairs of Black Kite; 60 pairs of Black Vulture and several Egyptian; eight pairs of Spanish Imperial Eagle, several pairs of Golden and Bonelli's, and no fewer than 50 pairs of Booted Eagles.

TIMING
Of year-round interest. Black Storks tend to congregate in July at the small reservoirs such as the *embalses* of Rincón de Ballesteros and Peña del Águila.

SPECIES
◆ *Resident* Red and Black-shouldered Kites, Buzzard, Black and Griffon Vultures, Spanish Imperial, Golden and Bonelli's Eagles, Goshawk, Sparrowhawk, Peregrine, Eagle Owl, Hoopoe, Thekla Lark, Great Grey Shrike, Blue Rock Thrush, Dartford Warbler, Azure-winged Magpie, Chough, Rock and Spanish Sparrows, Rock Bunting.
◆ *Breeding season* White and Black Storks, Black Kite, Honey Buzzard, Booted and Short-toed Eagles, Egyptian Vulture, Hobby, Lesser Kestrel, Red-necked Nightjar, Great spotted Cuckoo, Bee-eater, Roller, Red-rumped Swallow, Spectacled and Subalpine Warblers, Black-eared Wheatear.

Houbara Bustard

Little Shearwater

Bulwer's Petrel

Cream-coloured Courser

Blue Chaffinch

Barbary Falcon

White-tailed Pigeon

Canary Islands Chat

Madeiran Laurel Pigeon

Bolle's Pigeon

Crag Martin

Red-rumped
Swallow

Alpine Accentor

Subalpine Warbler

Olivaceous
Warbler

Marmora's
Warbler

Moustached Warbler

Spectacled
Warbler

Rock Thrush

Blue Rock Thrush

Black-
eared
Wheatear

Black
Wheatear

Trumpeter Finch

Citril Finch

Rock Bunting

Chough

Alpine Chough

Wallcreeper

Azure-winged
Magpie

Bee-eater

Hoopoe

Scops Owl

Roller

White-
rumped
Swift

Red-necked
Nightjar

Lesser Short-
toed Lark

Black
Woodpecker

Thekla Lark

Dupont's
Lark

Montagu's Harrier

Lesser Kestrel

Little Bustard

Great Bustard

Red-crested Pochard

Stone Curlew

Purple Gallinule

White-headed Duck

Crested Coot

Marbled Teal

Black-
shouldered
Kite

Black Kite

Red Kite

Spanish
Imperial Eagle

Booted Eagle

Bonelli's
Eagle

Egyptian Vulture

Black Vulture

Lammergeier

Griffon
Vulture

Avocet

Black-winged Stilt

Slender-billed
Gull

Audouin's Gull

Whiskered
Tern

Gull-billed Tern

Black-bellied
Sandgrouse

Pin-tailed
Sandgrouse

Eagle Owl

Great Spotted
Cuckoo

Little Egret

Purple Heron

Cory's
Shearwater

Squacco Heron

Spoonbill

White Stork

Glossy Ibis

Crane

Flamingo

Black Stork

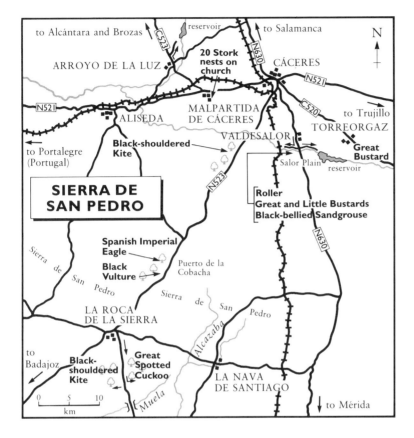

ACCESS

From Cáceres the N523 highway to Badajoz crosses the eastern end of the *sierra*, through almost continuous *dehesa*. Roads off into the area are few, but those that exist are definitely worth exploring, such as at Puebla de Obando, 45 km south of Cáceres. The road between La Roca de la Sierra and Montijo crosses Black-shouldered Kite country, about 10 km south of La Roca.

The Cáceres–Portalegre (Portugal) road forms the northern edge of the area, before crossing into the *sierras* towards Valencia de Alcántara. Some 30 km from Cáceres, at Aliseda, C521 cuts into the area. This road forks left towards Villar del Rey or right to the attractive hilltop fort town of Albuquerque. Either alternative is excellent. From Albuquerque to Valencia is another good road. There is accommodation at Albuquerque as well as at Valencia, Portalegre and, of course, Cáceres.

THE INTERNATIONAL TAJO

39°40N 07°20W

Several parts of the Spain/Portugal border run along portions of rivers. The international Duero was dealt with in the last chapter and now it is the turn of a rather better-known example, called in Spanish the Tajo or in Portuguese, the Tejo. We usually know it by its Roman name, the Tagus.

The Tajo at this point is not a river but a long, thin reservoir, like so many Spanish rivers in so many places. Its banks are steep with occasional cliffs. The vegetation along the river comprises typical Mediterranean scrub, with French lavender and holly oak, *dehesas* of cork and holm oak, and olive groves. This is one of the most important areas in western Europe for Black Stork, with at least ten pairs. Birds of prey are well represented, too, with a colony of Griffon Vultures, several pairs of Black-shouldered Kites, Bonelli's Eagles and Peregrines and plenty of Eagle Owls. The owls are hard to spot during the day, but a scan of the cliffs along the reservoir may reveal a roosting bird. Otherwise, listen for their low hooting call after dark.

TIMING
Black Storks and Egyptian Vultures arrive in mid–late March, when nesting is underway for the Griffons, Bonelli's Eagles and Eagle Owls. Ospreys pass through at this time, and have stayed all summer. White Storks arrive and leave early: February and late July respectively.

SPECIES
◆ *Resident*: Great Crested Grebe, Grey Heron, Red and Black-shouldered Kites, Buzzard, Griffon Vulture, Golden and Bonelli's Eagles, Goshawk, Sparrowhawk, Peregrine, Eagle Owl, Hoopoe, Thekla Lark, Grey Wagtail, Great Grey Shrike, Blue Rock Thrush, Black Wheatear, Dartford Warbler, Azure-winged Magpie, Chough, Rock and Spanish Sparrows, Rock Bunting.
◆ *Breeding season* White and Black Storks, Black Kite, Booted and Short-toed Eagles, Egyptian Vulture, Hobby, Lesser Kestrel, Little Ringed Plover, Red-necked Nightjar, Alpine Swift, Bee-eater, Roller, Red-rumped Swallow, Subalpine Warbler, Black-eared Wheatear, Rufous Bushchat.
◆ *Passage* Osprey.

ACCESS
The only road which crosses this part of the river is at Alcántara (*see* also page 91), which is not actually on the border. Between here and the border is an area of low hills and *dehesa* that is often rewarding. North of Alcántara is Zarza la Mayor, close to the Río Erjas, an international tributary of the Tajo. The Peñafiel reserve to the west, managed by ADENEX, is good. A road runs south-west from Alcántara (take a right turn off the C523 6 km south of the town) to Membrío. From Membrío one can either turn left to the main N521, or right to Santiago de Alcántara, following the southern boundary of the IBA. In Santiago there is another choice, a small local road that short-cuts across the area towards the Herrera road, or a dog-leg of some 26 km to the same point. Either way, from here to Herrera de Alcántara is an excellent route and very scenic; it eventually leads to the junction of the rivers Tajo and Sever. This road can be reached via the N521 at Casa del Empalme.
Access details are given for the Portuguese side on page 170.

BADAJOZ BORDERLANDS
38°48N 07°08W
The area south of Badajoz, close to the Portuguese border, is one of the most intact expanses of *dehesa* in the whole peninsula. The triangular area between Badajoz in the north and stretching from the Portuguese border east to Zafra is a fascinating mixture of dense stands of holm oak and dry plains. The area

Alpine Swift

north of Olivenza and east of Albalá is outstanding for Little Bustards: 100 breeding pairs with numbers swelling to 3000 in winter. Olivenza and the area on this east bank of the Guadiana changed hands between Spain and Portugal several times. This has kept the area relatively sparsely populated, even by Extremaduran standards.

The central portion of this site is important for breeding Black-shouldered Kites and wintering Cranes in the *dehesa*, and has a good range of grassland birds: 500 Great Bustards, 200 pairs of Little Bustards and a high density of Montagu's Harriers, both sandgrouse, and Stone Curlew. There is another important breeding ground for Great Bustards to the east, the Tierra de los Barros, around the town of Villalba de los Barros.

TIMING
The grassland birds congregate in flocks between August and late February. March to May finds them displaying and nesting, as the *dehesas* liven up with the arrival of summer raptors and passerines. Cranes arrive in November.
SPECIES
- *Resident* Red and Black-shouldered Kites, Buzzard, Great and Little Bustards, Stone Curlew, Pin-tailed and Black-bellied Sandgrouse, Calandra Lark, Great Grey Shrike, Azure-winged Magpie, Cirl Bunting.
- *Breeding season* White Stork, Black Kite, Montagu's Harrier, Lesser Kestrel, Red-necked Nightjar, Bee-eater, Roller, Hoopoe, Tawny Pipit, Orphean Warbler.
- *Winter* Griffon and Black Vultures, Peregrine, Merlin, Common Crane, Golden Plover, Lapwing.
ACCESS
From Badajoz, any of the roads radiating south afford access to some part of this area. The C436 leads to Olivenza; after about 12 km a right turn leads to Albalá through good Little Bustard country. From Olivenza a road runs north-west to the river Guadiana and the Portuguese border through prime habitat.

The C423 from Olivenza to Almendral via Valverde is good; Valverde can also be reached by driving south from Badajoz through 25 km of *dehesa* and farmland. The N432 leads to La Albuera and, after 46 km to Santa Marta. The roads between here and Villalba de Los Barros are good for bustards.

DEHESAS OF JERÉZ DE LOS CABALLEROS
38°15N 06°50W

The vast oak groves around Jeréz de los Caballeros hold a healthy population of Booted Eagle, Black Kite and Azure-winged Magpie. Jeréz itself is an attractive little town with a few pairs of Lesser Kestrels in the three interesting churches.

The N435 between Barcarrota and Jeréz runs through undulating land where the oak cover is very dense. To the north-west, a minor road runs to the Portuguese border at Cheles, via Villanueva del Fresno. This and another road from here back to Barcarrota encircle the most interesting area. Short-toed Eagles, Black-shouldered Kites, and, in more open country, Great and Little Bustards, Pratincoles and Stone Curlews are all plentiful. Another circular route of around 60 km takes in Jeréz, Burgillos del Cerro along the C4311, thence to Salvatierra de los Barros to the north and back to Jeréz along a minor road. There are three good *hostales* in Jeréz.

From Villanueva it is a short drive across the border to Mourão (page 180).

LA SERENA
38°50N 05°30W

Among the most important areas in the world for grassland birds, this vast 100,000 ha plain is a must for any Extremaduran itinerary. There may be as many as 20,000 Little Bustards here, with 4000 recorded in a single winter flock. Some 500 together is not at all unusual. There are hundreds of Great Bustards and in summer Montagu's Harrier is abundant.

Black-bellied and, especially, Pin-tailed Sandgrouse are common. There is a good wintering population of Stone Curlew, many of which stay to breed, and of Golden Plovers and Lapwings, visitors from the north.

Between November and February, it is worth getting up at first light to witness a spectacular flypast of Cranes from their roost at the Zújar and Orellana reservoirs to their feeding ground in the *dehesas* to the south. A good vantage point is at the radar station about 9 km east of Castuera near Puerto Mejoral. A path leads to the top of the rocks above the road. The Cranes pass low overhead, provided observers keep below the skyline. The return flight at dusk is equally spectacular. This area is rather scrubby, and has a good population of Dartford and Sardinian Warblers.

TIMING

Winter is the best time to see large numbers of bustards, Stone Curlews, Cranes and small birds. Spring is also excellent, with the arrival of Lesser Kestrels and Montagu's Harriers. Rollers appear from late April.

SPECIES

◆ *Resident* Great Crested Grebe, Black-shouldered Kite, Buzzard, Great and Little Bustards, Stone Curlew, Pin-tailed and Black-bellied Sandgrouse, Short-toed, Dupont's and Calandra Larks, Great Grey Shrike.

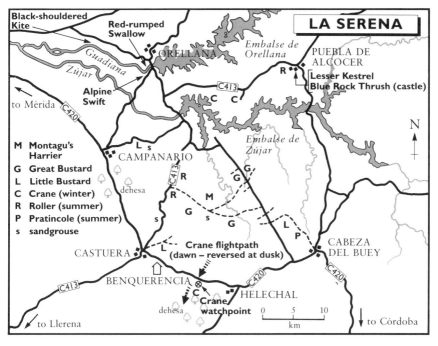

- *Breeding season* White Stork, Black Kite, Montagu's Harrier, Lesser Kestrel, Pratincole, Red-necked Nightjar, Bee-eater, Roller, Hoopoe, Tawny Pipit, Spectacled Warbler, Black-eared Wheatear.
- *Winter* Cormorant, Grey Heron, wildfowl, Hen Harrier, Griffon and Black Vultures, Peregrine, Merlin, Common Crane, Golden Plover, Lapwing, Meadow Pipit.

ACCESS
There are good roads from which to explore La Serena but if possible it is best to come off the tarmac. Signs denoting private hunting estates, *Coto Privado de Caza*, do not imply that entry is barred, but it is advisable to pass the time of day with anyone who looks like they own the place. The C413 from Castuera to Puebla de Alcocer is good, and has Roller nestboxes along much of its length. Tracks which cut east from this road afford excellent birdwatching. Inexpensive accommodation is available at Castuera.

SOUTHERN BADAJOZ
38°20N 05°40W
The area between Castuera on the edge of La Serena, south to Llerena and the Sierra Morena is a wonderfully scenic blend of *dehesa*, grassland and low *sierras*. The Sierra Grande de Hornachos supports an interesting raptor population, including a few pairs of Egyptian Vultures, Spanish Imperial Eagles, Golden and Bonelli's Eagles and a pair or two of Black Storks.

To the east, between Campillo de Llerena and Peraleda de Zaucejo, the land is gently undulating cereal fields and scattered pockets of *dehesa*. Cranes feed under the oaks and in the fields in winter, and both Great and Little Bustards and Pin-tailed Sandgrouse are present all year.

TIMING

Little Bustard flocks may number between 500 and 1000 from October to February. Black Storks and Egyptian Vultures arrive in mid-March; Montagu's Harrier a week or so later.

SPECIES

◆ *Resident* Red and Black-shouldered Kites, Buzzard, Spanish Imperial, Golden and Bonelli's Eagles, Griffon Vulture, Peregrine, Little Bustard, Stone Curlew, Pin-tailed and Black-bellied Sandgrouse, Eagle Owl, Calandra Lark, Great Grey Shrike, Azure-winged Magpie, Cirl Bunting.

◆ *Breeding season* White and Black Storks, Black Kite, Short-toed and Booted Eagles, Montagu's Harrier, Egyptian Vulture, Lesser Kestrel, Bee-eater, Roller, Hoopoe, Tawny Pipit, Rufous Bushchat, Orphean Warbler.

◆ *Winter* Hen Harrier, Peregrine, Merlin, Common Crane, Golden Plover.

ACCESS

Some 42 km south of Castuera is Campillo de Llerena. The fields immediately past the village on the Peraleda and Azuaga roads are very good for Cranes and bustards in winter. There is an information centre for the Sierra Grande in Hornachos, on the left about 200 m past the main crossroads on the road to Puebla de la Reina. This is usually open in the mornings when the Extremaduran group ADENEX can provide maps and information on the *sierra*.

The C413 leads on to Llerena, from where the N432 leads to Azuaga, 28 km to the east, so a profitable circular route is possible. The area around Ahillones is particularly good for grassland species. Accommodation is available in Llerena and Castuera.

SIERRA MORENA (WEST)

37°50N 06°00W

The Sierra Morena forms the boundary between Extremadura and Andalucía and stretches from the Portuguese border towards the city of Jaén, a distance of around 300 km. The westernmost set of hills are the Picos de Aroche, on the border with Portugal. The most important population of Black Vultures in Andalucía, around 30 pairs, is found here, along with a pair of Spanish Imperial Eagles. Farther east, in Sevilla province, the hills are more rugged, with steep valleys in which Griffon Vultures and a good selection of raptors nest.

TIMING

Morena is good for raptors all year round. In winter, Black and Griffon Vultures range widely and may be found throughout the range. Black Storks may arrive as early as the first week in March.

SPECIES

◆ *Resident* Red Kite, Goshawk, Buzzard, Spanish Imperial, Golden and Bonelli's Eagles, Griffon and Black Vultures, Peregrine, Eagle and Long-eared Owls, Hoopoe, Woodlark, Great Grey Shrike, Blue Rock Thrush, Black Wheatear, Dartford Warbler, Firecrest, Crested Tit, Hawfinch, Azure-winged Magpie.

◆ *Breeding season* White and Black Storks, Black Kite, Short-toed and Booted Eagles, Honey Buzzard, Scops Owl, Bee-eater, Roller, Woodchat Shrike, Orphean and Bonelli's Warblers, Rufous Bushchat, Black-eared Wheatear, Golden Oriole.

ACCESS
The Picos de Aroche and Sierra de Aracena are crossed by the N433 and
N435. A good circular route would be the N435 northwards from Zalamea
la Real, turning right after 30 km to Aracena. A right turn just inside Aracena
leads, after 33 km to a junction. Another right leads back to Zalamea.

For the Sierra Norte de Sevilla a good area is found farther west along the
N433, or along the N630 Seville–Zafra highway. Between El Ronquillo and
Santa Olalla del Cala there are roads leading east to Almadén de la Plata.
From here the minor road which runs north and then east to Cazalla de la
Sierra is good, as is the C433 between Cazalla and El Pedroso to the south.

SIERRA MORENA (EAST)
38°00N 05°15W
The Sierra Morena of Córdoba province is of great interest, with over 20
pairs of Black Vulture, 75 pairs of Griffon and a dozen or so pairs each of
Golden and Bonelli's Eagles. There is a newly created Natural Park there, the
Sierra de Hornachuelos. This is north of the C431: 45 km west of Córdoba,
near Palma del Río, is a turn to Hornachuelos village. From here there is a
spectacular 74-km circuit via San Calixto and Navas de la Concepción. All
along this road are tracks leading off left and right, which reward exploring
on foot.

Still more to the east the Sierra Madrona, in the provinces of Ciudad Real
and Jaén, has a similar range of species as well as a few pairs of Black Storks.
The eastern end of the Sierra Morena also includes the Sierras de Cardeña y
Montoro and Andújar. The minor road which runs south from Puertollano to
Andújar is an ideal route across the mountains.

SIERRA DE CAZORLA
38°00N 02°40W
A Natural Park of nearly a 250,000 ha, this rugged mountain range has
yielded several sightings of Lammergeier. Griffon Vultures are much more in
evidence, and Golden Eagles and Goshawks can often be seen on the scenic
road from Cazorla town up towards the Parador. Just above the town, Black
Wheatears can be found in the rocks by the side of the road.

TIMING
Winter can be troublesome from the point of view of access, but is a good
time to see the large raptors. Late spring is the best time for the other raptors
and songbirds, and summer is a good time to get onto the higher ground.
SPECIES
◆ *Resident* Red Kite, Goshawk, Buzzard, Golden Eagle, Griffon Vulture,
  Lammergeier, Peregrine, Rock Dove, Eagle and Long-eared Owls, Crag
  Martin, Great Grey Shrike, Blue Rock Thrush, Black Wheatear, Black
  Redstart, Crested Tit, Rock Bunting, Crossbill, Rock Sparrow, Chough.
◆ *Breeding season* White Stork, Black Kite, Short-toed and Booted Eagles,
  Honey Buzzard, Egyptian Vulture, Hoopoe, Alpine Swift, Red-rumped
  Swallow, Water Pipit, Woodchat Shrike, Spectacled, Subalpine, Orphean
  and Bonelli's Warblers, Rock Thrush.
◆ *Winter* Little Grebe, wildfowl, Avocet, Alpine Accentor.

*Juvenile and adult
Woodchat Shrikes*

ACCESS

On the way to Cazorla from the Jaén and Córdoba roads there is a small reservoir which has a surprising selection of waterfowl, often including Avocets, in winter. This is 9 km north-west of Peal de Becerro.

Once inside the park, there is a network of small tracks, many of which are gated. Check the closing times if you decide to take any of them, but avoid them if you cannot get hold of a large scale map.

The C323 from Quesada to Pozo clips the southern end of the park. This is also a good place for Black Wheatears and Blue Rock Thrushes. There is no shortage of accommodation in the town, and there is a *Parador* in the park.

SOUTH-EASTERN STEPPES

37°25N 03°10W

There are relatively few areas of steppe grassland in the far south of Spain, but between Granada and the Mediterranean coast two areas stand out. Perhaps the best area in Andalucía for Little Bustards and Black-bellied Sandgrouse is the Guadix depression, a semi-arid area with dry cereals and many ravines, stretching out north of Guadix, famous for its inhabited caves. Choughs, Peregrines and Eagle Owls haunt the rock faces, and Stone Curlew and Montagu's Harriers live in the wastelands and fields. Close by, to the east of Baza, is a very similar area which also holds an isolated population of Dupont's Larks.

TIMING

As with all steppe areas, birdwatching is less easy during June–September.

SPECIES

- *Resident* Buzzard, Peregrine, Little Bustard, Stone Curlew, Pin-tailed and Black-bellied Sandgrouse, Eagle and Long-eared Owls, Lesser Short-toed, Dupont's and Calandra Larks, Great Grey Shrike, Chough.
- *Breeding season* White Stork, Black Kite, Montagu's Harrier, Lesser Kestrel, Hobby, Red-necked Nightjar, Bee-eater, Roller, Hoopoe, Short-toed Lark, Tawny Pipit, Spectacled Warbler, Black-eared Wheatear.
- *Winter* Griffon Vulture, Golden Plover, Lapwing, flocks of seed-eaters.

ACCESS

The Guadix depression lies north of the N342 between Guadix and Baza. Several small roads and tracks lead into the area, and the road to Villanueva de las Torres crosses it. The Baza depression is east of and north of Baza, either side of the N342. The local road to Benamaurel is good, especially the area around the Ermita de la Virgen del Rosarito.

There is accommodation in Baza, Guadix, Granada and villages in the area.

CABO DE GATA

36°43N 02°15W

The coast of Almería province is very rugged for the most part, with small coastal *sierras* rising to overlook the sea at this south-east corner of Spain. Much of the coast east of Almería is semi-desert and of considerable botanical interest. Typical of the area is the Trumpeter Finch. This is a bird of the deserts and semi-deserts of North Africa and the Middle East and in Europe is known only from the Canary Islands and this small corner of Spain. There is also a good selection of steppe birds including Little Bustard, Stone Curlew, Black-bellied Sandgrouse and Dupont's Lark. SEO has set up a 900-ha steppe reserve at Las Amoladeras where all these species can be found.

At the coast near the village of El Cabo de Gata there are some saltpans where Flamingos have attempted to breed: up to 2000 are often to be found there. This is arid Almería's most important wetland. Avocets and Black-winged Stilts are present throughout the year. Spring and autumn migration brings large numbers of typical waders such as Little Stints and Curlew Sandpipers. Audouin's Gulls are regular visitors in spring and autumn.

TIMING

July and August are usually scorching months, although at the *salinas* things begin to get interesting towards the end of August and it is worth getting up early, before the heat haze makes watching waders difficult.

SPECIES

- *Resident* Flamingo, Buzzard, Bonelli's Eagle, Little Bustard, Black-winged Stilt, Stone Curlew, Black-bellied Sandgrouse, Eagle Owl, Lesser Short-toed, Thekla, Dupont's and Calandra Larks, Great Grey Shrike, Black Wheatear, Trumpeter Finch, Spanish Sparrow.
- *Breeding season* White Stork, Black Kite, Montagu's Harrier, Lesser Kestrel, Pratincoles, Little Tern, Red-necked Nightjar, Alpine and Pallid Swifts, Bee-eater, Roller, Hoopoe, Tawny Pipit, Spectacled Warbler, Rufous Bushchat, Black-eared Wheatear.

◆ *Passage* waders, Audouin's Gull.
◆ *Winter* wildfowl, Hen Harrier, Avocet, Audouin's Gull, Caspian Tern.
ACCESS
The Las Amoladeras reserve is 6 km along the road to El Cabo from the main
N344. A permit can be obtained from the Almería office of the Andalucían
Environment Agency (AMA): tel. 951 237680.
    The small road connecting the village of El Cabo with the cape itself runs
alongside the salt-pans to a hide. The local road to San José crosses the *sierra.*

SIERRA DE ALHAMILLA–CAMPO DE NÍJAR
37°00N 02°20W
The Sierra de Alhamilla is the most important area in Spain for Trumpeter
Finches, being reminiscent of their more accustomed north African habitat.
Black Wheatears are common and Thekla Larks abundant on the stony
wastelands. Some 5 km west of Tabernas a local road runs south from the
N340 the length of the Sierra de Alhamilla to Turillas. From here the road
runs left back to the main road, or right to Lucainen de las Torres.
    The Desierta de Tabernas could easily be mistaken for the wastes of
Arizona or southern California. Black-bellied Sandgrouse, Rollers, Thekla
Larks and Spectacled Warblers are common, along with yet more Trumpeter
Finches. The Tabernas desert is crossed by the C3326 road between Gérgal
and the N340, west of Tabernas. From the junction of these two roads a dry
river bed runs north for 6 km towards Tabernas and is worth exploring.

ROQUETAS DE MAR
36°40N 02°40W
It has to be said that the coast west of Almería city may not spring readily to
mind as a prime birdwatching area. There are, however, several large areas of
salinas and some seasonal lagoons which are protected under regional law
and which are a haven for wintering and migrating birds. Breeding birds
include White-headed Duck, Stone Curlew and Lesser Short-toed Lark.
    After breeding, many of the Flamingos of Fuente de Piedra come to these
coastal saltpans. The three main pans, south of Roquetas, hold up to 1000.
They are often joined by Audouin's and Slender-billed Gulls.
    In 1993 a small wetland reserve was established by SEO called La Cañada de
las Norias at Las Norias de Daza. Surrounded by a sea of plastic, it is an 80-ha
lagoon created from abandoned topsoil pits. In this unpromising habitat White-
headed Ducks have bred, producing in 1992 the second highest number of
fledged young anywhere in Europe: 33. Stone Curlew and Kentish and Little
Ringed Plovers breed and around 25 species of waders are recorded on
migration. Up to two dozen Marbled Teal are recorded, mostly in autumn.

TIMING
Migrating waders in spring and summer; Flamingos from July, along with the
two gulls mentioned. Little Gulls are common from November to May.
SPECIES
◆ *Resident* Shelduck, White-headed Duck, Little Bustard, Kentish Plover,
    Black-winged Stilt, Avocet, Stone Curlew, Lesser Short-toed, Thekla and
    Dupont's Larks.

♦ *Breeding season* Little Bittern, Montagu's Harrier, Pratincole, Little Tern, Red-necked Nightjar, Pallid Swift, Bee-eater, Roller.

♦ *Passage* Purple Heron, Spoonbill, Marbled Teal, Osprey, waders, terns.

♦ *Winter* Flamingo, wildfowl, Audouin's Gull, Caspian Tern, Bluethroat.

ACCESS
There are important saltpans and lagoons stretching between 6 and 12 km south of Roquetas and smaller ones just north of the town. The public roads provide a good view, but a permit can be obtained to enter the area from the Almería AMA: tel. 951 237680.

There is a small marsh about 10 km west of El Ejido, 7 km east of Adra. At km post 66 there is a track leading to the lagoons, where there are observation towers. An AMA permit is needed for these, too. Las Norias de Daza is on the back road between Roquetas and El Ejido.

SOUTH CÓRDOBA WETLANDS
37°25N 04°45W
These diverse lagoons are best treated as a group, although they are quite spread apart. Between them, they provide a good list of 'target' species: White-headed Duck, Purple Gallinule, Flamingo and so on. This is the main breeding area for the globally threatened White-headed Duck in Europe (outside Turkey) and there are several hundred in winter. Three of the lagoons have permanent water, but the other three dry up in summer.

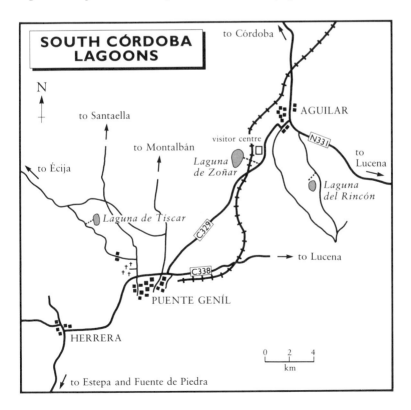

Laguna de Zoñar is the largest permanent lake, covering 38 ha. In winter there is a huge roost of Lesser Black-backed Gulls and good numbers of northern ducks. From a large, glass-fronted public hide, which is approached by crossing a railway line (see map), scan the reeds on the opposite side for Purple Gallinules. Black-necked, Great Crested and Little Grebes are common and White-headed Duck are found all year round.

Laguna de Tiscar is approached along a fairly rough road which leaves the village of Puerto Alegre through an olive grove. A path leads off right to a hilltop hide which looks down, over some distance, onto the salty lake. Flamingos are attracted away from Laguna de Fuente de Piedra (page 128), but do not breed. Black-winged Stilts and Avocets may be found at any time and duck numbers build up in winter.

Laguna del Rincón is a small, 4-ha lake fringed with reeds and surrounded by vegetation. There is a hide, but this is inside a closed boundary fence and the offices are not always manned, although it is possible to see White-headed Ducks by walking round the outside, asking permission if there are any farmers around.

TIMING
Normally 'endorreic' lagoons such as these would be dry between June and October: later in dry years.

SPECIES
◆ *Resident* Little Egret, Red-crested Pochard, White-headed Duck, Marsh Harrier, Purple Gallinule, Avocet, Redshank, Hoopoe, Lesser Short-toed Lark, Cetti's and Fan-tailed Warblers, Firecrest.
◆ *Breeding season* Little Bittern, Purple Heron, Black Kite, Short-toed and Booted Eagles, Black-winged Stilt, Pratincole, Bee-eater, Roller, Wryneck, Short-toed Lark, Red-rumped Swallow, Tawny Pipit, Woodchat Shrike, Black-eared Wheatear, Savi's and Great Reed Warblers, Golden Oriole.
◆ *Passage* Osprey, Honey Buzzard, waders, Whiskered Tern, Black Tern, Great Spotted Cuckoo, Pallid and Alpine Swifts, Wryneck, Redstart, Pied Flycatcher.
◆ *Winter* Grey Heron, wildfowl, Hen Harrier, Common Sandpiper, Water Pipit, Bluethroat.

ACCESS
At all the lagoons, there are other hides for permit holders, but these must be obtained from the Environment Agency (AMA) in Calle Tomás de Aquino, Córdoba (tel. 957 239000). There is a reception centre close to Laguna de Zoñar, just outside Aguilar de la Frontera and well marked from the Puente Genil road. Here the staff are helpful, at least if you have a few words of Spanish. Accommodation is not difficult to come by in Puente Genil, Lucena, Baena and Aguilar.

HUELVA MARSHES
37°15N 06°50W
The Atlantic coast of Andalucía combines the climate of the Mediterranean with the tidal influence of the ocean to create river estuaries almost unique in Europe. These are the *Rías*: there is a series of them from the Guadiana, which forms the border with Portugal, to the Guadalquivir, the world-famous

marshes of which are described overleaf. This section looks at the estuaries around the city of Huelva.

The most important marshes are found at the mouths of the rivers Tinto and Odiel. A thriving colony of Spoonbills, numbering about 300 pairs, nests on the ground on the Isla de Enmedio. There are also mixed heronries with Little Egrets, Grey and Purple Herons. Flamingos have bred, and there is also an important colony of Little Terns.

There are lagoons and saltpans which regularly attract Flamingos from Doñana and are important feeding areas for the Spoonbills.

At the very mouth of the river is Punta Umbría, where the juniper scrub is worth investigating for landfalls of warblers and other small birds. Seaduck, shearwaters and auks can be seen offshore here.

TIMING
The area is good for waders from late August to late May and for breeding waterbirds from February to July, so the whole year has something to offer.
SPECIES
◆ *Resident* Red Kite, Little and Cattle Egrets, White Stork, Spoonbill, Marsh Harrier, Water Rail, Black-winged Stilt, Avocet, Stone Curlew, Kentish Plover, Sandwich and Whiskered Terns, Hoopoe, Lesser Short-toed Lark.
◆ *Breeding season* Little Bittern, Night, Squacco and Purple Herons, Black Kite, Booted Eagle, Purple Gallinule, Pratincoles, Scops Owl, Red-necked Nightjar, Pallid Swift, Bee-eater, Roller, Short-toed Lark, Woodchat Shrike, Savi's and Great Reed Warblers.
◆ *Passage* Black-necked Grebe, Black Stork, Glossy Ibis, Osprey, waders, Audouin's Gull, Black Tern, Wryneck, Tawny Pipit.
◆ *Winter* Black-necked Grebe, Flamingo (some all year, and has bred), Red-crested Pochard, wildfowl, Osprey, Black-shouldered Kite, Hen Harrier, waders, Marsh Sandpiper, Little Gull, Caspian Tern, Bluethroat.

ACCESS
One of the best ways to see the Odiel marshes is by boat, and regular trips are organized by the Compañia Varela S.A., lasting between two and three hours, starting at Huelva port or Punta Umbría.

The main area of marsh is on the bank opposite the city, and access is via the N431 towards Portugal, turning left towards Alijaraque 11 km after crossing the Odiel river at Gibraleón. At Alijaraque a small road runs across the marshes to a long spit of land, the *Espigón Juan Carlos I*. The Isla de Enmedio is west of Bacuta island, over which this road runs, via a new information centre. There are good saltworks on Bacuta. The main road out of Alijaraque leads to Punta Umbría, turning left at the coast. A right turn here leads to Laguna del Portil, a protected lagoon.

A small tributary of the Río Tinto, the Estero Domingo Rubio, is a protected area. Just over the Río Tinto (or before it if coming from Doñana) there is a road leading to the Monastery of La Rábida which crosses the area. About 4 km farther along the C442 are the Laguna de los Palos and the Laguna de la Madre, just on the inland side of the road.

AYAMONTE AND PIEDRAS MARSHES
37°13N 07°25W
Farther west there are two more estuarine marshes, those of the Río Piedras and the Guadiana. They are smaller areas which are particularly important for migrant waders. The Piedras marshes are protected by a sand bar 10 km long which is an important resting area for waders, gulls and terns. Behind the spit the estuary is sheltered and rather lagoon-like.

From the Portil lagoon (above) the coast road leads to El Rompido. The left bank of the estuary can be explored from a track which leaves the road about 2 km beyond the settlement. From Lepe, 6 km to the west, another coast road leads to the right bank at Nueva Umbría

The Isla Cristina marshes near Ayamonte at the mouth of the Guadiana are internationally important for Kentish Plovers, have a good selection of breeding birds such as Pratincoles and hold post-breeding concentrations of Spoonbills and terns, including Caspian. They are reached via the fishing village of Isla Cristina, by turning south from the N431, 8 km west of Lepe, or 9 km from the border with Portugal. On the opposite bank is Castro Marim, in Portugal, which is described on page 188.

DOÑANA
37°00N 06°25W
The marshes, lagoons, sand dunes and woods at the mouth of the river Guadalquivir make up Spain's most famous natural area, and one of the best-known in Europe. At peak times perhaps 500,000 waterbirds are to be found there; its mixed heronries contain thousands of pairs; it is the world stronghold of the Spanish Imperial Eagle and one of the best places for Iberian lynx. At its centre is a National Park, Coto Doñana.

The extraordinary natural richness of Doñana was recognized more than a hundred years ago by Abel Chapman, who used to hunt in the marshes. His book *Wild Spain* was to inspire the famous expeditions of the 1950s, led by Guy Mountford, which are described in his *Portrait of a Wilderness*.

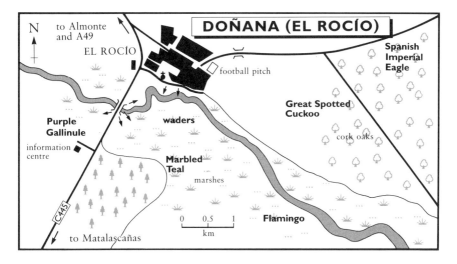

Over 340 bird species have been recorded on the Guadalquivir marshes and their surroundings. Of these, 125 breed. The list includes no fewer than eight species of global conservation concern: Marbled Teal, White-headed Duck, Black Vulture, Spanish Imperial Eagle, Lesser Kestrel, Great Bustard, Slender-billed Curlew and Audouin's Gull.

Within the National Park itself there is a rich mixture of habitats: seasonal marshes, *lucios* (deeper lagoons, the last areas to dry out), *matorral* of dry scrub, woods of oak and pine, sand dunes and beach. *La vera* is the only part of the park with guaranteed water all year. It is here, between the dry *matorral* and the flood marsh, that rabbits and other small mammals find sustenance during the summer drought. Without these, the park's 30 lynx, 15 pairs of Spanish Imperial Eagle and dozens of Booted Eagles would have little on which to feed. Close to the old Palace of Doñana, on the edge of the *vera* is an isolated group of ancient cork-oaks. This is 'la pajarera', one of Doñana's most famous images: a mixed colony of egrets, herons and, in particular, Spoonbills, more here than anywhere else in Europe. Spanish Imperial Eagles can often be seen perched in these old cork oaks or hunting over the fixed dunes and scrub. Another place to find them is the Coto del Rey, at the northern edge of the National Park.

The marshes are outstanding in winter, and hold 80,000 Greylag, 170,000 Teal, 120,000 Wigeon, 20,000 Pintail and 40,000 Black-tailed Godwits. The National Park headquarters and information centre, at El Acebuche, south of El Rocío, includes a small nature trail which, while providing only a snapshot of the great marshland wilderness beyond, is a surprisingly good way to see several of the speciality species. The hides here are one of the best places in Europe to see Purple Gallinules. They spend much of their time in the depths of the reeds and reedmace, but patience is usually rewarded, especially towards evening. The hides are also good for Marsh Harriers, Kingfishers, Ferruginous Duck (there is a reintroduction scheme) and Little Grebes. Great Spotted Cuckoos may be seen from the hides, and Savi's Warblers heard. The car park and picnic area at El Acebuche is good for Azure-winged Magpies and Serins.

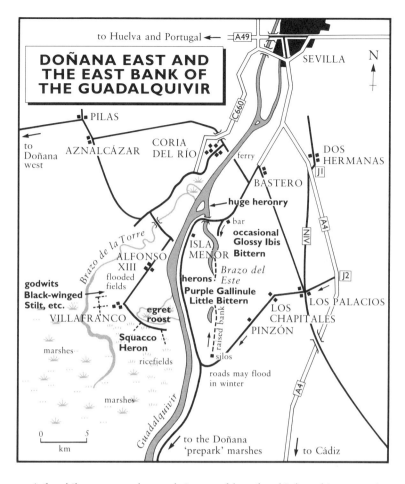

DOÑANA EAST AND THE EAST BANK OF THE GUADALQUIVIR

to Huelva and Portugal ← A49

SEVILLA N

PILAS

to Doñana west

AZNALCÁZAR

CORIA DEL RÍO

C660

ferry

DOS HERMANAS

J1

BASTERO

huge heronry

bar

occasional Glossy Ibis Bittern

Brazo de la Torre

ALFONSO XIII

ISLA MENOR

Brazo del Este

flooded fields

herons!

Purple Gallinule Little Bittern

A-IV

J2

LOS PALACIOS

godwits Black-winged Stilt, etc.

VILLAFRANCO

egret roost

LOS CHAPITALES

PINZÓN

raised bank

Squacco Heron

marshes

ricefields

silos

roads may flood in winter

A4

marshes

Guadalquivir

0   5
km

to the Doñana 'prepark' marshes

to Cádiz

A few kilometres to the north is one of best free birdwatching spots in Europe. The Matalascañas–El Rocío road crosses a small bridge over the La Rocina stream. Against a backdrop dominated by the white church of El Rocío, the marshes are alive with birds. The light is best in the afternoon here. In winter, there may be thousands of ducks and waders. Flamingos are frequent visitors, and Cattle and Little Egrets are permanent fixtures. A scan among the duck may reveal a few of the rare Marbled Teal. Black-winged Stilts, Avocets, Whiskered Terns and Garganey winter here, their numbers boosted from January by spring arrivals. Thousands of Ruff and Little Stints pass through, along with lesser numbers of Greenshank, Spotted Redshank, Marsh Sandpipers, Temminck's Stints and Whimbrels. Red Kites are common, and are joined in spring and summer by the equally abundant Black Kite.

The beach is accessible on foot and is a good sea-watching spot during the migration periods, when Gannets, Common Scoters and terns can be seen. Terns and gulls often rest on the beach itself, and Kentish Plovers and migrant waders, especially Sanderling, feed at the water's edge.

The eastern side of the area is a Natural Park, run by the Andalucian administration. This is working farmland around Villafranco del Guadalquivir but in winter many of the fields are flooded and can hold thousands of Black-tailed Godwits and hundreds each of Flamingo, Black-winged Stilt and Avocet. In late spring Pratincoles and Gull-billed Terns may breed here. A heron roost gathers towards dusk, especially outside the breeding season, at Villafranco.

TIMING
By mid-April the summer visitors are all in, and Black and Gull-billed Terns, Pratincoles, Bee-eaters, Rollers and Red-rumped Swallows can be seen throughout the area. By the end of May the water level has receded dramatically. Nevertheless, the La Rocina marshes are one of the few sites where there is something to see even in high summer. The track from El Rocío is usually impassable in winter.

SPECIES
- *Resident* Black-necked Grebe, Little and Cattle Egrets, Flamingo, Marbled Teal, Red-crested Pochard, White-headed Duck, Black-shouldered and Red Kites, Marsh Harrier, Griffon Vulture, Spanish Imperial Eagle, Avocet, Black-winged Stilt, Stone Curlew, Kentish Plover, Whiskered Tern, Hoopoe, Calandra, Lesser Short-toed and Thekla Larks, Dartford Warbler, Rock Sparrow, Hawfinch, Cirl Bunting, Azure-winged Magpie.
- *Breeding season* Spoonbill, White Stork, Little Bittern, Night, Squacco, Purple and Western Reef Herons (rare, late summer), Garganey, Black Kite, Short-toed and Booted Eagles, Montagu's Harrier, Lesser Kestrel, Quail, Baillon's, Little and Spotted Crakes, Pratincoles, Slender-billed Gull, Gull-billed and Little Terns, Pin-tailed Sandgrouse, Great Spotted Cuckoo, Red-necked Nightjar, Pallid Swift, Wryneck, Bee-eater, Roller, Short-toed Lark, Red-rumped Swallow, Tawny Pipit, Rufous Bush Chat, Savi's, Great Reed, Spectacled, Subalpine and Orphean Warblers, Golden Oriole.
- *Passage* Gannet, Black Stork, Glossy Ibis, Osprey, Honey Buzzard, waders, Audouin's Gull, Black, White-winged Black and Lesser Crested Terns (rare), Nightjar, Black-eared Wheatear, Moustached Warbler (rare).
- *Winter* wildfowl, Egyptian and Black Vultures, Bonelli's and Spotted Eagles (rare), Hen Harrier, Merlin, Crested Coot, Common Crane, Marsh Sandpiper, Jack Snipe, Slender-billed Curlew (very rare), Mediterranean and Little Gulls, Caspian Tern, Great Spotted Cuckoo, Water Pipit, Bluethroat, Firecrest, Penduline Tit.
- *Small numbers throughout the year* Spoonbill, White Stork, Little Bittern, Squacco Heron, Glossy Ibis, Black Vulture, Booted Eagle, Black Kite, Audouin's Gull, Caspian Tern, Red-necked Nightjar, Penduline Tit.

ACCESS
For years, the only official way to see the Park itself has been by guided Land Rover tour. These have often been booked up well in advance and the quality of the tour depends heavily on the driver. This is likely to change, and it is worth getting independent advice from SEO (*see* page 204). However, the advantage of taking the official tour is that it takes you to the heart of Doñana, to the 'pajarera', the *matorral*, the cork oaks. They leave from the Acebuche centre (tel. 955 448711).

From El Rocío there is a track to Palacio del Rey which is usually driveable with care but can be boggy or sandy. This leads from the north-east corner of the square, over two bridges to some excellent cork woodland. The track forks right in some eucalyptus trees along the northern edge of the marshes to Brazo de la Torre, 17 km further on. On the east side, the raised banks between the fields between Colonia de Alfonso XIII, Villafranco and the Brazo de la Torre river can be driven with relative ease. Through Villafranco there is a left turn in the road, onto a wide, unpaved track leading to a ferry (*barca*). A hundred metres or so down this road on the right is a reedbed where Cattle Egrets and Night Herons roost. Accommodation is plentiful in Matalascañas, although this is very much a package resort. El Rocío, Almonte and Mazagón are alternatives.

GUADALQUIVIR LEFT BANK

37°00N 05°50W

Much of the Guadalquivir marshland east of the river has long been converted to rice paddies or drained altogether. The rice fields are a mixed blessing: a favourite habitat of Squacco Herons and Little Egrets but, in some cases, heavily treated with pesticides. They are an important summer haunt of waterbirds, especially Marbled Teal, when the marshes are dry. The meandering tributaries have been canalized but some remnants remain, and in many cases these are as good as anywhere in the area for marsh birds.

South of Seville is a protected area, Brazo del Este, an eastern arm of the old Guadalquivir delta. Visitors to this area have reported remarkable sightings, such as the case of the 37 Purple Gallinules and 12 Purple Herons seen in the air together, flushed by a passing Short-toed Eagle! There is a huge heronry on an island here, perhaps the largest in the West Palaearctic, so the presence of Night and Squacco Herons and countless Little and Cattle Egrets is assured. Dark-phase Little Egrets and apparently genuine Reef Herons have been recorded with increasing regularity.

Close to the mouth of the river is part of the 'pre-park' of Doñana, a buffer zone for the National Park. Almost all of the species associated with Doñana can be found here. There are private saltworks at Bonanza which attract Avocets, Flamingos and Black-winged Stilts and very large wader numbers during migration. On arrival it is necessary to seek permission to enter the works. Note that at weekends the office may be closed, but prior permission may be possible by telephone (tel. 956 360719). There is a pine wood at nearby La Algaida, where Rollers and Azure-winged Magpies breed.

TIMING

This is an outstanding area all year. Winter flooding may cut off many areas, especially in the 'pre-park'.

SPECIES

- *Resident* Black-necked Grebe, Little and Cattle Egrets, Flamingo, White-headed Duck, Red Kite, Marsh Harrier, Griffon Vulture, Spanish Imperial Eagle, Purple Gallinule, Avocet, Stone Curlew, Kentish Plover, Hoopoe, Lesser Short-toed Lark, Dartford Warbler, Firecrest, Azure-winged Magpie.
- *Breeding season* Spoonbill, Little Bittern, Night, Squacco and Purple Herons, Garganey, Marbled Teal, Black Kite, Short-toed and Booted Eagles, Lesser Kestrel, Little and Spotted Crakes, Black-winged Stilt, Pratincole, Slender-billed Gull, Gull-billed and Whiskered Terns, Great Spotted Cuckoo, Red-necked Nightjar, Pallid Swift, Bee-eater, Roller, Short-toed Lark, Woodchat Shrike, Olivaceous, Savi's and Great Reed Warblers, Golden Oriole.

◆ *Passage* Glossy Ibis, Osprey, Black Tern, Nightjar, Wryneck, Tawny Pipit.
◆ *Winter* Red-crested Pochard, wildfowl, Black-shouldered Kite, Egyptian
and Black Vultures, Hen Harrier, Crested Coot, Mediterranean Gull,
Caspian Tern, Great Spotted Cuckoo, Bluethroat, Penduline Tit.
ACCESS
Brazo del Este is west of Los Palacios y Villafranca, which is 25 km south of
Seville on the NIV. A road leads west via Los Chapatales and Pinzón, and
after 15 km crosses a raised bank which affords good views over the marshy
areas. The road continues to the Guadalquivir, where a right turn leads to Isla
Menor village, close to the heronry island, and on to Seville. A left turn
instead would lead to Sanlúcar.
    The 'pre-park' area is just upstream of Sanlúcar de Barrameda. From the
nearby village of Bonanza there are tracks leading to the pine woods at La
Algaida and into the pre-park.
    Accommodation is plentiful in the area at Sanlúcar, Jeréz, Cádiz, Los
Palacios and Seville.

UTRERA, LAS CABEZAS
AND ESPERA LAGOONS
36°53N 06°47W
Huge cotton fields and vineyards extend either side of the fast road which
takes you from Seville to Cádiz, but there are dozens of endorreic lagoons,
grouped in three or four complexes, to lift the monotony. The most northerly
group are on the Seville/Cádiz boundary, between Utrera and Arcos de la
Frontera. Three species on most birdwatchers' hit-lists here are Purple
Gallinule, White-headed Duck and Crested Coot, which are around most of
the year and probably breed. The gallinule certainly breeds, with about ten
pairs at the Las Cabezas lagoons. The nearby Espera Lagoons are particularly
good for these species and Marbled Teal are also found there on migration.
Avocets and Flamingos frequently drop in from Cádiz bay and Doñana,
especially in winter.
    The Utrera lagoons are 12 km south of the town of that name, just south
of El Palmar de Troya. They are reached on foot from there, or from the road
between El Palmar and the reservoir a few kilometres to the east.
    The road between Las Cabezas de San Juan, on the A4 toll road, and
Espera crosses the NIV Seville–Cádiz road. Immediately afterwards is Laguna
del Charrodo to the left of the road. A little farther on is a left turn followed
closely by a fork. The first road off left leads to Laguna del Taraje,whereas
the right fork farther on leads to several seasonal lagoons to the right of the road.
    Doubling back to take what was the left fork would lead to the Espera
group of lagoons. There are minor roads off right to the lagoons, about 3 km
after the sign marking the provincial boundary.

BAHÍA DE CÁDIZ
36°35N 06°20W
The cosmopolitan port of Cádiz gives its name to the whole ornithologically
rich province east of the Guadalquivir, as well as to the small bay it
dominates. This, too, is of great importance for birds, with the biggest

Gull-billed Tern

breeding population of Little Terns in Spain, and huge concentrations of salt-loving birds. There is a vast complex of saltpans, although many are rapidly being turned into fish-farms under generous grants from the EU. This piece-meal destruction is happening almost unnoticed around the Mediterranean, and Spain and Portugal have been particularly affected.

Nonetheless, the saltpans of the Bahía de Cádiz hold up to 600 Avocets and 1200 Flamingos in late summer and through the winter, breeding Black-winged Stilts and Kentish Plovers, and up to 5000 Wigeon, 1700 Ringed Plovers and 1800 Kentish Plovers in winter. There are extensive salt-marsh and intertidal areas, which are important for wintering waders and egrets.

TIMING
Important all year round.

SPECIES
- *Resident* Little and Cattle Egrets, Flamingo, Marsh Harrier, Avocet, Stone Curlew, Kentish Plover, Whiskered Tern, Hoopoe, Lesser Short-toed Lark.
- *Breeding season* Garganey, Black Kite, Lesser Kestrel, Black-winged Stilt, Pratincole, Slender-billed Gull, Little and Gull-billed Terns, Red-necked Nightjar, Pallid Swift, Short-toed Lark.
- *Passage* Osprey, waders, Black Tern.
- *Winter* Black-necked Grebe, Spoonbill, wildfowl, Hen Harrier, Crested Coot, Marsh Sandpiper, Mediterranean Gull, Caspian and Sandwich Terns, Bluethroat.

ACCESS
The best salt-marsh areas are in the bay at El Trocadero, east of Puerto Real, and south of Cádiz, at Sancti Petri, which is reached via the coast road out of Chiclana de la Frontera. The saltpans are all round the bay and alongside the NIV. Cádiz and the towns around the bay have plenty of accommodation.

LAGOONS OF CÁDIZ AND JERÉZ
36°37N 06°03W

Four further complexes of endorreic lagoons (that is, they have no outlet but evaporation), each an Important Bird Area, are found in the region of Cádiz city and the sherry town of Jeréz de la Frontera.

The best known is the Laguna de Medina, near Jeréz, which is one the most reliable places for White-headed Duck. A few pairs of Crested Coots breed and many more winter there, but they are hard to pick out from the masses of ordinary Coots. Most people look for the red, fleshy knobs on the top of the head, but I find the shape of the white head plate is more distinctive at a distance. Purple Gallinules nest here as well as at Laguna de Taraje, near Puerto Real, and Lagunas de Terry to the north.

TIMING

Laguna de Medina usually stays wet all year, except in drought years such as 1993. All the lagoons dry out to some extent in summer.

SPECIES

- *Resident* Little Egret, White-headed Duck, Marsh Harrier, Purple Gallinule, Crested Coot, Kentish Plover, Avocet, Lesser Short-toed Lark.
- *Spring* Little Bittern, White Stork, Osprey, Black Kite, Short-toed Eagle, Pratincole, Black-winged Stilt, waders, Whiskered and Black Terns, migrant songbirds.
- *Autumn* Flamingo, Marbled Teal, Red-crested Pochard, Osprey, Hobby, waders, migrant songbirds and hirundines.
- *Winter* Flamingo, Greylag, Shelduck, Marbled Teal, Hen Harrier.

ACCESS

Laguna de Medina is 10 km from Jeréz, close to the Medina–Sidonia road. A footpath circles the lagoon. The Puerto de Santa María complex is reached by taking the NIV from El Puerto towards Jeréz, and turning left after 3 km towards the Casino Bahía de Cádiz. At the bend in the road, a right turn along an irrigation canal leads, after 1.5 km, to the first of the lagoons.

Laguna de Taraje and the Puerto Real complex are east of the town of that name. A local road leaves the town to the east, joining the C440 after 21 km, but after 12 km a track crosses this road. Laguna del Taraje is to the left, about 3 km down this track (NB this is different to the Laguna del Taraje near Espera). The other lagoons are close by, to the south and east.

There are further lagoons near Chiclana. A track leaves the C346 6 km from the town, heading north. There are lagoons either side of this track.

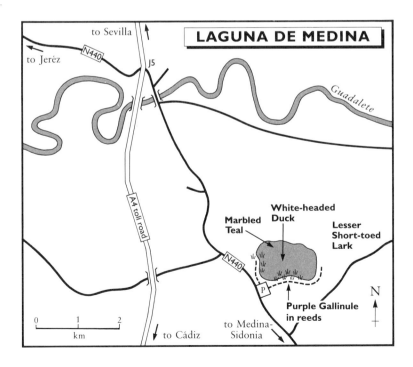

LOS ALCORNOCALES

36°25N 05°35W

Los Alcornocales is a 170 km² park which includes seven small *sierras* which abut the Ronda and Grazalema hills, extending northwards from Algeciras and Tarifa. The higher ranges of Las Cabras, El Aljibe and Montecoche, with their rocky outcrops towering over a forest cover of oak, constitute a largely uninhabited area to the east of Alcalá de los Gazules; to the south are the gentler slopes of el Bujeo, Ojén, el Niño and Blanquilla.

Like the Ronda hills, the area is of great importance for raptors. In addition, the extensive forests contain a diverse and abundant passerine fauna, a pair or two of Spanish Imperial Eagles and plentiful wildcats, genets, red deer and wild boar. White-rumped Swifts breed in some of the gorges.

TIMING
The mild winters and proximity to Africa allow resident, and even migrant, birds to breed early, so February to May is the best season. Depending on the weather conditions, migrating raptors and storks may concentrate in the area.

SPECIES
◆ *Resident* Goshawk, Buzzard, Bonelli's and Spanish Imperial Eagles, Griffon Vulture, Peregrine, Rock Dove, Eagle Owl, Crag Martin, Great Grey Shrike, Dartford Warbler, Firecrest, Blue Rock Thrush, Black Wheatear, Black Redstart, Crested Tit, Rock and Cirl Buntings, Rock Sparrow, Hawfinch, Chough.

◆ *Breeding season* White Stork (some resident), Black Kite, Booted Eagle, Egyptian Vulture, Lesser Kestrel, Scops Owl, Hoopoe, Red-necked Nightjar, Alpine and White-rumped Swifts, Red-rumped Swallow, Tawny Pipit, Bonelli's, Melodious, Olivaceous and Orphean Warblers, Rock Thrush, Black-eared Wheatear, Rufous Bush Chat, Ortolan Bunting.

◆ *Passage* Black Stork, raptors.

ACCESS
Driving the C440 from Algeciras to Alcalá de los Gazules with frequent stops at likely-looking spots is as good a way as any of exploring the area. The C221 runs west over Puerto de Ojén to Facinas, and 16 km farther on another runs between Puerto del Castaño and Benalup. Alcalá de los Gazules has a particularly good Lesser Kestrel colony in the town.

The Algeciras–Ronda road (*see* below) passes by Jimena de la Frontera. From here a smaller road, the C3331, leads off into the hills over the Puerto de Galis and on to Ubrique. About 8 km beyond the *puerto* towards Ubrique there is a left turn onto a local road which rejoins the C3331.

RONDA AND GRAZALEMA

36°40N 05°00W

Goya and Hemmingway were among the many artists and writers who have fallen in love with Ronda, perched as it is above a 90-m deep gorge in the southern Andalucian *sierras*. They have since been followed by thousands of birdwatchers, seduced by the charm of the place and the outstanding birdwatching that is to be had in the town and its surrounding hills.

Within the town, the gorge is spanned by three bridges, which make good look-out posts for Rock Sparrows, Lesser Kestrels, Peregrines and Alpine Swifts.

There are several *sierras* surrounding Ronda and each of the five roads leading into town crosses a different range. They are all of limestone, with abundant cliffs and oakwoods.

Several hundred pairs of Griffon Vultures soar along the cliff edges and are often to be seen thermalling over the many picturesque villages. The area is a stronghold of the Bonelli's Eagles and of raptors generally. The Serranía de Ronda, stretching south-east to Marbella, is also important for interesting passerines, such as Hawfinch, Olivaceous, Orphean and Dartford Warblers and Tawny Pipits. Alpine Accentors are occasionally recorded during the breeding season. There are numerous reservoirs and small natural marshes in the area, which are worth stopping at.

One of the specialities of the region is the White-rumped Swift, which breeds in disused Red-rumped Swallow nests under bridges or on buildings close to water.

TIMING
In spring and early summer night-time walks should reveal the sound, and perhaps a glimpse, of Eagle and Scops Owls, Stone Curlews and Red-necked Nightjars. White-rumped Swifts are unlikely to be seen before mid-May.

SPECIES
◆ *Resident* Cattle and Little Egrets, Goshawk, Buzzard, Bonelli's and Golden Eagles, Griffon and Black Vultures, Peregrine, Stone Curlew, Rock Dove, Eagle and Long-eared Owls, Crag Martin, Great Grey Shrike, Dartford Warbler, Firecrest, Blue Rock Thrush, Black Wheatear, Black Redstart, Alpine Accentor, Crested Tit, Rock and Cirl Buntings, Rock Sparrow, Hawfinch, Chough.
◆ *Breeding season* White Stork (some resident), Little Bittern, Purple Heron, Black Kite, Honey Buzzard, Booted Eagle, Egyptian Vulture, Lesser Kestrel, Scops Owl, Hoopoe, Red-necked Nightjar, Alpine and White-rumped Swifts, Red-rumped Swallow, Tawny Pipit, Bonelli's, Melodious, Olivaceous and Orphean Warblers, Rock Thrush, Black-eared Wheatear, Redstart, Ortolan Bunting.

ACCESS
Ronda is reached via any of three roads up from the coast (from Málaga, Marbella and Algeciras) and two others from Jeréz, Granada, Córdoba and Seville. These five roads are all very scenic and all cross at least one of the four IBAs surrounding the town.

The C344 from Málaga and Torremolinos cuts through the Serranía de Ronda. A side road to Tolox, 15 km beyond Coín, leads into a National Reserve. The southern part of the Serranía can be explored via the C337 Marbella–Coín road or at Istán, on a small road north of Marbella. The C339 unites Marbella (at nearby San Pedro de Alcántara) and Ronda via several viewing points overlooking the Serranía to the right (coming from the coast) and the Sierra Bermeja to the left of the road.

The C341 Algeciras–Ronda road is particularly rewarding as it winds gradually higher through the Sierras de Ubrique and Bermeja. A local road from Estepona joins this road at Algatocín from across the Sierra Bermeja. From the west, the N342 from Jeréz passes through Algonodales, a village at the southern end of the Sierra de Líjar. A detour towards La Muela, off the

Morón de la Frontera road, should be good for cliff-nesting birds. At Algonodales the road to Ronda turns right off the main road skirting the lovely Sierra de Grazalema. Alternatively, a smaller road (the C344) runs from Arcos de la Frontera to Ronda via Grazalema.

There is plenty of accommodation in Ronda, Grazalema, Toxon and Istán.

Fuente de Piedra

37°10N 04°45W

Mention Fuente de Piedra to anyone in Spain and if they know nothing else, they know that it is here that the Flamingos live. In 1990 there were a record 14,000 pairs, the only regular breeding site in the country. The numbers fluctuate: if the conditions are not just right they may not breed at all.

Fuente de Piedra is a huge lagoon surrounded by several complexes of much smaller endorreic lagoons set in the wheat fields and olive groves of Málaga province. In addition to the Flamingos, breeding species usually include Kentish Plovers, Slender-billed Gulls and Gull-billed Terns. Montagu's Harriers and Stone Curlews breed in the fields around the lagoons.

In winter the lagoons are important for Greylags and other wildfowl, including Red-crested Pochard. Avocets and Black-winged Stilts often winter at the Laguna de la Ratosa, if water and salinity levels are suitable.

TIMING

These lagoons, including Fuente de Piedra, start to dry out in spring and are usually completely dry from May to October, and often until late January.

SPECIES

◆ *Breeding season* Great Crested and Black-necked Grebes, Little Egret, Flamingo, Black Kite, Marsh and Montagu's Harriers, Lesser Kestrel, Common Crane, Little Bustard, Avocet, Black-winged Stilt, Pratincole, Slender-billed Gull, Gull-billed Tern, Bee-eater, Hoopoe, Lesser Short-toed and Thekla Larks, Cetti's, Fan-tailed and Spectacled Warblers.

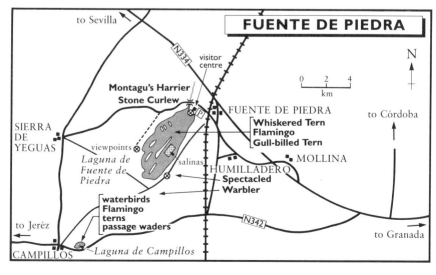

- *Passage* Osprey, waders, Whiskered and Black Terns, Great Spotted Cuckoo, Pallid and Alpine Swifts, Wryneck, Redstart, Pied Flycatcher.
- *Winter* Grey Heron, Greylag, Shelduck, Red-crested Pochard, wildfowl, Hen Harrier, Black-tailed Godwit, Green Sandpiper, Avocet, Black-winged Stilt, Thekla and Lesser Short-toed Larks, Water Pipit.

ACCESS

Laguna de Fuente de Piedra is close to the small town of that name which is on the N334, 20 km from Antequera and 60 km west of Granada. A track encircles the lagoon from the road which crosses the railway by the station. There is an information centre close to the road, and hides.

SIERRA NEVADA
37°05N 03°10W

Ranging between 1000 and 3481 m in altitude, the Sierra Nevada is permanently snow-capped and largely treeless. It is botanically one of Europe's hot spots, with over 40 alpine species found nowhere else in the world. This is one of the best places in Spain to find Alpine Accentors, since they spend much of their time hopping around in the ski resorts and are generally tame. The area around the *Parador* hotel and the University hostel is a reliable spot. Other passerines include Rock Buntings, Ortolans and Black Wheatears.

Among the raptors, the Golden Eagle has a healthy population of some ten pairs, and there are Bonelli's Eagles, Peregrines and Eagle Owls present.

TIMING

The road as far as the ski resort is kept open all year round, and winter can be a good time to find the Accentors.

SPECIES

- *Resident* Goshawk, Buzzard, Bonelli's and Golden Eagles, Griffon Vulture, Peregrine, Rock Dove, Eagle and Long-eared Owls, Crag Martin, Great Grey Shrike, Blue Rock Thrush, Black Wheatear, Black Redstart, Alpine Accentor, Crested Tit, Rock Bunting, Chough, Raven.
- *Breeding season* Black Kite, Honey Buzzard, Booted Eagle, Egyptian Vulture, Hoopoe, Red-rumped Swallow, Water Pipit, Subalpine, Spectacled, Orphean and Bonelli's Warblers, Rock Thrush, Black and Black-eared Wheatears, Ortolan Bunting.
- *Winter* Ring Ouzel, Siskin.

ACCESS

Europe's highest road runs from Granada to the *Parador* hotel above the ski resort at Solynieve, and, in August, on up to the Pico de Valeta and down the other side to the Alpujarras. The rest of the year it is likely to be blocked just above the resort. The walk from here in any direction is rewarding and you soon leave the hordes behind. Beware, however, the weather changes, which can occur at any time of the year, and keep the buildings in sight if you do not have maps, compasses and the knowledge to use them. There is plenty of accommodation at Solynieve during the ski season (December to May) but this needs to be booked well in advance. Granada or the Alpujarras, in the southern foothills, make perfectly good bases for a day trip into the mountains. A long (two-day) hike is possible in summer between Solynieve and Capileira in the Alpujarras.

TARIFA AND LA JANDA
36°05N 05°35W

Above all, the southern tip of Europe, at Tarifa in Cádiz province and across the bay in Gibraltar, is the point at which Europe and Africa become linked, twice a year, by a tide of migrating birds. With only 14 km of sea to cross, millions choose this as the place to make their European landfall in spring or embark on their African adventures in autumn.

When and where to observe this phenomenon depends largely on wind direction, and varies according to species. Gibraltar ornithologist Clive Finlayson has studied this in detail and his results are set out in his book *Birds of the Straits of Gibraltar*. In general, Tarifa has a greater share of southward migrants when an easterly wind is blowing, but during a westerly more birds choose Gibraltar. This effect is more pronounced for some species (Black Kite, Honey Buzzard, Osprey for example) than others. Spring birds tend to head east of Tarifa, arriving around Punta de Carnero during westerly winds or nearer to Tarifa during easterlies.

For the White Stork, Tarifa is of immense importance in late July and August, the peak time for southward flight. Many congregate at the ornithological reserve at Los Lances to await the right conditions, especially during strong easterlies. Huge flocks can be seen at La Janda, once one of Spain's most important wetlands until it was drained in the 1950s. This event was one of the great conservation tragedies of recent times.

La Janda is now farmland, periodically flooded in winter, but there are small numbers of breeding Great Bustards, Pratincoles and Montagu's Harriers and a large colony of Cattle Egrets. Along with the storks, over 400 Montagu's Harriers may gather in late August prior to crossing the Strait. Griffon Vultures and Booted Eagles hunt at La Janda from their nearby breeding grounds at the Sierra de la Plata. This latter site is also a breeding area for White-rumped Swifts.

There are two small estuaries in Algeciras bay, the Palmones and the Guadiaro. They are important for Ospreys in winter and on migration, and have small communities of marsh birds including Little Bitterns, wintering Penduline Tits and Bluethroats and visiting Flamingos. In late summer Audouin's Gulls and sometimes Lesser Crested Terns are seen.

TIMING
For peak migration periods for each species, *see* Gibraltar.

SPECIES
◆ *Breeding season* Little Bittern, Red-necked Nightjar, White-rumped and Pallid Swifts.
◆ *Autumn* Audouin's Gull, Lesser Crested Tern.
◆ *Winter* wildfowl, Bonelli's Eagle, Griffon Vulture, Common Crane, Great and Little Bustards, Kentish Plover, Golden Plover, Sanderling, Audouin's Gull, Lesser Crested Tern, Black Wheatear, Blue Rock Thrush, Bluethroat.

ACCESS
Tarifa is 25 km south-west of Algeciras. Several small roads lead to the coast off the N340, which links these two towns. Punta del Carnero is reached via a good road 3 km from Algeciras. The Playa de Los Lances reserve is west of Tarifa. A turn off the N340 near the hotel Dos Mares leads to the beach.

La Janda is farther along the N340, east of the road between Tahivilla and Vejer. There are smaller roads off into the agricultural land, and the fields around Tahivilla are the best area for Great Bustards.

The Palmones marshes are off the N340 between Algeciras and Gibraltar. The left bank of the river is reached via Palmones village, the right via El Rinconcillo. The estuary of the Guadiaro is east of San Roque. The right bank of the river can be found by taking a small side road marked Sotogrande off the N340 and crossing the bridge over the river.

GIBRALTAR

36°17N 05°21W

Since the border with Spain was reopened in 1985, Gibraltar has been available to add to a southern Spanish birdwatching itinerary. This means two things: Barbary Partridge and an alternative migration watchpoint. The Partridge, whose only other European haunts are in the Canary Islands and Sardinia, likes open, steppe-like habitat and garrigue on the Rock itself.

The Straits of Gibraltar are an important passage bottleneck for east–west migration of seabirds as well as north–south migration of raptors, storks and small birds. Passage over the Rock can be spectacular, when a westerly wind pushes birds east of Tarifa. The Rock of Gibraltar is particularly important for Honey Buzzard passage which, being concentrated in a short space of time, can be an incredible sight at watchpoints such as the Cable Car Top Station. The following list indicates the numbers of birds migrating through the area and the peak migration times. For species that have a long migration period, a range and peak month (in **bold**) are given.

Species	Northward migration	Southward migration	Numbers (southward)
White Stork	Oct–**Jan**–Mar	Jul/Aug	40000
Black Stork	Feb–**Mar**–May	Sept/Oct	600
Osprey	Feb–**Mar**–May	Sept	100
Honey Buzzard	Apr/May	Aug/Sept	100000
Black Kite	Feb–**Mar**–Jun	Jul/Aug	60000
Egyptian Vulture	Jan–**Mar**–May	Aug/Sept	3000
Short-toed Eagle	Feb–**Mar**–May	Sept/Oct	4000
Marsh Harrier	Feb–**Mar**–May	Aug–**Sept**–Oct	200
Montagu's Harrier	Mar–**Apr**–May	Jul–**Aug**–Sept	1500
Buzzard	Feb–**Mar**–May	Aug–**Oct**	2500
Booted Eagle	Mar–**Apr**–May	Sept	4000
Scops Owl	Mar–**Apr**	Aug–Oct	?
Swift	Mar–**Apr**–May	**Jul**–Oct	400000
Bee-eater	Mar–**Apr**–Jun	Sept	40000
Roller	Apr/May	Jul–Sept	small nos.
Hoopoe	Nov–**Mar**–Apr	Aug/Sept	?
Wryneck	Feb–May	Sept/Oct	?
Swallow	Jan–May	Jul–**Oct**–Dec	100000
Red-rumped Swallow	**Feb**–May	Sept–Nov	5000
House Martin	Jan–**Feb**–Jun	Sept/Oct	14000

Honey Buzzard

Seabird numbers in the Straits of Gibraltar are greatest in October to March and least from May to August. There is a peak in November due to large numbers of Cory's Shearwaters migrating into the Atlantic. In terms of species diversity, March–May and July–October are best. Peak times in the Strait for selected seabirds are:

Cory's Shearwater	Mar, Jun/Jul, Nov
Yelkouan Shearwater	Jun, Nov-Jan
Storm Petrel	Apr-Sept
Mediterranean Gull	Nov-Mar
Audouin's Gull	Feb/Mar, Jul/Aug
Lesser Crested Tern	Mar-May, Aug-Oct
Auks	Mar/Apr

Europa Point is the favourite sea-watching point and is best in late afternoon and evening. For the Barbary Partridge, the Upper Rock area is best, where firebreaks and other open areas often reveal coveys in the early morning and at dusk. In particular, Windmill Hill, within the military base, is outstanding. A permit must be obtained well in advance from the Adjutant, Gibraltar Regiment, Lathbury Barracks, Gibraltar. The eastern cliffs and Mediterranean Steps area is good for wintering Alpine Accentors, and resident Blue Rock Thrushes.

ACCESS
Gibraltar is served by regular scheduled flights from the UK, and is now easily reached by road from Málaga, Cádiz and elsewhere in southern Spain, on production of a valid passport. There is a tourist office in Gibraltar (tel. 74982). The Straits of Gibraltar are crossed by ferries plying between Gibraltar and Tangiers, and between Algeciras, Tangiers and the Spanish North African enclaves of Ceuta and Melilla. At suitable times these boats provide good seabird- and dolphin-watching opportunities.

BALEARIC ISLANDS

The Balearic Islands, and Mallorca in particular, have probably welcomed more British birdwatchers on their first foreign trip than anywhere else. So geared up for cheap travel are they, that they are ideal for a first contact with typical Mediterranean species, as well as one or two specialities.

There are around 500 pairs of Eleonora's Falcon in the Balearics, mostly on the coast of Mallorca and its associated islands. Ospreys are present all year round and the islands' small breeding population is almost unique in southern Europe. Marmora's Warbler is confined to Corsica, Sardinia and the Balearics. All the islands are important for seabirds, including the rare Audouin's Gull. The Balearic Shearwater is now regarded as a race of Yelkouan Shearwater.

The Balearic islands differ between themselves in interesting ways. For example, Red Kites are fairly common in Menorca but uncommon in Mallorca. Egyptian Vultures breed only on Menorca, Black Vultures only on Mallorca. Dartford Warblers appear to have replaced Marmora's on Menorca, whereas they are rare on Mallorca. Menorca tends to have a more peaceful, slower pace than its larger neighbour, which for many makes up for its slightly less varied birdlife. Ibiza scores relatively low on both counts, but with Formentera, makes an interesting speciality location.

Mallorca is certainly the most diverse of the Balearic islands and is almost unique in southern Europe in having a fairly well-developed birdwatching infrastructure, almost reminiscent of Norfolk. Many of the hotels in the north-east are accustomed to receiving and advising birdwatchers and there is a resident expatriate, Graham Hearl, who gives advice and runs twice-weekly evening meetings to allow visitors to find out what's about. These are held in the Hotel Pollentia, Port de Pollença, on Mondays and Fridays, starting at 9 p.m. in spring and autumn. Graham can be reached at Apto 83, Sa Pobla, Mallorca (tel. 862418). If writing, send an addressed envelope and international reply coupon.

As has already been mentioned, the Balearics are easy to reach, with scheduled and charter flights, as well as a vast choice of package tours, available. Formentera is reached by sea from Ibiza. On Mallorca a hired car is essential, but relatively inexpensive. The same goes for Menorca and Ibiza, although at a pinch taxis or public transport can be used for the occasional day out if birdwatching is not the main purpose of the holiday. On Menorca hire car insurance does not cover damage to wheels and tyres – an indication of the quality of some of the roads. Many towns are reverting to their original, local names. On Menorca in particular this has led to some substantial changes: Maó for Mahón and Eivissa for Ibiza are not too difficult, but the change from San Cristóbal back to Es Migjorn Gran and from Villa Carlos to Es Castell is rather confusing.

BIRDWATCHING SITES

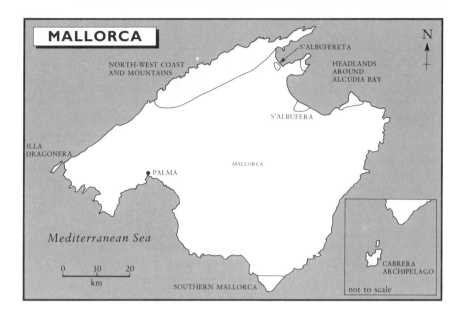

S'ALBUFERA DE MALLORCA
39°47N 03°06E
The Parc Natural de S'Albufera is Mallorca's best-known birdwatching area. Its reedbeds, lagoons, sand dunes and saltpans are now protected both under Balearic law and the EU Birds Directive, which, given the relentless growth of tourism development on the island, is a relief for the many Mallorquín and foreign campaigners who have spent years fighting for its survival.

In bird conservation terms, S'Albufera's importance lies in its hundred or more pairs of Little Bittern and 50 pairs of Purple Heron, as well as Spain's largest population of Moustached Warbler, a real Mediterranean speciality. Spotted and Little Crakes are common, but share the Little Bittern's frustrating shyness. They are, however, quite vocal and can readily be located if you know their calls. Another denizen of the reeds is the recently reintroduced Purple Gallinule, which can sometimes be seen feeding or loafing at the edge of the reeds or, in winter and spring, fighting noisily.

The marsh starts at the southern edge of Alcudia, where a series of lagoons can be viewed from a green bridge. Confusingly, British birdwatchers who have been visiting Mallorca regularly always refer to this site as the Orange Bridge (it was, once), and it is very bad form to refer to it by any other name. Crossing the bridge is not allowed (there is usually a gate across in any case) but nor is it necessary. In summer it is a good spot for Purple Herons, Whiskered Terns and, during migration, waders.

Eleonora's Falcon is another attraction at Albufera. It breeds on the in rockier parts of the coast, but often comes to hunt over the marsh, especially spring, before breeding starts. Occasionally, there may be ten or a dozen in the air together. The reedbeds hold a good population of Moustached Warblers, which are best sought out just after dawn in spring.

The saltworks to the south of the Albufera are easily viewed from the road. Kentish Plovers and Black-winged Stilts breed, and the saltpans are a great attraction for migrating waders in the spring and late summer. This can also be a good time for looking for the less common migrants such as White-winged Black and Gull-billed Terns and Pratincole.

TIMING

This area is a magnet for visiting foreign birdwatchers in April and May. This is certainly the best time, but the tendency for British birdwatchers to ignore the Albufera at other times does not do justice to the place.

SPECIES

◆ *Resident* Little Egret, White-headed Duck, Marsh Harrier, Osprey, Peregrine, Spotted Crake, Purple Gallinule, Kentish Plover, Scops Owl, Hoopoe, Thekla Lark, Crag Martin, Cetti's, Moustached and Fan-tailed Warblers, Firecrest, Crossbill.

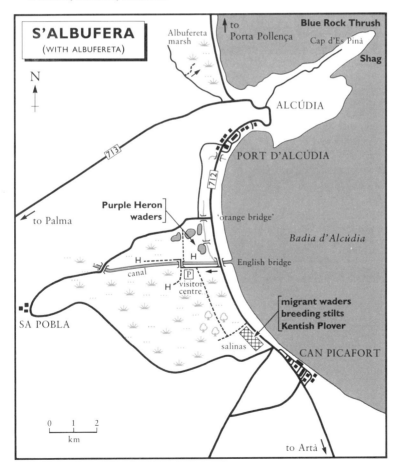

- ◆ *Breeding season* Little Bittern, Night and Purple Herons, Black Kite, Hen Harrier, Booted Eagle, Eleonora's Falcon, Avocet, Black-winged Stilt, Pallid and Alpine Swifts, Bee-eater, Wryneck, Short-toed Lark, Tawny Pipit, Woodchat Shrike, Great Reed and Melodious Warblers, Golden Oriole.
- ◆ *Passage* Squacco Heron, Garganey, Honey Buzzard, Red-footed Falcon, Quail, waders, Pratincole, Whiskered and Black Terns, Red-throated Pipit, Red-rumped Swallow, Black-eared Wheatear.
- ◆ *Winter* wildfowl, Hen Harrier, Water Pipit, Bluethroat, Penduline Tit.

ACCESS

The Orange (green) Bridge is behind the shops off the main 712 coast road just past the Sa Pobla turn. A morning visit is recommended, to take advantage of the light from behind. The coast road crosses another bridge ('English Bridge') a kilometre or so farther south. This marks the entrance to the reserve proper, where a visitor centre, car park and toilets are found.

Permits are available from the visitors' centre (tel. 89 22 50), which is open daily from 9 a.m., closing at 5 p.m. in winter and 7 p.m. in summer. Groups are required to book in advance during peak periods. Nearby Alcudia and Can Picafort have plentiful accommodation.

NORTH-WEST COAST AND MOUNTAINS OF MALLORCA

39°50N 02°45E

The rocky north-west coast of Mallorca is a far cry from the tourist traps of the southern part of the island. Its limestone cliffs are almost continuous and beaches are few. The most accessible part of this coast is the Formentor peninsula, north-east of Port de Pollença. At the cape, Blue Rock Thrushes, Peregrines and Eleonora's Falcons are fairly common, and below, over the sea, Cory's and Yelkouan Shearwaters pass close inshore.

One of the target birds at Formentor is the Marmora's Warbler. The scrubby hillside at Casas Veyas is a fairly reliable spot, as is the scrub around the km 17 road marker. There is a well-watched track leading from Port de Pollença to the north coast at Cala Boquer which is a migration route for raptors such as Honey Buzzard and a favourite hunting area for Eleonora's Falcons. It may be possible to watch the falcons at their cliff face nesting grounds from the sea. At Cala Sant Vicenç some hotels can arrange short trips, or advise on availability.

The Sierra (*serra* in Mallorquín) de Tramuntana runs along the length of this coastline: a mountainous, largely uninhabited region, the last haunt in the islands of the Black Vulture. Only a few pairs of this huge bird remain, but several immature or non-breeding birds range widely over the hills. Route 710 runs, somewhat tortuously, along the length of the *serra* and the Lluch monastery, 21 km west of Pollença, is a good place to watch for the vultures and also Booted Eagles as is the viewing area at Escorca to the west.

The reservoir at Cuber, between Lluch and Soller is outstanding. Ospreys fish there and Rock Thrushes nest in a small quarry west of the dam. Black Vultures often put in an appearance and Eleonora's Falcons hunt over the water and bathe at its edge. Spectacled Warblers are now regular breeders in the area to the left of the track leading to the dam.

Yelkouan Shearwater

TIMING
Spring is the best time to seek out small birds such as Marmora's Warbler, and is good for raptor migration. Eleonora's Falcon arrives late, in May.

SPECIES
◆ *Resident* Shag, Osprey, Egyptian and Black Vultures, Peregrine, Crag Martin, Blue Rock Thrush, Sardinian and Marmora's Warblers, Firecrest, Cirl Bunting.
◆ *Breeding season* Cory's and Yelkouan Shearwaters, Red and Black Kites, Booted Eagle, Eleonora's Falcon, Pallid and Alpine Swifts, Wryneck, Short-toed Lark, Tawny Pipit, Rock Thrush, Spectacled Warbler.
◆ *Passage* migrant passerines.
◆ *Winter* Gannet, Alpine Accentor.

ACCESS
From Port de Pollença eastwards there is a road along the Formentor Peninsular with regular stopping points and a car park at the headland. The Boquer valley footpath starts in Port de Pollença along the Formentor road. Avenida Bocharis is opposite the start of the track, which passes through a farm and into the valley. There is a gate at the entrance to the farm but at present access is not restricted. However, the land is private and access is allowed on condition that visitors do not wander from the path. Very occasionally the gate is locked to enable the farm to operate, such as during sheep shearing.
    Port de Pollença and Alcudia have ample accommodation.

S'ALBUFERETA, MALLORCA
39°52N 03°05E
Albufera is a word derived from the Arabic *Al-Buhaira* meaning lake or marsh. S'Albufereta, then, is the Little Marsh, a small wetland between Alcudia and Port de Pollença. Half way along the Port de Pollença–Alcudia road there is a smaller road near C'an Cuarassa leading north-west towards Pollença (as opposed to Port de Pollença). About 2.5 km along this road another road runs left along a stream and behind the marsh, eventually joining the 713 road to Palma close to its junction with the coast road. Rough tracks off the back road enable the marsh to be approached on foot, but they are mostly private and per-mission should be sought. The coast road runs along one edge of the marsh.
    The tamarisks along the stream are a favourite roost of Night Herons, and the trees around the marsh are worth scanning for herons of all species,

including Squacco. In spring there is often a good selection of rarer migrants such as Red-footed Falcon (especially following easterly winds) and Red-throated Pipit. At the Alcudia end of Pollença bay the road crosses a small river which forms a small estuary where Kentish Plovers, Black-winged Stilts and migrant waders can be seen. A rough track runs off this road to the left at the bridge. Take this track as far as a small raised area from which the whole marsh can be seen. This is a good area for Quail, pipits, Marsh Harrier and Osprey. A further left turn leads to another good viewpoint.

HEADLANDS AROUND ALCUDIA BAY, MALLORCA

39°52N 03°01E

The north-east coast of Mallorca comprises two bays, the *Badias* de Pollença and Alcudia, which are bounded by headlands at, from north to south, Cap Formentor, Cap d'es Pinà, Cap de Ferrutx and Cap del Freu.

These are important breeding grounds for the Mediterranean race of Shag and, in the case of Cap de Ferrutx and Cap del Freu, for Audouin's Gull. Rock Doves and Ravens also share these cliffs with Blue Rock Thrushes.

The Artà massif, north of routes 712 and 715, is particularly well conserved and beautiful. Booted Eagles are relatively common here, and Thekla Lark, a relatively infrequent bird in the northern half of Mallorca can also be found. These can be seen along the road to the Ermita de Betlem, along with Alpine Swifts and the occasional Black Vulture. This is also a good area for passing migrant raptors and passerines. Marmora's Warblers breed in the scrub along the eastern edge of the Badia d'Alcudia, between San Pedro, the Ermita de Betlem and the headland.

SOUTHERN MALLORCA

39°19N 03°05E

Since most birdwatchers, justifiably, base themselves in the north of the island, the south generally receives less attention, being usually covered in a long day trip. The main attraction in the far south are the Lagunas del Salobrar de Campos, also known as the Salinas (in Mallorquín *Salines*) de Levante. There is abundant Mediterranean scrub in what is a generally much dryer region than the more familiar north. The combination of natural lagoons, and both abandoned and working saltpans presents a variety of wetland habitats and salinity grades, appealing to a similar diversity of birds.

Black-winged Stilts are the most characteristic birds of the *salines*, with over 100 pairs. Kentish Plovers are also common, and in spring and late summer there is a sizeable throughput of migrating waders and terns. Whiskered, Black and Gull-billed Terns are regular, Slender-billed Gulls less so and Avocets and Flamingos, although somewhat unpredictable, are frequently recorded. There are pine woods and dunes between the *salines* and the sea where Firecrests, Crossbills and, in the open areas, Stone Curlew are common.

The headland at Cap de Ses Salines is a good sea-watching point, with Cory's and Yelkouan Shearwaters passing by throughout the day, especially with southerly or easterly winds, and Audouin's Gull are regular. Stone Curlew and Thekla Lark are common in the dry hinterland.

Sardinian Warbler

Round the coast to the west, the cliffs between Cala Pí and Cap Enderrocat are important for Shag and gulls, and have Stone Curlew and Thekla Lark in the open spaces.

TIMING
April/May and August to October are peak months for migration at the *salines* and spring birdwatching is enhanced by the abundant breeding birds.
SPECIES
◆ *Resident* Shag, Peregrine, Kentish Plover, Hoopoe, Thekla Lark, Blue Rock Thrush, Sardinian Warbler, Firecrest, Crossbill, Raven.
◆ *Breeding season* Cory's and Yelkouan Shearwaters, migrant waders, Stone Curlew, Black-winged Stilt, Audouin's Gull, Scops Owl, Pallid Swift, Bee-eater, Short-toed Lark, Tawny Pipit, Marmora's Warbler.
◆ *Passage* Flamingo, Pratincole, waders, Little Gull, passerines.
ACCESS
The town of Campos is on route 717. From here, there is a road leading south to Colonia de Sant Jordi. After 8 km there is a crossroads. A left turn here would lead to Ses Salines village but to reach the *salines*, stay on the Sant Jordi road for another kilometre or so to Banyos de Sant Joan. A track leading to Es Trenc beach skirts the area and passes through the pinewoods. The *salines* are private, but the views from the public roads are good. Cap de Ses Salines is reached by turning right 3 km beyond Ses Salines village.

ILLA DRAGONERA, MALLORCA
39°35N 02°18E
Sa Dragonera is an uninhabited island of 288 ha off the north-west tip of Mallorca. Its very high limestone cliffs are home to some 75 pairs of Eleonora's Falcon, one of the most important colonies in Spain, and a similar number of Audouin's Gulls. Ospreys fish in the island's inshore waters but do not breed on the island. Both shearwaters breed on the island along with Storm Petrels. The seabird colonies extend to the Mallorcan mainland across the sound at the Andratx headland near Sant Telm (San Telmo), which is a good place to watch them passing close inshore towards dusk. A reception

centre is planned for Sant Telm, which is 8 km along a scenic side road west of Andratx town, in turn 30 km from Palma along route 719. A ferry to Sa Dragonera currently runs four days a week, several times a day from Sant Telm (reservations tel. 24 66 98).

CABRERA ARCHIPELAGO, MALLORCA

39°09N 02°55E

Cabrera is an archipelago off the southern tip of Mallorca, and one of Spain's newest National Parks. Its 18 islands cover a total land area of 1836 ha, but the protected area also includes over 8000 ha of sea. It is thus Spain's first terrestrial-maritime National Park and as such a potential model for the rest of maritime Europe. Its sudden conversion from a military garrison to a protected area owes much to the tenacity of the growing environmental movement in the Balearics, notably the Grup Ornitologic Balear. As a result, some of the most interesting seabird islands in the Mediterranean can be managed to maintain and enhance their great beauty and natural importance.

The main island is covered with a thick *maquis* of wild olive, juniper and pine. This makes the island an important stop-over for migrant warblers, flycatchers and chats, enabling them to rest and feed before continuing their journey. The cliffs and islets are inhabited by the two shearwaters, Audouin's Gull, Storm Petrel, Shag, Peregrine and Eleonora's Falcon. A pair of Ospreys can sometimes be seen fishing in the clear, shallow waters of the islands' many sheltered coves. A small population of Marmora's Warblers inhabits the scrubland of the main island.

In summer there are daily crossings to the island as well as non-landing excursions. These depart from the harbour at Colonia de Sant Jordi. The crossing passes by some of the smaller islands before landing, and most of the seabirds can be seen *en route*, including rafts of Cory's and Yelkouan Shearwaters. Private landings are by permit only, obtainable from the ICONA headquarters in Palma (tel. 971 465507 or 467105). It is not possible to stay overnight, but accommodation is available in Colonia de Sant Jordi.

NORTH-EAST COAST OF MENORCA: CAVALLERIA–FORNELLS

40°03N 040°00E

The north-east coast of Menorca includes several favourite birdwatching locations, comprising rocky cliffs, offshore islands and headlands. Breeding birds include Cory's Shearwater, Audouin's Gull and the Mediterranean race of Shag. There are several peninsulas, the most notable being Cap de Cavalleria and Fornells. Cavalleria can be a good sea-watching point with Yelkouan Shearwaters passing close by throughout the summer. The drive to the point passes through rich flower meadows with Quails calling all around. Egyptian Vultures and Booted Eagles are common on both peninsulas and Blue Rock Thrushes are easily seen in the rockier areas. Audouin's Gulls may be seen at almost any time, but especially between April and October.

Fornells bay and cliffs are home, respectively, to breeding Ospreys and Cory's Shearwaters. There are *salines* at the southern end of the bay which are good for migrating waders, raptors and Tawny Pipit.

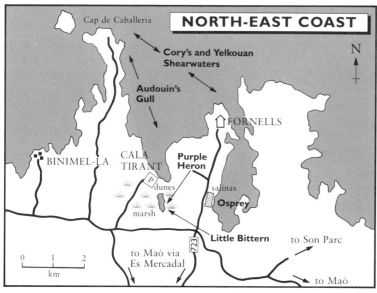

Behind Cala Tirant beach there is a freshwater marsh, which varies in extent according to the season and weather. The reedbeds and open water are good for herons, rails and waders and can be superb if conditions are right.

TIMING
The headlands are important for migrating passerines in April/May and September/October and for sea-watching between April and October.

SPECIES
♦ *Resident* Shag, Red Kite, Marsh Harrier, Peregrine, Scops Owl, Thekla Lark, Blue Rock Thrush, Fan-tailed and Dartford Warblers.
♦ *Breeding season* Cory's and Yelkouan Shearwaters, Purple Heron, Little Bittern, Little Egret, Egyptian Vulture, Booted Eagle, Osprey, Quail, Black-winged Stilt, Kentish Plover, Stone Curlew, Audouin's Gull, Pallid and Alpine Swifts, Hoopoe, Bee-eater, Short-toed Lark, Tawny Pipit.
♦ *Passage* Squacco Heron, Montagu's Harrier, migrant waders and passerines, Black-eared Wheatear.

ACCESS
The Fornells *salines* are on the 723 road from Es Mercadal to Fornells, about 1 km north of the right turn to Port d'Addaia and Maó. They can be viewed from the road at various points. A good vantage point for both the *salines* and bay can be reached via a new development just to the north. Access is forbidden to the 'la Concepció' *salines* at the southern end of the bay.

Cala Tirant is reached by following the road to Cavalleria from Fornells. This road skirts the marsh to the south, and after 2 km the right turn to Cala Tirant has good marshland either side of the road.

There is accommodation at Fornells and in the various resorts between there and Maó (Mahón), as well as camping at Cala Tirant.

NORTH-EAST COAST OF MENORCA: PORT D'ADDAIA AREA
40°00N 04°10E

East of Fornells is another rewarding area between Son Parc and Port d'Addaia. The coast here was marshy, and indeed still is, but the extent of freshwater marsh has declined with the spread of tourist hotels and apartments. Son Parc marsh is still good for raptors and herons such as Little Bittern and Night Heron.

Arenal d'En Castell is a couple of kilometres to the east along rewarding clifftop footpaths. Peregrines, Blue Rock Thrushes and Rock Doves breed along the cliffs, and Audouin's Gulls are frequent. The clifftops are good for wild flowers, Tawny Pipits and Dartford Warblers.

To the south of Port d'Addaia is an interesting wetland area formed mainly of old salines. These, however, are not accessible from Addaia itself (some maps suggest otherwise). This area has rewarded visitors with some spectacular sightings during migration, such as a dozen Red-footed Falcons recorded together in May. To reach the Salines d'Addaia, turn off the Maó to Fornells road towards Cap de Faváritx and after about 2.5 km there is a left turn onto a track, opposite a striking gateway with four white pillars. After a further 2 km there is a gate on the right leading to the reserve. Signs prohibit entry, but appear to refer to motor vehicles, and the area can be easily approached on foot from here. The Cap de Faváritx is a good place to see Audouin's Gull and Blue Rock Thrush, along with spring passage visitors such as Black-eared Wheatear. A small lake – the Basse de Morella – near the lighthouse has Little Bittern and a good selection of waders. Ospreys fish in the fjords and bays in this area.

S'ALBUFERA DES GRAO, MENORCA

39°55N 04°15E

Between Faváritx and the capital, Maó (Mahón), lies a small marshland area, or *albufera*, comprising a coastal lagoon with emergent vegetation, *maquis* and low cliffs. Osprey is a characteristic bird here, with local breeding birds dropping in to fish, and several birds congregating after nesting.

Booted Eagles are common and they, with Marsh Harriers and Red and Black Kites are the raptors most frequently encountered. Rarer birds of prey, such as migrating Red-footed Falcons or visiting Eleonora's Falcons turn up regularly. Little Egret is a non-breeding resident in small numbers, and Whiskered and other terns and herons are often present. A good range of waders passes through in spring and autumn and in winter there may be 5–7000 ducks of several common species.

Behind the beach at Es Grao there are pinewoods where Night Herons roost. Firecrest is common here, along with an often amazing selection of migrant birds during May and September.

TIMING

April/May and September/October are good for passing migrants, large and small. Wildfowl numbers build up in October and remain high until March.

SPECIES

◆ *Resident* Shag, Little Egret, Red Kite, Marsh Harrier, Booted Eagle,
   Peregrine, Scops Owl, Blue Rock Thrush, Dartford Warbler, Firecrest.

Short-toed Lark

- *Breeding season* Black Kite, Egyptian Vulture, Osprey, Stone Curlew, Scops Owl, Pallid Swift, Bee-eater, Short-toed Lark, Tawny Pipit.
- *Passage* Black-necked Grebe, Squacco, Night and Purple Herons, Red-footed Falcon, migrant raptors, waders, Whiskered Tern and passerines.
- *Winter* wildfowl, Cattle Egret.

ACCESS

From the village of Es Grao the sand bar separating the lagoon from the sea, the pine woods and the lagoon itself are readily accessible. There is little in the way of accommodation at Es Grao, but Maó (Mahón) is not far away and there are several new resorts in the area.

CIUTADELLA–ALGAIARENS, MENORCA

40°03N 03°50E

There is a Natural Area of Special Interest east of Cala Morell, known as La Vall d'Algaiarens, with meadows, oak woods and cliffs. Several small rivers run through the area to the sea where a small marsh is formed. This is often good for waterfowl. There is a large bee-eater colony and a good range of raptors typical of Menorca: Red Kite, Booted Eagle and Egyptian Vulture.

The Ciutadella–Cala Morell road is very rewarding, and can be profitably cycled (bikes are available for hire in Cala Blanca) to allow frequent stops along the narrow road. Rather than turn north to Cala Morell, keep going to reach La Vall d'Algaiarens. Access in summer is prohibited by the owners, and there is often a lot of heavy traffic serving the sand quarries there. If entry is barred, good areas with easier access can be found nearby, although in theory access to the beach is allowed from here on foot.

WEST COAST OF MENORCA

39°55N 03°55E

The west end of the island is dominated by Menorca's second town, Ciutadella. Two capes are worth visiting for seabird migration: Cap d'Artrutx in the south-west corner and Punta Nati in the north-west. Punta Nati often has Cory's Shearwaters passing by from April to October, as well as Yelkouan Shearwaters, which leave the area a month earlier. The landward parts of this headland are also interesting: a dry, windy, steppe-like area with abundant Stone Curlew, Thekla Lark and Blue Rock Thrush. Tawny Pipits, Short-toed Larks and Spectacled Warblers can be found in the hinterland. In the Balearics the last is generally a bird of passage, but they breed here and at one or two other sites in Menorca.

The coast north of Ciutadella has abundant breeding Cory's Shearwaters, which can be seen passing close inshore at sunset. South of the town the coast is a favourite haunt of Audouin's Gull, especially on the cliffs at Cala Blanca, where Pallid Swifts are also common.

TIMING

April to September is the best period for seabirds, but April to June are overall the best birdwatching months.

SPECIES

- *Resident* Shag, Red Kite, Booted Eagle, Peregrine, Osprey, Stone Curlew, Thekla Lark, Blue Rock Thrush, Dartford Warbler, Raven.

◆ *Breeding season* Cory's and Yelkouan Shearwaters, Black Kite, Egyptian Vulture, Audouin's Gull, Pallid and Alpine Swifts, Short-toed Lark, Tawny Pipit, Black-eared Wheatear, Spectacled Warbler.
◆ *Passage* Red-footed Falcon, migrant passerines.

ACCESS
Punta Nati is 5 km west of Ciutadella. Between here and Cala Morell on the north coast are several roads leading to the cliffs and headlands. There is similar regular access to the coast south of Ciutadella to Cap d'Artrutx. There is accommodation in Ciutadella, Cala Morell and Cala Blanca.

SOUTH COAST OF MENORCA

39°50N 04°07E

Menorca's long south coast is officially protected along much of its length, although needless to say pressure from tourists and the developments they spawn is considerable. There are two small wetland areas of particular interest, at Son Bou and Santa Galdana. Son Bou is an extensive reedbed, the only site on the island for breeding Moustached Warbler.

Farther west is the unplanned and ugly resort of Cala Santa Galdana, named after the beautiful and rewarding river valley at whose mouth it lies. Here and at Cala Turqueta, farther west still, is lush riverine vegetation where Cetti's Warblers betray their presence with their explosive song. These valleys – *barrancs* – have steep sides where Egyptian Vultures and Alpine Swifts nest. During autumn migration the trees and scrub can be dripping with warblers, flycatchers and chats. As Cala Santa Galdana resort expands, Cala Turqueta and, in between, Cala Macarella, may prove to be more interesting sites.

TIMING
Spring is the best time for the wetlands, although autumn migration – late September and early October – can be spectacular.

Marsh Harrier (female)

SPECIES
- *Resident* Little Egret, Red Kite, Marsh Harrier, Booted Eagle, Peregrine, Water Rail, Scops Owl, Blue Rock Thrush, Moustached and Dartford Warblers, Firecrest.
- *Breeding season* Black Kite, Egyptian Vulture, Pallid and Alpine Swifts, Bee-eater, Short-toed Lark, Tawny Pipit, Great Reed Warbler, Golden Oriole.

ACCESS
Son Bou is just to the east of Sant Jaume. From Alaior on the 721 road take the Sant Jaume road, but instead of turning right after 2 km carry on to Son Bou hamlet. Santa Galdana *barranc* is west of the town of that name, via the small road to Es Moli de Dalt, a right turn on entering the town from the north. A rewarding clifftop walk links Cala Santa Galdana with Cala Macarella. Cala Turqueta is approached from Ciutadella.

There are several archaeological sites, perhaps the most fascinating being the *talaiots*, megalithic constructions on the road to Sant Tomàs.

IBIZA
39°20N 01°30E

Ibiza and Formentera are the two southernmost Balearic islands, 220 km from Africa. They are rocky with numerous offshore islands, and are especially important for Yelkouan Shearwater, Audouin's Gull and Eleonora's Falcon.

For other species, the pine-clad larger island, Ibiza, has more diversity, but in view of the small size of the island, the lack of much in the way of variety in its habitats and the general lack of water and wetlands, it is somewhat limited. The pine woods are home to Crossbills and areas of bare ground often have Short-toed Larks on them. Hoopoes, Crested Larks, Stonechats, Sardinian Warblers and Fan-tailed Warblers are generally common throughout the island and Woodchat Shrikes are usually to be seen perched on overhead cables. The rocky coastal areas are home to Rock Sparrow, which is often seen around Portinatx lighthouse in the north, and Blue Rock Thrush, which is also found inland in hilly areas.

There are ancient saltworks on the southern tip of Ibiza: the island was once named 'Island of Salt'. This is the only wetland area on the island, although the *salines* are very dry from late spring until autumn. Black-winged Stilts and Kentish Plovers breed there, and Little Egrets are common visitors. Flamingos are irregular, but fairly frequent, especially in autumn and winter. Recently Shelduck has begun to colonize the area. Spectacled Warbler breeds in glasswort scrub in and around the old saltworks, but is rare. Nearby, Punta de Ses Portes is an excellent sea-watching promontory looking across to Formentera and the islands in the sound. Towards dusk Yelkouan and Cory's Shearwaters pass by the headland.

TIMING
Between mid-April and mid-June summer migrants are in evidence, and from late July to October return passage of, first, waders and then passerines can be outstanding. All the seabirds are around from April to September.

SPECIES
- *Resident* Shag, Shelduck, Peregrine, Kentish Plover, Blue Rock Thrush, Sardinian Warbler, Crossbill, Rock Sparrow.

◆ *Breeding season* Cory's and Yelkouan Shearwaters, Stone Curlew, Black-winged Stilt, Audouin's Gull, Scops Owl, Pallid Swift, Short-toed Lark, Tawny Pipit, Spectacled Warbler.

◆ *Passage* Flamingo, migrant waders and passerines.

ACCESS

Package and flight-only deals are readily available to Ibiza from northern Europe. There are flights from several Spanish cities and ferry services from Palma de Mallorca, Alicante and València.

Ses Salines is south of Eivissa (Ibiza) town, and the road to Sa Canal passes through the area. Interesting parts of the island's interior can be explored by taking the roads from the main town west to Sant Josep de la Talaia or north to Sant Miquel de Balansant. There are numerous hotels around the island.

ISLANDS AND HEADLANDS OF IBIZA

38°52N 01°14E

There are several small islands lying just off the coast of Ibiza. Vedrà and Vedranell are a pair of islands off the south-west coast with high densities of Yelkouan Shearwater and Eleonora's Falcon. Farther round the west coast there is a group of islands off Sant Antoní bay, and the adjacent headland at Cala Bassa, where Audouin's Gull can be seen, along with Peregrines. One of the largest colonies of Storm Petrel in the Balearics breeds on these islands, and can sometimes be seen at dusk from the headland.

The north-west coast between Cabo Nonó and the Illa Murada, near Punta de Sa Creu is an area of limestone cliffs and pinewoods where Storm Petrel, Shag and a few dozen pairs of Eleonora's breed. There are Eleonora's Falcons on the north-east coast, on the Illa Tagomago, and the adjacent headland at Cabo Roig.

There are no regular, formal arrangements for visiting the islands, but it is worth checking at the various harbours and hotels for information on occasional boat-trips. Some of the headlands are difficult to reach, but the following can be approached by car: Cap Llentrica, Cala Bassa, Cabo Nonó, Punta de Sa Creu, Cabo Roig, Punta de Ses Portes.

FORMENTERA

38°40N 01°30E

The much smaller island of Formentera is separated from Ibiza by a chain of islands, the Illas dels Freus, which are very important for seabirds, the two shearwaters and Audouin's Gull in particular. The islands and their birds can be viewed with ease, from the daily Ibiza–Formentera ferry,. Formentera itself is important for seabirds, with the best population of the Balearic subspecies of Yelkouan Shearwater in the world, at the eastern promontory known as La Mola. A road runs the length (21 km) of the island to Punta de Sa Ruda and some small tracks lead to other parts of the promontory.

The northern peninsula of Formentera is dominated by ancient *salines* andtwo large pools, or *estanys*. One of the largest winter concentrations of Black-necked Grebes in Europe congregates here, with over 4000 recorded. In spring and summer Black-winged Stilts and Kentish Plovers breed. The lagoons can be good during April/May and August–October for migrant waders and occasional groups of Flamingos.

CANARY ISLANDS

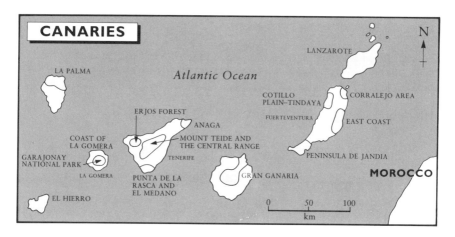

The Canary Islands are a subtropical outpost of Spain, a volcanic archipelago as much a part of Africa as of Europe. As with most oceanic island groups, they are a speciality birdwatching destination; what the bird life lacks in diversity it makes up for in uniqueness and rarity. From a conservation point of view, therefore, the islands are of immense importance. They form Europe's most important centre of endemism (in other words, an unusually high number of plant and animal species and subspecies are unique) and, as might be expected, several of the birds found here are either globally threatened or of international conservation concern. To 'clean up' on the specialities, you need to visit at least two islands, but this is not difficult.

Four Canarian species are found nowhere else in the world (Bolle's and White-tailed Pigeons, Canary Islands Chat and Blue Chaffinch, all of which are globally threatened) and two are found only in the Canaries and Madeira (Plain Swift and Berthelot's Pipit). Another globally threatened species, the Houbara Bustard, has its only European foothold here and is represented by an endemic subspecies. As for the local kinglet, no one really knows whether it is a Firecrest, a Goldcrest, or qualifies as a separate species in its own right. Even some of the familiar birds are worth a second look: Robin, Blue Tit and Chaffinch are represented here by very distinctive and attractive races.

Several other species are found here but are almost unknown on mainland Europe: Barbary Falcon, Cream-coloured Courser, Barbary Partridge and Trumpeter Finch. Huge numbers of Cory's Shearwaters nest in the islands, along with, in summer, Bulwer's Petrel and Little Shearwater. Clearly the Canary Islands are an outstanding destination for more experienced birdwatchers whose aim is for quality rather than quantity.

Package deals and charter flights from northern European abound and are fairly cheap. Hire cars are easy to come by, and there are inexpensive local firms as well as the usual international ones. Hired cars are a target for theft, so never leave equipment on show, and remove belongings overnight. The car ferry from Cádiz is a relaxed way of covering the distance over some 48 hours, with the added advantage of deck-based seabird watching in some of the best waters Europe has to offer. In particular, the waters around the Portuguese Selvagens group, just to the north of the Canaries, will be good territory for oceanic rarities (see page 196).

BIRDWATCHING SITES

LANZAROTE

28°55N 13°50W

On Lanzarote you know instinctively that the Sahara desert is not far away. Its famous beaches are lava black, except for one or two tiny ones in the east where the sand has drifted across from Africa. Drifting across from Europe is a tourist horde the island cannot cope with; there is not enough water. However, it means that Lanzarote is easy and cheap to get to, and can be used as first base *en route* to nearby Fuerteventura and beyond.

Lanzarote still holds a reasonable population of some of the birds more usually sought on Fuerteventura, including the Houbara Bustard and Cream-coloured Courser. These can be found in the plains between La Corona and Las Honduras and the plains in the south-west of the island.

Lanzarote is probably the best island in the whole archipelago for Barbary and Eleonora's Falcons. The Mirador del Río, at the far north-eastern corner of the island is good for both species and for sea watching. Red-billed Tropicbirds sometimes turn up and there may be a chance of Madeiran Storm Petrel here.The Famara area has impressive cliffs where Ospreys, Barbary Falcons, Cory's Shearwaters and Egyptian Vultures nest.

Timanfaya National Park is an extraordinary landscape of multi-coloured volcanic cones and lava fields. The coast here holds an impressive colony of Cory's Shearwaters, which can be seen passing along the coast from El Golfo. Just to the south are the saltpans of Janubio, important for waders on migration. It is likely that the occasional American vagrant would turn up here in October. Trumpeter Finches breed in the wildlands around the lagoons.

TIMING

Seabirds and Eleonora's Falcons are at their best from July to September, but this is the hottest period and therefore less good for land-based birdwatching. Some package travel deals increase in price during the Christmas and mid-winter peak period.

SPECIES
- *Resident* Cory's Shearwater, Osprey, Egyptian Vulture, Barbary Falcon, Barbary Partridge, Cream-coloured Courser, Stone Curlew, Houbara Bustard, Plain Swift, Lesser Short-toed Lark, Berthelot's Pipit, Spectacled Warbler, Trumpeter Finch.
- *Breeding season* Little Shearwater, Bulwer's and Storm Petrels, Eleonora's Falcon.
- *Passage* Eleonora's Falcon, possible rare American and African migrants.

ACCESS
Timanfaya National park and the plains of La Geria are crossed by the Yaiza–Tinaja road. There are numerous tracks off this road but in the interests of the ground-nesting birds and fragile flora, only clearly 'official' tracks should be used. The Janubio saltworks, to the south, is bordered by the El Golfo road. Famara beach is north of La Caleta, but the cliffs are accessible only on foot from here.

EAST COAST OF FUERTEVENTURA
28°28N 13°54W

Fuerteventura, like Lanzarote to the north, is windswept, almost treeless, rocky and dry. If this sounds uninviting, perhaps the thought that it is the only place in the world where the Canary Islands Chat is found helps make amends. It looks like a cross between a Stonechat and a Whinchat and can be found within a few minutes of landing at the airport. Some 2–3 km to the

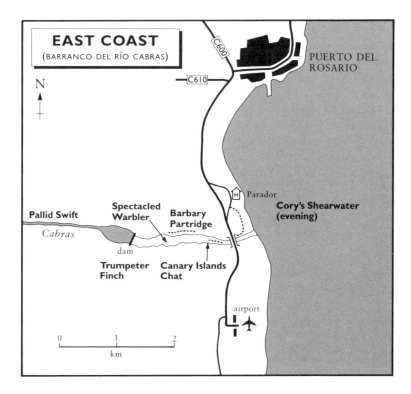

north is a dry, steep-sided river bed or *barranco*, the Barranco del Río Cabras. A pair or two of Canary Islands Chats breed here, and Trumpeter Finches, Barbary Partridges and Black-bellied Sandgrouse are also to be found. About 12 km south of the airport is the Barranco de la Torre, another Chat site.

The coast between Barranco de la Torre and Gran Tarajal is rocky with hills ranging inland. The area is crossed by tracks of varying quality. Barbary Falcon can be found in this area, along with a typical range of other species.

TIMING
Seabirds are best in summer, but October to April is the best time for Houbaras and other plains birds.

SPECIES
◆ *Resident* Cory's Shearwater, Egyptian Vulture, Barbary Falcon, Cream-coloured Courser, Stone Curlew, Black-bellied Sandgrouse, Plain Swift, Lesser Short-toed Lark, Berthelot's Pipit, Canary Islands Chat, Spectacled Warbler, Trumpeter Finch.

ACCESS
The Barranco del Río Cabras is reached by turning off the highway at the sign for the Parador, then down a track to the right. The Parador itself is a handy base for exploring the whole island over a two- or three-day visit, if it suits your price range. The sea-facing rooms have balconies from which Cory's Shearwaters can be watched each evening as they return from their feeding forays out to sea. A kilometre or two to the north is Puerto del Rosario, which has less expensive accommodation, and 5 km farther on is Barranco de la Monja, which may hold more chats.

COTILLO PLAIN–TINDAYA, FUERTEVENTURA
28°35N 14°00W
The other speciality of Fuerteventura is the Houbara Bustard, of which there are perhaps three hundred on the island.From Puerto del Rosario it is a 20-km drive north-west to the rambling village of Tindaya. Between here and Cotillo at the north-west corner of the island is a rough stony plain which holds a healthy population of Houbaras, along with Black-bellied Sandgrouse and Cream-coloured Coursers. It is essential to scan constantly for these difficult birds, and heat haze can be a problem from late morning to late afternoon. However, the sandgrouse are more likely to be seen in flight, especially in the mornings and towards dusk.

The whole coastal plain south of the Tindaya area is good, too. The road to Los Molinos, on the coast, is a good detour which should produce Egyptian Vultures, Chats, Coursers, Black-bellied Sandgrouse and Trumpeter Finches. The more accessible headlands on this west coast are good sea-watching points and Punta del Salvaje, north of Los Molinos, and Punta de Paso Chico, reached via Tindaya, are in a good breeding area for Cory's Shearwaters.

TIMING
Houbaras, Sandgrouse and Coursers tend to be easiest to see in winter, but they are around all year and only mid-summer is difficult, because of the heat haze and high winds.

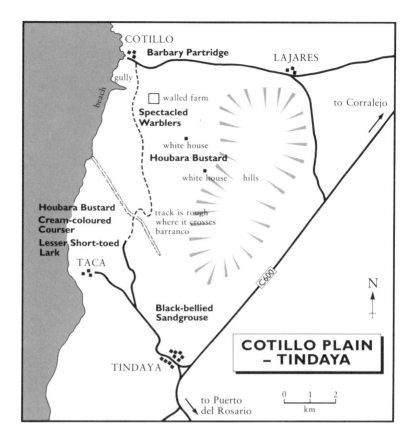

SPECIES
◆ *Resident* Egyptian Vulture, Barbary Partridge, Cream-coloured Courser, Stone Curlew, Houbara Bustard, Plain Swift, Lesser Short-toed Lark, Berthelot's Pipit, Spectacled Warbler, Trumpeter Finch.
ACCESS
Drive through Tindaya village on the tarmacked road. After about 2.5 km an unpaved (and unmarked) track runs off to the right. This eventually leads to Cotillo. The tarmac otherwise carries on for another couple of kilometres before running out. This portion of road is worth scanning from before taking the Cotillo track. It is important not to leave the track, since in recent years the over-use of four-wheel drive vehicles off the road has contributed to the growing problems faced by the Houbaras.

Cotillo is some 8 km on. The track has a rough section about half way along, but is negotiable with care. Within sight of the village, the landscape begins to be dotted with buildings and scarred with other tracks and may soon become less rewarding than the Tindaya end.

North of the turning to Tindaya from the main road, is a turning eastwards to Vallebrón. This valley holds a very high density of Canary Islands Chat. Vallebrón can also be reached (via a better road) from the east coast, turning west to Caldereta.

PENÍNSULA DE JANDÍA, FUERTEVENTURA

28°09N 04°16W

The rugged, semi-arid massif at the southern end of the island includes the Pico de Zarza, at 807 m the highest peak on the island. It is linked to the main part of the island by a sandy plain. There are unique plant communities here, including *Euphorbia handiensis*, endemic to this small area. It is the globally threatened Houbara Bustard which is the main attraction, the most important population in the archipelago. As part of a conservation scheme alfalfa fields are planted in the area, and in summer these are good places to sit at first light, waiting for the Houbaras to come and feed.

The area is protected as a Natural Park, but has been the scene of considerable controversy since the EU granted funds to a wind energy project in the middle of the core area. Several windmills have been built, causing serious damage to the vegetation and disturbing the bustards and other birds. The SEO and RSPB are currently fighting this both locally and in Brussels.

This is also one of the best areas in the island for Canary Islands Chat, Cream-coloured Courser, Black-bellied Sandgrouse and Trumpeter Finch. Egyptian Vultures and Barbary Falcons range widely over the area.

TIMING
Most of the key species are resident. On the shore, migration peaks in April and October.

SPECIES
- *Resident* Cory's Shearwater, Egyptian Vulture, Barbary Falcon, Barbary Partridge, Cream-coloured Courser, Stone Curlew, Kentish Plover, Houbara Bustard, Plain Swift, Lesser Short-toed Lark, Berthelot's Pipit, Canary Islands Chat, Spectacled Warbler, Trumpeter Finch.
- *Passage* Grey and Ringed Plovers, Whimbrel, Bar-tailed Godwit, Sanderling, rarities.

ACCESS
The main access route is the road to Morro Jable. There is also the road to the Jandía lighthouse and the Cofete road. Accommodation is available in Jandía, Morro Jable and Tarajalejo.

CORRALEJO AREA, FUERTEVENTURA

28°45N 13°55W

This sprawling, unplanned tourist town is not at first sight an obvious bird-watching haunt, but first appearances can be deceptive. Sea-watching from the pier early in the morning or at dusk is bound to produce Cory's Shearwater. The beach to the south-east is often good for waders during migration, and Kentish Plovers at all times. To the south is a lava plain, which has Houbara Bustards, Canary Islands Chats and Barbary Partridges. The area around Peña Azul, reached off the main La Oliva–Corralejo road, is worth scanning.

Offshore from Corralejo there is an important seabird island with colonies of Bulwer's Petrels, Cory's and Little Shearwaters, Storm Petrels and, possibly, Madeiran Storm Petrels. Sea-watches from across the sound may prove rewarding, but a good close-up is needed to separate the last two species. Occasionally boat-trips are organized to the island, but the best bet may be to negotiate a tailor-made trip round the island towards dusk, without landing.

MOUNT TEIDE AND THE CENTRAL RANGE, TENERIFE

28°11N 16°39W

There are very few places on Tenerife where the peak of mount Teide cannot be seen. It even dominates the seascapes of neighbouring La Gomera and Gran Canaria. The mountain itself is of relatively limited bird interest, but is geologically and botanically priceless. Several plant species are found nowhere else in the world. Among the most characteristic are the towers of bugloss, *Echium wildpretii,* which are very reminiscent of the giant lobelias and senecios of Kilimanjaro and Mount Kenya. The ubiquitous Berthelot's Pipit and rarer Trumpeter Finch share this habitat with a sparse but important flora and precious archaeological remains from the era of the *guanchos,* the original inhabitants of the islands.

An information centre at El Portillo explains all about these aboriginals and the geology and wildlife. A small garden is planted with the most interesting and noticeable plants of the park. Little artificial ponds here attract wild Canaries as well as the distinct Tenerifan subspecies of Chiffchaff and Blue Tit. Occasionally a Blue Chaffinch will appear from lower altitudes.

The lower slopes of the range are cloaked in Canary pine, where the Blue Chaffinches are found. The picnic site at Las Lajas is a particular hot-spot. The Blue Chaffinches, along with Berthelot's Pipits, Turtle Doves and the Tenerife race of Great Spotted Woodpecker regularly come to the drinking-water taps. At the base of each tap is a stone depression where water gathers.

TIMING
The area is of interest all year round, but weekends are best avoided.

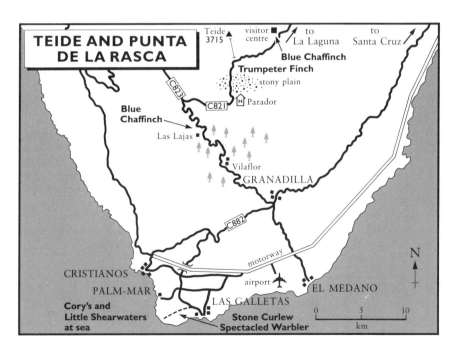

SPECIES
◆ *Resident* Barbary Partridge, Plain Swift, Great Spotted Woodpecker,
Berthelot's Pipit, Blue Tit, Chiffchaff, 'Canaries Kinglet', Chaffinch, Blue
Chaffinch, Canary, Trumpeter Finch.
ACCESS
The picnic site at Las Lajas is 9 km north of Vilaflor, on the south-west slopes
of the Teide range. East of Teide, the road to La Esperanza and La Laguna
runs through equally good pine forest. The forest is divided into *montes* or
forest estates and the Monte de la Victoria, about 15 km west of La Laguna,
is particularly good for Blue Chaffinch, 'Canaries Kinglets' and Plain Swift.

ANAGA, TENERIFE
27°48N 15°25W
The Anaga peninsula is the mountainous north-eastern part of Tenerife. Its
fearsome peaks at first suggest impenetrable terrain. Below the peaks,
however, are good, if slow, roads which offer access to one of the few
remaining laurel forests on Tenerife. This is the habitat of Bolle's and White-
tailed Pigeons. Both species are dependent on the *laurisilva* which once
covered great expanses of Tenerife, La Gomera, El Hierro and La Palma.

Bolle's Pigeon is more frequently encountered than the White-tailed,
which is particularly rare on Tenerife. Both species are best found by
watching over the forest canopy from above, since this affords a wider field
of view. Bolle's Pigeon should present no difficulties, and small groups
frequently fly from one side of the valley to the other. From above the dark
blue-grey appearance is distinctive, reminiscent of dark Stock Doves. The
rarer White-tailed Pigeon requires more patience, but should be seen,
especially at either end of the day. Its pale tail is obvious, as is its overall
brownish-burgundy coloration. The forest at Erjos (page 156) has a better
population, but is harder to reach, so it is worth trying here first.

TIMING
The area is of interest all year round. The pigeons breed in most months of
the year except August.
◆ *Resident* Sparrowhawk, Barbary Partridge, Bolle's and White-tailed
Pigeons, 'Canaries Kinglet', Canary.
ACCESS
The road out of La Laguna into the peninsular, via Las Mercedes, winds up
the mountains towards a series of lookout points. Of these, the Mirador del
Inglés is best. Even though it can be crowded at weekends, the mirador looks
out over the forest some hundreds of feet below, where the birds are
oblivious. It is then a matter of waiting. The north coast of the Anaga
peninsular is reached by continuing on this road and turning left after 12 km
to Taganana. Two offshore islets, the Roque de Fuera and the Roque de
Dentro hold one of the most important seabird colonies in the islands. They
are inaccessible but an evening sea-watch from the adjacent headland should
reveal Cory's and Little Shearwaters, Bulwer's, Storm and Madeiran Storm
Petrels, although the last two would be inseparable at any distance without
considerable experience of both species' flight patterns. There is always a
chance of negotiating a boat-trip offshore for a closer look.

ERJOS FOREST, TENERIFE

28°20N 16°49W

Near Erjos in the north-west part of the island there is a larger expanse of laurel forest with good populations of both pigeons. Access is, however, more difficult that at Anaga. Erjos lies south-west of Icod on the C820. Before the village (driving north) there is a left turn down a track, opposite the *casa forestal*. Eventually this track enters the forest. A rocky outcrop on the right after about 5 km signals an open area from which to watch over the canopy, and other similar watchpoints can be found along the way. It is not a good track, especially for the first 500 m, but passable.

PUNTA DE LA RASCA AND EL MEDANO, TENERIFE

28°00N 16°20W

The Protected Landscape of Malpaís de la Rasca is a magnificent example of land claimed from the sea by volcanic action, and is therefore geologically very important. Botanists will be delighted by the impressive stands of *Euphorbia canariensis*. This is one of the best places in the island to see Trumpeter Finch, Berthelot's Pipit, Barbary Partridge and Lesser Short-toed Lark. In recent years a roost of Long-eared Owls has collected in the trees at the entrance to the area, to the right of the gate. From here it is a 20-minute walk to the lighthouse at the coast. On the way, the low hills are good for Barbary Partridge. At the coast, Cory's and Little Shearwaters can be watched from the headland, along with Bulwer's and 'Storm' Petrels.

Round the coast to the east is the expanding town of El Medano. West of here are coastal ponds which are good for waders during spring, late summer/autumn and to some extent winter.

TIMING

Seabirds are present from April to September (Cory's all year). Wader migration peaks in April–May and again in late August–October.

ACCESS

Take the Las Galletas exit from the southern coastal motorway. 2 km before Las Galletas, after a series of walled banana plantations is a service station on the right. A track immediately afterwards leads behind the plantations, to an old farmstead and a gate, which is usually locked. Recently there have been 'no entry' signs here, but access is not supposed to be barred, and local birdwatchers are trying to get this sorted out. Punta de la Rasca is reached on foot from here. Alternative access to the point is found by taking the road to Palm-Mar (right at the first crossroads after the motorway exit), driving left along the shore for 400 m and walking the last kilometre. For El Medano lagoons, take the road that runs along the coast towards Los Abrigos. A track leads south of the airport towards the coast and the first large pond. The coast here is dominated by a great red rock, Montaña Roja, which looks like a mini Gibraltar. The other side of the rock are more ponds, where at high tide a typical selection of migrating or wintering waders may be found. Montaña Roja itself is a protected area and the area around is worth exploring for Stone Curlew, Trumpeter Finch and, allegedly, Cream-coloured Courser.

Barbary Partridge

CROSSING TO LA GOMERA

28°20N 17°00W

This delightful island could hardly be a greater contrast with the bustle of the tourist traps of Tenerife. There are few tourists, and the island's economy is dominated by bananas and other tropical fruit. This may change as La Gomera gets its first airport, due to open in the mid-1990s.

There are currently two ways to get to the island from Tenerife, and both entail suffering Los Cristianos, a monument to brash, unashamed sun-worship. It is from the little harbour here that the jet-foil and the car ferry sail for La Gomera. Unless you are in a great hurry, the jet-foil is not advisable. The ferry, however, is a birdwatcher's delight. Cory's are abundant, with very close views of a hundred or so the norm. Little Shearwaters are harder to pick up, partly because they do not seem to come so close, but also, of course, on account of their size. Bulwer's Petrels are usually seen flying away from the boat, but are instantly recognizable by their all-dark appearance, long tail and tern-like (or better, Pratincole-like) flight. Madeiran Storm Petrels are around, but spotting them is a matter of good eyesight and luck. In August and September Great and Sooty Shearwaters are likely. Non-bird interest includes dolphins, which are pretty reliable, the occasional turtle and the amazing flying fish, which leap out of the boat's bow wave.

July to September are the best months for seabirds, although Cory's Shearwaters are seen all year. Most birdwatchers note that the evening crossings are more productive than in the morning.

GARAJONAY NATIONAL PARK, LA GOMERA

28°07N 17°13W

Some of the best preserved laurel forest in the Canaries is to be found in this 4000-ha national park. Festooned with lichens and moss, and usually dripping with condensation, there is a distinctly tropical feel to Garajonay. Indeed, it is a genuine cloud forest reminiscent of central America. It is a strange experience to walk in this cool, dark forest in the rain, knowing that the rain is created by the trees themselves.

A sea of cloud, which usually hovers at between 600 and 1500 m around each island, sometimes obscures the forest and the height of the cloud determines how best to watch for the two laurel pigeons. Ideally, the best way to see them is by viewing over as wide an expanse of canopy as possible. On the many occasions when the cloud is low and dense, it is worth getting into the forest itself and seeking out resting birds – by no means an easy task.

TIMING
The area is of interest all year round. The pigeons breed in most months of the year except August.

SPECIES
◆ *Resident* Buzzard, Woodcock, Bolle's and White-tailed Pigeons, Plain Swift, 'Canaries Kinglet', Canary.

ACCESS
Garajonay is reached quickly and easily from San Sebastian, along some 25 km of excellent road. There are several vantage points worth trying. Soon after entering the Park on the San Sebastian–Valle Gran Rey road there is a *mirador*, or viewpoint, on the right overlooking three great basalt plugs. If it is not windy, White-tailed Pigeons may be seen flying around over the trees below. The best area, however, is a little farther on, after turning right towards Hermigua. Bolle's Pigeon can be seen along this road, but the best area is down a track leading off left (signposted 'El Cedro'). On misty mornings, all seems quiet down here. A Woodcock may wander along the track: the species is present at a very high density in the *monte*. After about 1 km this dirt track forks. Taking the right fork a short way, the canopy opens out and if the cloud has lifted, the pigeons may fly to and fro overhead.

The coast of La Gomera

28°06N 17°21W

Much of the rocky coast of La Gomera is difficult to reach, except by rough tracks out of the few coastal towns, or on foot. In several places there are good seabird populations, along with Ospreys and Barbary Falcons. Two of the best sectors are between Punta Falcones and Playa de Santiago in the south, and Costa de Majona, in the north-east. In both cases, driving to the nearest coastal village and walking some distance along the coast is the best bet. Thus, a walk west from Playa de Santiago or west from Tagaluche (10 km west of Hermigua) may be productive.

Alternatively, there are occasional organized boat-trips to interesting parts of the coast, such as the spectacular Protected Landscape of Los Órganos. These cliffs take the form of vertical stones like great organ pipes and are the haunt of Ospreys. Enquire at the harbour at San Sebastian about possible trips. An evening trip in summer should be good for seabirds.

Gran Canaria

28°03N 15°41W

The Canary Islands are generally divided between the hot, dry islands of the east and the more oceanic and humid islands in the west. Gran Canaria is somewhere in the middle and as such has an unusual combination of habitats and features. The main town is Las Palmas, which has a colony of Bulwer's Petrels and breeding Barbary Falcons on a volcanic outcrop known as La Isleta, to the north of the town. After about 30 km, the main coast road south of the town passes close to the Costa de Arinaga, which has breeding Kentish Plovers and Lesser Short-toed Larks, and good wader passage.

There are few fine examples of Canary Pine forest on the island, but the forest reserve of Inagua, Ojeda and Pajonales is an exception. This is an important area for the Blue Chaffinch and the Canarian subspecies of Great Spotted Woodpecker. The wooded valley can be explored from El Juncal, by taking the road opposite the church. The Gran Canaria subspecies of Blue Chaffinch is distinctive, with paler underparts and more prominent wing bars than the Tenerife version. Unlike the Tenerife race, it is highly endangered.

The road running south-west from Agaete crosses another important forest area, Tamadaba, with similar species, although the Blue Chaffinch is harder to find here. The coast here is worth checking for breeding Barbary Falcons and Ospreys. Similarly a pine forest in the south-west, near Mogán, is worth checking. This area, the Macizo de Tauro Protected Landscape, also has large areas of scrub and semi-desert where Trumpeter Finches can be found. There is a minor road between Mogán and Ayacata, with tracks off, which affords access to the area.

La Palma

28°43N 17°52W

La Palma stands out from the other islands in the Canaries group because of its fertility and lushness. It is here that Spain produces fruit more usually associated with the tropics – not that the Tropic of Cancer is that far away. Thus there is an extensive network of roads serving the farm areas where bananas, avocados, pineapples and papayas grow.

La Palma's chief claim to fame is the relative abundance of the two laurel pigeons, which are more common here than on the other islands where they may be found. Apart from this, the main natural attraction is the National Park of La Caldera de Taburiente. This pine-cloaked crater is an impressive reminder of the archipelago's volcanic origins.

The coast of La Palma has scattered seabird colonies, the most important of which is at the Roques de Garafía, a group of stacks and islets at the northern end of the Costa de Puntagorda. Cory's Shearwaters and Bulwer's Petrels nest here.

SPECIES
◆ *Resident* Cory's Shearwater, Short-eared Owl, Stone Curlew, Bolle's and White-tailed Pigeons, Plain Swift, Berthelot's Pipit, Spectacled Warbler, 'Canaries Kinglet', Canary, Chough.
◆ *Breeding season* Manx Shearwater, Bulwer's and Storm Petrels.
ACCESS
The island can be reached by air and sea from all the other islands. Good areas of laurel forest exist at Monte de los Sauces y Puntallana. There are various forest roads which penetrate this area off the Santa Cruz–Barlovento and Santa Cruz–Roque Los Muchachos roads. The seabird areas are not easy to reach but the road between Los Llanos and Garafía has tracks leading off to the coast at intervals. There are hotels in Santa Cruz de la Palma, Puerto Naos and Tazacorte.

EL HIERRO
27°44N 18°01W
This is the smallest and least well known of the main islands. It is also the southern- and westernmost. It is essentially a mountain rising from the sea bed, and shows traces of a volcanic crater. In places the mountain, which rises to 1500 m, slopes almost vertically to the sea and its covering of pine and laurel forest clings on precariously.

The entire western part of the island is the Natural Park of El Hierro and within this, four areas are recognized Important Bird Areas. The Monte Verde de Frontera is an area of heath, scrub and laurel forest and inland cliffs. Cory's Shearwaters breed on the cliffs along with Ospreys. Bolle's Pigeons inhabit the forested area, but are believed to be restricted to ten pairs or so. The rocky south-west coast also has Cory's Shearwaters and Ospreys, as well as Little Shearwaters nesting. Along the cliffs of the west coast these species can all be found along with Bulwer's and Storm Petrels.

SPECIES
◆ *Resident* Cory's Shearwater, Osprey, Stone Curlew, Short-eared Owl, Bolle's Pigeon, Plain Swift, Berthelot's Pipit, Spectacled Warbler, Canary.
◆ *Breeding season* Little Shearwater, Bulwer's and Storm Petrels.
ACCESS
There are ferries to the island from Tenerife, La Palma and La Gomera. The Park can be explored from the road that runs between Valverde and El Golfe; there is a turning off this road to La Restinga as well. Otherwise, there are numerous estate roads and tracks which can be followed with care.

PORTUGAL

P ortugal comprises three autonomous regions: continental Portugal, Madeira, an archipelago off the Moroccan coast north of the Canaries, and the Azores, in mid-Atlantic. This chapter deals with continental Portugal, which covers an area of 92,000 km² along Europe's Atlantic seaboard.

The River Tejo may be said to divide Portugal: the country to the north is rather mountainous with some original oak forest, heathland and plenty of pine plantations and other coniferous cover; the country to the south is mostly undulating plains cultivated with cereals, grazed with sheep, goats and cattle, or covered with Mediterranean forest, particularly cork oak.

The long Portuguese coastline is broken by a number of major estuaries, where four of the five great Iberian rivers meet the Atlantic after flowing though great stretches of Spanish and Portuguese countryside. Otherwise the coast is largely sandy withdunes and marshes, although there are stretches of cliffs and offshore rocky islands.

Tourism is concentrated along the Algarve, but there are good facilities along the west coast and in the historic centres. There is a network of state-approved hotels, the *Pousadas*.

IMPORTANCE FOR BIRDS

For a small country, continental Portugal has its fair share of global rarities. Great and Little Bustards can be found in many parts of the country, sharing the plains with the seriously declining Lesser Kestrel and large numbers of Montagu's Harriers. In the remote border regions there are other international rarities, such as Red Kite, Black Vulture and Spanish Imperial Eagle. Here, too are important populations of Black Storks and Egyptian Vultures. In the wetlands of the south, the Marbled Teal has a fragile foothold.

The Black-shouldered Kite has its European stronghold in southern Portugal, being especially associated with mixed farming and scattered cork oaks, a characteristic landscape.

The river estuaries and lagoons are important for passage and wintering waders, especially Avocets, and for large numbers of migrant passerines.

CONSERVATION

All of Portugal's four main rivers rise in Spain, where there are radical plans to maximize the use of their water, by building dams and irrigation networks. Portugal will get what is left over. This, added to Portugal's own water shortage problems is leading in the near future to serious degradation of her riverine Important Bird Areas and estuaries.

Other problems include the rapid march of eucalyptus afforestation into areas once occupied by prime habitat and the intensification of agriculture. Portugal has seen many of its small wetlands converted into fish farms or drained in recent years. The fish-farm boom, largely funded by the European Union, has also led to the wholesale conversion of ancient saltworks. This piecemeal, and largely unnoticed, loss of habitat has been disastrous.

However, Portugal is starting to benefit from recent reforms in EU policy that will enable farmers to receive subsidies for maintaining agricultural systems which are good for conservation. This is very largely due to the hard work of the country's small conservation movement. The Portuguese Nature Protection League, supported by the RSPB, and the government's Nature Conservation Institute have been the prime movers in cataloguing and conserving the country's bird wealth.

Hunting is legally practised over vast areas of private land on Thursdays, Sundays and public holidays, and illegally at other times.

GETTING THERE AND GETTING AROUND

Lisbon is served by a growing number of direct flights from European and North American cities. There is an international airport in Porto, which has direct flights from some parts of Europe, such as London. The other main point of entry by air is Faro on the Algarve, which receives charter flights from northern Europe as part of the thriving package holiday trade.

Driving from Spain is very straightforward, and many border posts are unmanned. The main roads from Seville to the Algarve, and from Madrid via Badajoz/Elvas are the most used crossings, but other main highways, such as those from Salamanca and Vigo are equally convenient. Some border posts, particularly in mountainous areas, are open only in the summer.

Within Portugal, public transport is an acceptable way of getting from town to town, but a hire car is essential for most birdwatching sites and it is best to book one in advance to be picked up at the airport. Road maps are readily available, but there is a massive road-building programme which renders all maps rapidly out of date. Most of the new roads are excellent, however. In remote rural areas the maps are often slightly, but significantly, inaccurate. Older roads are often in poor condition, and journeys take longer than might be expected. Security is not usually a problem, although the usual precautions are advisable, especially in the busier parts of the Algarve. A bigger problem, frankly, is the standard of Portuguese driving, which can verge on the suicidal. It is also worth bearing in mind that car insurance in Portugal often does not cover hitch-hikers.

BIRDWATCHING SITES

MINHO AND COURA ESTUARIES

41°55N 08°50W

Although less spectacular than the Tejo and Sado estuaries, the mouths of the Minho, Portugal's northernmost river, and of its tributary, the Coura, are important staging posts for many of the waders which congregate in their thousands farther south.

The Mata Nacional do Camarido at the mouth of the river downstream from Caminha is an area of dunes and pine woods, which attracts passerines on migration and which serves as an important high-tide roost.

TIMING

As this is not an area of great importance for breeding birds, late May to early September is the least interesting period, and is in any case a period of heavy human pressure.

SPECIES

- *Resident* Sandwich Tern, Fan-tailed, Dartford and Sardinian Warblers, Crested Tit, Short-toed Treecreeper, Waxbill, Cirl Bunting.
- *Breeding season* Montagu's Harrier, Hobby, Golden Oriole.
- *Passage* Osprey, Marsh Harrier, waders, terns, passerines.
- *Winter* divers, Little Egret, Red-breasted Merganser, Avocet, Sanderling.

ACCESS

The N13 runs the length of the southern shore of the estuary. There is a border crossing over the river to Tui, from where the Spanish side can be explored (see page 15), and there is a ferry crossing from Vila Nova de Cerveira to Goián. The quay at Seixas is good for observing roosting waders and gulls at high tide and the whole coast down to Viana do Castelo can be good for seaducks and divers in the winter.

PENEDA-GÊRES NATIONAL PARK

41°49N 08°07W

The north of Portugal contains an interesting variety of upland habitats, combining both Mediterranean and Atlantic characteristics. Several of the bird species found here are essentially northern European. The Peneda-Gerês National Park is Portugal's only site for several of them: Whinchat, Red-backed Shrike and Bullfinch.

   The National Park rises to 1500 m and is covered with oak, pine, mountain heathland and pasture. It is important for breeding raptors such as Honey Buzzard, Hen and Montagu's Harriers, Golden, Short-toed and Booted Eagles. Rock Thrushes and Choughs inhabit the higher, rockier parts and Great Spotted Cuckoos the scrubbier areas.

TIMING

The ideal time to visit would be late spring, when all the summer migrants have arrived, although late winter is good for raptors.

SPECIES

- *Resident* Goshawk, Golden Eagle, Hen Harrier, Peregrine, Eagle Owl, Dartford Warbler, Crested Tit, Cirl and Rock Buntings, Crossbill, Chough.
- *Breeding season* Honey Buzzard, Short-toed and Booted Eagles, Montagu's Harrier, Hobby, Scops Owl, Great Spotted Cuckoo, Tawny Pipit, Crag Martin, Red-rumped Swallow, Red-backed Shrike, Rock Thrush, Black-eared Wheatear, Whinchat, Subalpine and Bonelli's Warblers, Firecrest.

ACCESS

Peneda-Gerês is situated on the border with Galicia. The frontier post on the road from Ourense in Spain also marks the border of this mountain park, and is open in the summer months only. Approaching from the south, the park boundary is 35 km from Braga, which is in turn about 40 km from the northern city of Porto. A good road runs through the National Park north from Caniçada, off the 103 road from Braga, to the Gerês spa, where there is an information centre. There are numerous smaller roads and forest tracks leading through the forest to above the tree-line from this road. At Caniçada there is a *Pousada*, one of a chain of inexpensive state hotels, which affords superb views of the valleys and has Scops Owls in and around the grounds.

MONTESINHO NATURAL PARK

41°55N 06°50W

In the north-east corner of the country is another mountain area, the Montesinho Natural Park. It is relatively unexplored ornithologically, and would certainly yield a good selection of northern oak-wood species such as

Red-backed Shrike

Redstart, Garden Warbler and Pied Flycatcher. More typical of Iberian oak woods is Bonelli's Warbler, which is common here. Species found here but not in Peneda-Gerês include White Stork and Egyptian Vulture.

The international border area east of Bragança is formed by the river Macãs, a tributary of the Douro (see below). This area holds Portugal's most northerly populations of some of the species, including Bonelli's Eagle, which are typical of the remote border region.

TIMING
See Peneda-Gerês

SPECIES
- *Resident* Goshawk, Golden Eagle, Peregrine, Blue Rock Thrush, Dartford Warbler, Dipper, Cirl and Rock Buntings, Rock Sparrow.
- *Breeding season* White Stork, Short-toed Eagle, Montagu's Harrier, Scops Owl, Great Spotted Cuckoo, Water and Tawny Pipits, Crag Martin, Red-rumped Swallow, Rock and Blue Rock Thrushes, Black-eared Wheatear, Subalpine, Dartford and Bonelli's Warblers, Firecrest, Ortolan Bunting.

ACCESS
The ancient walled town of Bragança is on the southern edge of the park and the 103 road from Bragança to Braga and Porto forms the southern boundary. Roads running north into the park from Bragança or Vinhais to the west are all good. There are information centres in both towns.

UPPER DOURO VALLEY
41°10N 06°45W

About 130 km of the border with Castilla y León is formed by the Douro (Duero) river, and its tributary the Águeda. Both the Portuguese and Spanish banks are outstanding for birds, and the Spanish side is described on page 69. The northern part of the area, from Miranda do Douro to Bemposta, supports a high density of Bonelli's Eagle, Peregrine and Eagle Owl. In the south, from Bemposta to the river's confluence with the Águeda, Egyptian and Griffon Vultures are common. Black Storks and Golden Eagles are relatively common throughout. Blue Rock Thrush, Black and Black-eared Wheatears, Chough, Rock Sparrow and Rock Bunting add to the variety of this little-known area. The surrounding scrublands and woods are good for Red-necked Nightjar, Dartford, Spectacled and Subalpine Warblers.

TIMING
The International Douro is of interest all year round, with early spring being particularly good for stork and raptor migration and nesting.

SPECIES
- *Resident* Great Crested Grebe, Grey Heron, Red Kite, Buzzard, Griffon Vulture, Bonelli's Eagle, Goshawk, Sparrowhawk, Peregrine, Eagle Owl, Hoopoe, Thekla Lark, Grey Wagtail, Great Grey and Woodchat Shrikes, Blue Rock Thrush, Black Wheatear, Orphean and Dartford Warblers, Azure-winged Magpie, Chough, Rock Sparrow, Rock Bunting.
- *Breeding season* White and Black Storks, Black Kite, Booted and Short-toed Eagles, Egyptian Vulture, Hobby, Lesser Kestrel, Little Ringed Plover, Red-necked Nightjar, Alpine Swift, Bee-eater, Roller, Red-rumped Swallow, Spectacled, Subalpine and Bonelli's Warblers, Black-eared Wheatear

ACCESS
In the north, Miranda do Douro on the border is a good base for exploring the area. The villages of Picote and Bemposta to the south along the N221 afford access to two of the steep reservoirs along the border. The more varied and accessible southern part can be appreciated by taking the roads between Torre de Moncorvo and Vila Nova de Foz Coa and from there to Figueira de Castelo Rodrigo, then north to the river at Barca de Alva. Almeida, on the N332 is a good base for the Águeda and Turones river valleys, and has a *Pousada* and other accommodation available.

SERRA DA MALCATA

40°12N 07°15W

Sixty km north of Castelo Branco is the Serra da Malcata, a Natural Reserve of 21,000 ha which is contiguous with the Sierra de Gata in Spanish Extremadura (page 71). Inhabitants include Portugal's few remaining lynx. There are 30–40 pairs of Black Vultures on the Spanish side, and they range widely into Malcata, especially in winter. The same is true of Griffon Vulture and Spanish Imperial Eagle. The Serra da Malcata has its own breeding populations of Booted Eagles, Red Kites, Egyptian Vultures, Sparrowhawks and Goshawks. Small bird interest includes Ortolan, Rock and Cirl Buntings.

TIMING

Late April to late June sees these hills at their best; winter temperatures can drop to zero.

SPECIES

◆ *Resident* Red Kite, Goshawk, Buzzard, Bonelli's and Golden Eagles, Griffon Vulture, Peregrine, Eagle Owl, Blue Rock Thrush, Crested Tit, Rock Bunting, Rock Sparrow, Chough, Raven, Azure-winged Magpie.
◆ *Breeding season* White and Black Storks, Black Kite, Short-toed and Booted Eagles, Honey Buzzard, Egyptian Vulture, Hobby, Great Spotted Cuckoo, Hoopoe, Red-rumped Swallow, Woodchat Shrike, Melodious and Bonelli's Warblers, Black-eared Wheatear.
◆ *Winter* Spanish Imperial Eagle, Black Vulture.

ACCESS

Few roads penetrate the Serra da Malcata. The N233 from Castelo Branco leads to Penamacor, where the Park Headquarters are (in Rua dos Bombeiros: tel. 077 94467). The park boundary is a 6 km farther on, where a minor road heads through the park, rejoining the N233 24 km farther on. Alternatively, the village of Malcata is along a minor road which leaves the N233 3 km south of Sabugal. From Malcata there are tracks into the *serra*. Accommodation is available in Castelo Branco.

SERRA DA ESTRELA

40°25N 07°35W

This area, slightly to the west of Malcata, contains Portugal's highest mountains (1991 m) and is home to Rock Thrush and Subalpine Warbler, characteristic birds of higher altitudes. The Serra da Estrela has Short-toed and Booted Eagles, Red Kites, Montagu's Harriers and Goshawks, as well as Ortolan, Rock and Cirl Buntings, Blue Rock Thrushes and Choughs.

The mountain roads between the villages of Gouveia, Seia and Manteigas, where there is an information centre, cover a range of habitats above the tree-line for Ortolan Buntings, Black Redstart and Tawny Pipit, and below, where Great Spotted Cuckoo, Crested Tit and Firecrest may be found.

RIA DE AVEIRO

40°40N 08°40W

Some 250 km to the north of Lisbon is Aveiro, lying at the mouths of several small rivers. This is a small, marshy estuary with extensive areas which have been converted for rice growing, fish farming or grazing.

Little Bittern

Up to 1800 Avocets winter along with 400 Black-tailed Godwits. During migration, from late August to late October and again in spring, the mudflats and saltpans are alive with shorebirds. Little Stints, Ruff, Curlew Sandpipers and Ringed Plovers are particularly common.

In the salt-marshes and reedbeds, Purple Herons and Little Bitterns breed. Fan-tailed, Savi's, Reed and Great Reed Warblers are found along the margins of the marshes and in the reeds. There is a nature reserve at the end of a long dune spit which all but encloses the estuary. The São Jacinto reserve includes a plantation of stone pines and sand dunes and is botanically interesting. The pines hold good numbers of Crested Tits and Serins. In late April and May, and, especially, late September and October, there can be spectacular passerine migration. Chats such as Redstart and Whinchat, Spotted and Pied Flycatchers, and warblers of several species can descend during a 'fall'.

TIMING
In March and April there is a particularly good passage of waders, especially Whimbrel. In winter Common Scoters congregate offshore, with counts reaching 4000.

SPECIES
- *Resident* Red Kite, Goshawk, Marsh Harrier, Hoopoe, Fan-tailed Warbler, Great Grey Shrike.
- *Breeding season* Little Egret, Little Bittern, Purple Heron, White Stork, Black Kite, Montagu's Harrier, Black-winged Stilt, Little Tern, Great Spotted Cuckoo, Pallid Swift, Bee-eater, Short-toed Lark.
- *Passage* Squacco Heron, waders.
- *Winter* seaduck, Osprey, Merlin, Avocet, Black-tailed Godwit.

ACCESS
The main marsh is north of the town, but the network of creeks and embankments makes access difficult. The best bet is to drive right round to São Jacinto where the road from Ovar runs alongside the river for 25 km and frequent stops should reveal a good selection of shorebirds. There are hides overlooking the estuary, lagoons and ocean, nature trails and an information centre with knowledgeable English-speaking staff. Aveiro town, which has been compared to a small-scale Venice, has a fascinating network of canals and attractive late medieval buildings. Boat-trips are available into the Ría, aimed mainly at anglers, but a birdwatching trip could possibly be negotiated.

PAÚL DE ARZILA
40°10N 08°33W
This small fresh-water marsh is located close to the ancient university town of Coimbra in the Mondego floodplain. Most of the once extensive riverine marshes downstream of Coimbra have been drained, or converted to paddies and fish farms.

Paúl de Arzila is protected as a natural reserve, mainly for its breeding populations of herons, notably Little Bitterns and Purple Herons. There are also Savi's and Great Reed Warblers in summer and Spotted Crakes in winter.

TIMING
The heronries are active between February and August. July and August can be very dry, depending on the amount of water taken for agriculture.

SPECIES
- *Resident* Cattle Egret, Marsh Harrier, Hoopoe, Fan-tailed and Cetti's Warblers, Waxbill, Cirl Bunting.
- *Breeding season* Little Bittern, Purple Heron, White Stork, Black Kite, Booted Eagle, Whiskered Tern, Savi's and Great Reed Warblers, Golden Oriole.
- *Passage* Night and Squacco Herons, Black Stork, Red Kite, waders, warblers, Bluethroat.
- *Winter* Little Egret, ducks, Osprey, Goshawk, Hen Harrier, Spotted Crake.

ACCESS
The village of Arzila is 13 km west of Coimbra on the N341. The marsh, or *paúl*, is south and west of the village. From the N341 there are drainage ditches and paths which penetrate the area.

UPPER RIVER TEJO

39°40N 07°15W

The steep-banked Tejo river forms, like the Minho and the Douro, part of Portugal's border with Spain. The Spanish side is described on page 106. This is one of Portugal's remotest areas, and its natural vegetation has been allowed to remain unaltered in many places, save by the grazing of an occasional passing goat flock. Thus an aromatic Mediterranean scrub community dominates, with *Cistus* and French lavender ringing with the songs of Sardinian, Dartford and Spectacled Warblers. There is an important population of Black Stork with at least ten pairs, as well as a colony of Griffon Vultures several pairs of Golden and Bonelli's Eagles, Peregrines and Eagle Owls. This is one of the few places in Portugal where the three European kites can be found together.

TIMING

The cliff-nesters tend to breed early, so February to May is peak time. Spring is suberb for both birds and flowers, for which this area is outstanding.

Goshawk

SPECIES
- *Resident* Great Crested Grebe, Grey Heron, Red and Black-shouldered Kites, Buzzard, Griffon Vulture, Golden and Bonelli's Eagles, Goshawk, Sparrowhawk, Peregrine, Eagle Owl, Hoopoe, Thekla Lark, Grey Wagtail, Great Grey Shrike, Blue Rock Thrush, Black Wheatear, Dartford Warbler, Azure-winged Magpie, Chough, Waxbill, Rock and Spanish Sparrows, Rock Bunting.
- *Breeding season* White and Black Storks, Black Kite, Booted and Short-toed Eagles, Egyptian Vulture, Hobby, Lesser Kestrel, Little Ringed Plover, Red-necked Nightjar, Alpine Swift, Bee-eater, Roller, Red-rumped Swallow, Subalpine and Spectacled Warblers, Black-eared Wheatear, Rufous Bushchat.
- *Passage* storks and raptors including Osprey

ACCESS
There are numerous small roads and estate tracks which penetrate the area. The N240 from north of Castelo Branco to the border, and small roads running off it, is also worth exploring, especially the 353 road to Rosmaninhal.

The N18 from Castelo Branco south to Portalegre crosses the Tejo at Vila Velha de Ródão. From the bridge or either bank a good selection of cliff-dwelling passerines and occasional raptors can be seen. Waxbills occur in the scrub along the river bank here.

There is a Natural Park on the border a little to the south of the Tagus, in the Serra de São Mamede near Portalegre. A similar range of species is to be found by exploring the road which runs east to the hermitage of São Mamede, close to the 1000-m peak of the same name. The castle at Marvão is good for Lesser Kestrels while the one at Alegrete is a good vantage point from which to try for Bonelli's Eagle.

PAÚL DO BOQUILOBO
39°23N 08°32W
This fresh-water marsh by the Rio Almonda, surrounded by willow carr, contains one of Portugal's most important heronries and has been declared a Natural Reserve, an EU Special Protection Area, and, most recently, a listed wetland under the Ramsar Convention. There are 156 species listed.

Five species of heron breed: Night and Squacco Herons, Cattle and Little Egrets and Little Bittern. There are usually a few non-breeding Purple and Grey Herons around as well. Whiskered Terns and Red-necked Nightjars are also among the breeding species. In winter several thousand ducks arrive with the abundant flood waters, and Ospreys are usually to be seen at this time.

Despite its paper protection, the *paúl* suffers from excessive drainage and pollution. The extent of the problem varies according to the rainfall; wet years show a marked decrease in pollution and good water levels, often all year.

TIMING
The heronry begins to liven in February and is active until September. July and August are the driest months.

SPECIES
- *Resident* Cattle and Little Egrets, Hoopoe, Fan-tailed and Cetti's Warblers, Great Grey Shrike.

◆ *Breeding season* Little Bittern, Night, Squacco and Purple Herons, White Stork, Spoonbill, Black Kite, Booted Eagle, Whiskered Tern, Red-necked Nightjar, Great Spotted Cuckoo, Bee-eater, Great Reed Warbler, Woodchat Shrike.
◆ *Passage* Purple Heron, Black Stork, Red Kite, waders.
◆ *Winter* ducks, Osprey.

ACCESS

The Paúl do Boquilobo is in the Tejo valley, 30 km upstream of Santarém. The entrance track is south-west of Golegã, running right from the N365 if heading towards Azinhaga and Santarém. There is a left turn after about a kilometre, before a rise, to the reserve centre, from where there are footpaths. The heronry is most active at either end of the day.

Accommodation is plentiful in Santarém and in towns along the valley.

BERLENGAS ISLANDS

39°25N 09°37W

The few small, rocky islands off the coast at Peniche, are home to continental Portugal's most important seabird colonies, and continental Europe's only colony of Madeiran Storm Petrel. There are around 50 pairs of them on the Farilhões islands, the more northerly cluster in the archipelago. There are also 200 pairs of Cory's Shearwaters, 70 pairs of Shag and a similar number of the threatened Iberian race of Guillemot. A pair of Peregrines breeds. The islands are also important for their flora, which includes two endemic species.

The islands can be visited in summer: there are three return trips a day from Peniche. For birds the boat trip itself is more rewarding than the landing, and a crossing towards late afternoon in summer should yield at least Cory's Shearwater. Peniche can be a good sea-watching point between August and May, especially during north-westerlies. Accommodation is available in Peniche or in the delightful walled village of Óbidos. The Lagoa de Óbidos, to the north-west of the village, is an estuarine inlet which can hold a good selection – in small numbers – of waders, herons and wildfowl.

TEJO ESTUARY

38°45N 09°05W

Lisbon is a surprisingly well-placed city from the birdwatcher's point of view. Within a few kilometres are some of the richest feeding grounds for waders in Europe. As a migration staging post for waders the Tejo estuary is a vital link in a chain which stretches, for some species, from South Africa to Russia.

The Tejo estuary is important in winter for its Avocet, Flamingo and Black-tailed Godwit populations. It was only recently discovered that the rice fields here hold a staggering number of Godwits – up to 75,000 in December, which is harvest time in the rice paddies of Mauritania and Senegal.

The northern half of the area is a state nature reserve of 14,560 ha, although there are many excellent areas of considerable importance outside the reserve. There are several areas of salt-pans, where Little Terns breed and which during the migration season are alive with waders.

There are salt-marshes and reedbeds, especially in the north of the reserve, where Purple Herons breed along with the Little Bittern, although this species is rare. Fan-tailed, Savi's, Reed and Great Reed Warblers are characteristic.

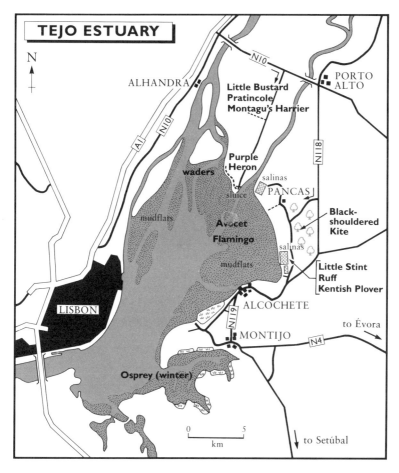

The drier, farmed parts of the floodplain hold good breeding populations of Pratincole, Little Bustard and Montagu's Harrier and smaller grassland inhabitants such as Calandra and Short-toed Larks. In winter the bustard population rises to around 500. On the east bank is a fine expanse of cork oak *montado* – a parkland or savannah-like habitat where Black-shouldered Kites can be found. Other raptors here include Short-toed and Booted Eagles, Black Kite and Buzzard.

The Tejo estuary is the subject of a range of conservation problems. Many of the smaller rivers flowing into the area are seriously polluted with sewage and heavy metals. A bridge is to be built across part of the estuary with as yet unquantified, but certainly serious, consequences for the birds. This has been the subject of a vigorous campaign by LPN in Portugal and the RSPB in the United Kingdom.

TIMING

The Tejo estuary has year-round interest on account of its diversity. For waterbirds only late June to mid-August is a relatively poor time. The *montado* is best in spring and winter.

173

SPECIES
- *Resident* Cattle and Little Egrets, Black-shouldered Kite, Marsh Harrier, Little Bustard, Stone Curlew, Kentish Plover, Hoopoe, Calandra Lark, Fan-tailed Warbler, Great Grey Shrike, Azure-winged Magpie.
- *Breeding season* Little Bittern, Purple Heron, White Stork, Black Kite, Short-toed and Booted Eagles, Montagu's Harrier, Quail, Black-winged Stilt, Pratincole, Little Tern, Great Spotted Cuckoo, Pallid Swift, Bee-eater, Orphean Warbler, Woodchat Shrike.
- *Passage* Flamingo, waders, terns, passerines.
- *Winter* Flamingo, ducks, Osprey, Avocet, Black-tailed Godwit, Bluethroat.

ACCESS
There are many access and viewing points, taking in the full range of habitats. From the A-1 highway the N10 branches off over the bridge at Vila Franca. After 8 km an unpaved but mostly good road runs south across a floodplain to the headland. The cereal fields here are the best place to find Little Bustards. Pratincoles breed in the unsown fields along this stretch. After some 11 km there is a large sluice and a little farmhouse. You can park at the sluice and take a track which runs from here westwards round the point. The salt-marshes and mud-flats here are among the best areas.

Tracking back to the N10, continue eastbound for 3 km before turning right onto the N118. This road runs though the *montado*. After about 10 km there is a right turn signposted 'Pancas'. Take this and then the estate track off to the right a few km on. Eventually this leads to the estuary again, after cutting through excellent cork woodland.

Back to the N118, a right turn leads to Alcochete. *En route* are some excellent saltpans which can be viewed from the road. Alcochete is on the river, and there are numerous vantage points. The Reserve has its headquarters here, where information material can be obtained.

This is the southern limit of the reserve, but farther south are some excellent spots. Between Montijo and Almada are a series of small bays, which can be easily worked. This is the main area for wintering Avocets.

SADO ESTUARY
38°32N 08°50W

Only a few kilometres to the south is another excellent estuary reserve, on the Sado river. There are several good birdwatching spots, especially on the south and east banks. The Lagoa de Bem Pais is a quiet, reed-fringed lagoon where herons and egrets breed, Marsh Harriers quarter the lake edge, and Kingfishers fish. In winter Penduline Tits can be found in the reeds and willows, and flocks of seed-eaters assemble in the salt-marshes and river banks.

At Murta on the southern shore there is an irrigation reservoir which has a large mixed colony of Little and Cattle Egrets. There are also a few pairs of Purple Herons and Little Bitterns. These birds feed in the saltmarsh and rice paddies to the north of the road and are often joined by Spoonbills, especially in spring and autumn. Portugal's only known breeding Bitterns, a species in serious decline in Europe, also nest here.

TIMING
See Tejo estuary.

SPECIES
- *Resident* Cattle and Little Egrets, Black-shouldered Kite, Marsh Harrier, Stone Curlew, Kentish Plover, Hoopoe, Fan-tailed Warbler, Great Grey Shrike, Cirl Bunting, Azure-winged Magpie.
- *Breeding season* Little Bittern, Purple Heron, White Stork, Black Kite, Short-toed and Booted Eagles, Montagu's Harrier, Black-winged Stilt, Pratincole, Little Tern, Great Spotted Cuckoo, Pallid Swift, Bee-eater, Orphean Warbler, Woodchat Shrike.
- *Passage* Spoonbill, Flamingo, waders.
- *Winter* Flamingo, ducks, Osprey, Avocet, Black-tailed Godwit, Bluethroat.

ACCESS
The Sado estuary lies south and east of Setúbal, which is only 40 km along the highway from Lisbon. There are numerous observation points in the course of a 107-km clockwise circuit of the whole intertidal basin. At least the first 80 km from Setúbal are recommended.

The northern estuary can be appreciated by taking the right turn off the N10 to Gâmbia and on to the point at Pontal de Musgos. This road runs through pine and cork woods to an extensive area of salt-marsh. The area can be busy at weekends. The Lagoa de Bem Pais is reached by turning right 4 km beyond Marateca towards Pinheiro. This road leads on to the estuary and then, via Monte Novo, back to the main road. There are three lagoons along this road: Bem Pais is about 7 km from the turn. At Pinheiro there is a good view over the mud-flats and the Ilha do Cavalo, where waders roost at high tide.

Beyond Alcácer do Sal a right turn towards Comporta and Tróia takes you along the southern shore of the estuary. The Murta dam is about 20 km after the turn. A few kilometres farther, the fishing port of Carrasqueira is worth a visit in its own right, and also affords access to good salt-marsh.

Whilst Setúbal has plenty of accommodation, a better strategy might be to stay in Alcácer do Sal, an ancient and attractive town, which is better placed for the south and east banks. The north and west could be explored from Lisbon. There is a ferry across the mouth of the river from Setúbal to Tróia. West of Setúbal is the beautiful Natural Park of the Serra de Arrábida.

SANTO ANDRÉ AND SANCHA LAGOONS

38°06N 08°49W

These two lagoons, on the Alentejo coast north of Sines, are still in use as fishing grounds, commercial reed- and sedge-beds and summer grazing. The link with tradition ends there, however, since they are coming under pressure from over-fishing, pollution and tourist use. Nevertheless, these brackish wetlands, surrounded by extensive reedbeds and coastal scrub and, in the case of Santo André, pine and cork woods, still offer excellent birdwatching *en route* between Lisbon and the south-west.

Santo André, at 900 ha, is much the larger and more diverse, Sancha being only 50 ha in extent. Santo André is the most important area for Red-crested Pochards in Portugal. Both have breeding Little Bitterns, Purple Herons and Marsh Harriers. Black-winged Stilts, Little Terns and, possibly, Baillon's Crake are added at Santo André.

Great Reed Warbler

TIMING
There is considerable hunting pressure between October and February.
SPECIES
◆ *Resident* Cattle and Little Egrets, Red-crested Pochard, Black-shouldered Kite, Stone Curlew, Kentish Plover, Hoopoe, Fan-tailed, Cetti's and Dartford Warblers, Crested Tit, Great Grey Shrike, Cirl Bunting.
◆ *Breeding season* Little Bittern, Purple Heron, Marsh Harrier, Hobby, Little and Whiskered Terns, Red-necked Nightjar, Bee-eater, Short-toed Lark, Red-rumped Swallow, Savi's and Great Reed Warblers, Woodchat Shrike.
◆ *Passage* Night and Squacco Herons, White Stork, Black Kite, Booted Eagle, waders, Pratincole, Great Spotted Cuckoo, Bluethroat, warblers.
◆ *Winter* ducks, including Red-crested Pochard, Osprey, Bluethroat.
ACCESS
Lagoa de Santo André is 23 km north of Sines along a highway. From the Sado estuary, it is 50 km south of Tróia on the N261 and 55 km south of Alcácer do Sal on the N120. Some 6 km north of Santo André village on the N261 a road runs west to Brescos where tracks afford access to the lagoon and marsh. A local road south out of Brescos leads to other access points.

The Sancha lagoon is west of the Sines highway, and is reached by passing under the highway along a rural road which leads off the N261-3 through Bêbeda. There is accommodation in Sines and all the towns of the area, as well as a campsite at the Santo André lagoon.

ELVAS PLAINS
38°55N 07°19W
The Elvas plains lie close to the Spanish border and are home to a small population of Great and Little Bustards. There are also pockets of lightly wooded country which are a stronghold of the Black-shouldered Kite. This species is found, along with Little Bustards and Montagu's Harriers, a few kilometres to the south-east of Elvas town. This border area along the Caia and Guadiana rivers also has irrigated croplands and rice paddies. Pratincoles, Black-winged Stilts and passage waders are common.

About 16 km to the north is Campo Maior, along a road which runs through cereal country where both bustards, Black-bellied Sandgrouse and Pratincole can be found. To the north of Campo Maior, the countryside around Arronches contains some good *montado* which should be explored for Black-shouldered Kite and Roller, and the scrubby hillsides searched for *Sylvia* warblers. East of Arronches, towards Esperança, there is a good chance of seeing Bonelli's Eagles, Black Storks and Griffon Vultures. West of Campo Maior is a reservoir, the Barragem do Caia, where in winter the occasional Osprey and a few hundred Red-crested Pochard assemble.

TIMING
Both bustards are much in evidence in early spring, when display takes place. In winter, they roam in flocks and may be more difficult to find.
SPECIES
◆ *Resident* Little and Cattle Egrets, Red and Black-shouldered Kites, Great and Little Bustards, Stone Curlew, Black-bellied Sandgrouse, Calandra Lark, Azure-winged Magpie, Waxbill.

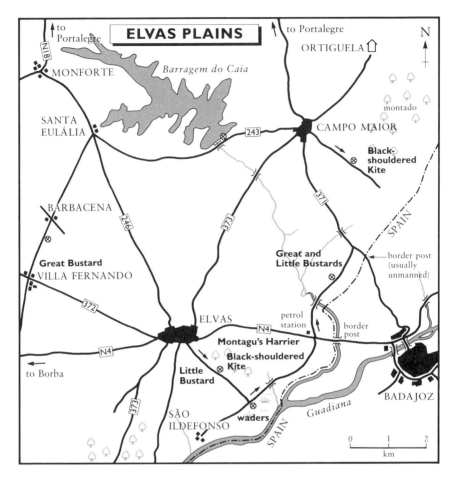

- *Breeding season* White Stork, Black Kite, Montagu's Harrier, Lesser Kestrel, Pratincole, Black-winged Stilt, Red-necked Nightjar, Great Spotted Cuckoo, Bee-eater, Roller, Hoopoe, Tawny Pipit, Rufous Bushchat, Orphean Warbler.

ACCESS

The minor road leading out of Elvas to the south-east joins up with another, which runs parallel to the border between the Caia border post on the N4 and São Ildefonso. These roads should be explored for Black-shouldered Kite, Little Bustard and Pratincole. Just before the border post on the N4 a minor road heads north to Campo Maior. This is better than the main N373 road between the two towns, and the N372 from Elvas to Veiros is good.

ALTER DO CHÃO AND MONFORTE PLAINS
39°08N 07°30W

There are further areas of wheatfields and dry pasture immediately to the north-west of the previous area, south of Portalegre. The plains around Alter do Chão hold around 40 Great Bustards, numerous Little Bustards and other typical grassland species such as Montagu's Harrier and Calandra Lark. The plains around Monforte have a similar range of species.

Good roads to try are the 369 between Alter do Chão and Monforte, the N245 south of Alter do Chão and the Monforte–Barbacena road. Black-shouldered Kites are in the cork oak *montados* in the south-east of this area.

ÉVORA
38°34N 07°54W
Évora is one of the main towns of the Alentejo and dates back to the Roman era. The land around the town is sparsely populated, with extensive areas of wheat and grassland, and woodlands of cork and holm oak.

White Storks and Lesser Kestrels are a feature of the town itself, while the grasslands around hold Great and Little Bustards, Montagu's Harrier, Stone Curlew and larks. Pratincoles and, occasionally at least, Whiskered Terns, are to be found in summer near some of the small irrigation dams and the marshy ground which punctuate the landscape. These are also good for breeding wildfowl, including some of Portugal's few breeding Gadwall and Shoveler. Cranes spend the winter feeding under the oaks and roosting at these reservoirs. North of Alcáçovas there is a small, reedy dam that occasionally has both Crested Coot and Marbled Teal, and is one of the few places in the country for these species more often associated with Andalucía.

TIMING
The variety of habitat helps ensure that the area has something to offer throughout the year.
SPECIES
◆ *Resident* Red and Black-shouldered Kites, Great and Little Bustards, Stone Curlew, Black-bellied Sandgrouse, Calandra Lark.
◆ *Breeding season* White Stork, Black Kite, Montagu's Harrier, Lesser Kestrel, Pratincole, Black-winged Stilt, Whiskered Tern, Bee-eater, Roller, Hoopoe, Red-necked Nightjar, Tawny Pipit, Black-eared Wheatear.
◆ *Winter* Common Crane, Golden Plover.
ACCESS
The N254 from Viana do Alentejo to Évora crosses some good grassland areas. After 23 km, or about 6 km from Évora, there is a right turn to Vale da Moura, where an irrigation reservoir, or *açude*, is worth checking.

Alcáçovas is south-west of Évora on the N2. The small lake by the roadside a few kilometres to the north is one of several in the area which often hold a good selection of waterbirds and migrants.

CENTRAL GUADIANA VALLEY
38°13N 07°28W
For 65 km downstream of Elvas, the Guadiana forms the border with Spain then flows entirely within Portuguese territory for 150 km, before becoming international again for the last 45 km of its journey to the Atlantic ocean at Castro Marim (page 188). For much of this central portion it forms a long, steep-sided valley rich in birdlife. The portion from Alqueva upstream almost as far as Elvas is set to become Portugal's largest reservoir as a controversial dam is built with EU funds. This will flood, among other treasures, a huge

Cattle Egret

heronry in mid-stream on the border with Spain and the beautiful ornithological reserve at Monte Nova de Roncão, near Montes Juntos.

The plains around Mourão, only 7 km from the border, hold up to 200 Great Bustards in winter of which about 40 stay to breed. Little Bustards and Montagu's Harriers are also common and there are breeding Black-bellied Sandgrouse. The cork oaks in this area have a few pairs of Black-shouldered Kite and up to 1000 Cranes in winter. There is a good population of raptors and Black Storks in the area between Portel, Vidigueira and Moura.

TIMING
The valley is at its best in the breeding season, and the migration periods bring influxes of small migrants, storks and raptors, which navigate along the river course.

SPECIES
- *Resident* Cattle and Little Egrets, Grey Heron, Red and Black-shouldered Kites, Buzzard, Bonelli's Eagle, Goshawk, Peregrine, Great and Little Bustards, Stone Curlew, Black-bellied Sandgrouse, Eagle Owl, Hoopoe, Calandra and Thekla Larks, Grey Wagtail, Blue Rock Thrush, Black Wheatear, Dartford Warbler, Azure-winged Magpie, Chough, Waxbill, Rock and Spanish Sparrows, Rock Bunting.
- *Breeding season* Little Bittern, Night and Purple Herons, White and Black Storks, Black Kite, Booted and Short-toed Eagles, Egyptian Vulture, Montagu's Harrier, Hobby, Lesser Kestrel, Red-necked Nightjar, Great Spotted Cuckoo, Bee-eater, Roller, Red-rumped Swallow, Subalpine and Spectacled Warblers, Black-eared Wheatear, Rufous Bushchat
- *Passage* storks and raptors.
- *Winter* Black Vulture, Common Crane.

ACCESS
Mourão is on the N256 east of Évora. From here the N385 leads south to Safara; from here to Moura to the west the N258 completes a triangle of outstanding grassland and raptor country. The Guadiana immediately east of Moura is one of the best stretches for raptors and Black Storks, and there is a heronry a few kilometres downstream of the bridge. A good area of wooded country is the Safara–Barrancos-Amareja triangle, close to the border.

Farther south, the villages of Serpa, Brinches and Pias form another triangle, which can be explored in a couple of hours.

Many of the larger villages and towns, such as Beja, Vidigueira, Moura, Serpa and, to the south, Mértola, can provide accommodation.

MÉRTOLA

37°30N 07°10W

Mértola is a fine old hilltop town that overlooks the river Guadiana from an elevated perch between two gorges. Its castle and convent have nesting Lesser Kestrels, which hunt over the river and the nearby fields. The Oeiras, a tributary of the Guadiana, flows in from the west, through a gorge where Crag Martins, Blue Rock Thrushes and Rock Buntings nest.

Mértola is 70 km north of Castro Marim (page 188) along the N122. The road from Mértola east towards the border, the N265, leads to Serpa via the Serra de Mértola and the Serra de Serpa (see above), where Black Stork, Black-shouldered Kite and a good selection of raptors can be sought by making occasional stops in likely-looking areas along the road. Open areas should readily yield Roller, Stone Curlew, Little Bustard and Calandra Lark, whereas scrubland and *montado* will be good for Great Spotted Cuckoo, Bee-eater, Orphean, Sardinian and Dartford Warblers, Rufous Bushchat and Azure-winged Magpie. Around Mina de São Marcos is good sandgrouse country.

Guided bird tours can be arranged at the tourist information office in Mértola, as part of a scheme to develop the economic potential of the rich natural and cultural heritage of the town. A remote and impressive spot upstream that should not be missed is the Pulo do Lobo gorge, which can be reached by taking the N122 north from Mértola and taking the right turn after 3 km to Corte Gafo de Cima and Amendoeira. Here you can see Black Storks, Short-toed Eagles and Egyptian Vultures.

The main N122 to Beja crosses the Ribeira de Cobres at the northern edge of the Castro Verde plains. This small gorge is worth checking.

CASTRO VERDE

37°40N 08°05W

The gently undulating plains of Castro Verde have for generations been farmed in the traditional way, with low-intensity cereal production and sheep grazing predominating. The area holds over half Portugal's Great Bustards, around 600, and they are joined by up to 1000 pairs of Little Bustards and several pairs of Lesser Kestrels. It is the most important grassland area in the country. Other typical species include Black-bellied Sandgrouse, Stone Curlew, Roller and Calandra and Thekla Larks. Towards dusk in late July a roost of Montagu's Harriers assembles, with over 150 counted roosting on the ground in a single field. Dusk is also the best time to see the sandgrouse, flighting in in small parties to drink at the many small dams in the area.

There are also scattered patches of *Cistus* scrub and holm oak which have a good selection of small birds in spring and summer, and small reservoirs. These hold ducks in winter and passage waders in spring and autumn. Red-crested Pochard is regular in small numbers in winter and spring on many of them. Abandoned farm buildings are scattered about the plains and are often the haunt of Lesser Kestrels, Rollers and Barn Owls.

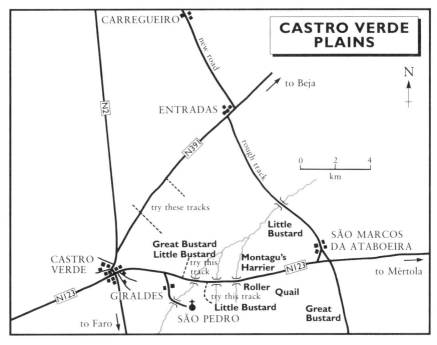

Recently, large expanses were bought by the state-run cellulose companies with a view to planting the grassland with eucalyptus. The process has been halted following pressure from conservation groups. The EU has stepped in with grants for land purchase and subsidies for farmers, aimed at encouraging the continued use of traditional systems.

TIMING

April and May are superb months, when the grassland is vibrant with flowers. The crop becomes too tall to see the birds with any ease by mid-May, and heat haze makes matters much worse in summer. An early morning visit is recommended at this time.

SPECIES

◆ *Resident* Red and Black-shouldered Kites, Great and Little Bustards, Stone Curlew, Black-bellied Sandgrouse, Calandra and Thekla Larks, Azure-winged Magpie.

◆ *Breeding season* White Stork, Black Kite, Short-toed Eagle, Montagu's Harrier, Lesser Kestrel, Quail, Pratincole, Black-winged Stilt, Bee-eater, Roller, Hoopoe, Tawny Pipit, Red-rumped Swallow, Black-eared Wheatear.

◆ *Winter* Red-crested Pochard, Common Crane, Lapwing, Golden Plover.

ACCESS

The best area is between Castro Verde and the village of São Marcos de Ataboeira, 14 km to the east. Tracks cross the area off the N391 and the N123, but these can be rough in places. There are plans for an information centre in the near future. The new road off the N391 from Entradas to Carregueiro is worth exploring.

Other worthwhile areas can be explored by scanning periodically from the road between Almodôvar and São João dos Caldeireios, and from here north-west to Penilhos.

SOUTH-WEST COAST
37°27N 08°48W

At the western end of the Algarve is Cabo São Vicente, which has recently been found to be a good migration watchpoint in autumn, especially during easterly winds. Eleonora's Falcon is regularly seen at this time, possibly non-breeding birds in search of migrating passerines. Recently a three-week count revealed over 800 Booted Eagles, 500 Sparrowhawks and over a hundred each of Egyptian Vultures, Short-toed Eagles, Honey Buzzards and Black Kites. Rarer migrants included two Spanish Imperial Eagles, four Lanner Falcons and three Long-legged Buzzards. The last species is also a regular visitor in early spring.

The cliffs to the north have breeding Choughs and Blue Rock Thrushes can be seen at the clifftops. Little Bustard and Stone Curlew are found in the fields just inland. The cliffs northwards up the coast have a few pairs of breeding Ospreys.

In recent years visiting birdwatchers have organized pelagic trips out of Sagres in August and September. These have turned up a good selection of petrels such as Storm, Madeiran and Wilson's; and Cory's and Yelkouan Shearwaters. Sabine's Gull and Grey Phalarope are also often recorded. This is an option only really viable for groups, but in practice the many deep-sea fishing trips which are available have been perfectly adequate for those who have tried them. North-westerly winds may bring some of these birds close enough for a spot of sea-watching at the cape. Ponta da Sagres, 6 km to the south-east, has lower cliffs better suited to sea-watching.

TIMING
This area gets very crowded during summer and at weekends, although tends to be quiet in the early morning. Peak raptor migration is usually in the last week of September and the first week of October.

SPECIES
◆ *Resident* Shag, Cattle Egret, Osprey, Little Bustard, Stone Curlew, Quail, Peregrine, Lesser Short-toed and Thekla Larks, Black Redstart, Blue Rock Thrush, Fan-tailed, Dartford and Subalpine Warblers, Waxbill, Rock Bunting, Chough.

◆ *Breeding season* White Stork, Short-toed and Booted Eagles, Lesser Kestrel, Quail, Red-necked Nightjar, Pallid and Alpine Swifts, Bee-eater, Tawny Pipit, Black-eared Wheatear, Spectacled Warbler, Woodchat Shrike.

◆ *Passage* Honey and Long-legged Buzzards (especially spring), Short-toed , Booted and Bonelli's Eagles, Egyptian Vulture, Eleonora's Falcon, warblers, flycatchers, Ortolan Bunting.

◆ *Winter* Alpine Accentor.

ACCESS
Sagres is a good base for the cape area, and the road between here and Cabo São Vicente is good for cliffs and scrub. There are some tracks leading inland off this road which allow access on foot to the fields.

MONCHIQUE
37°27N 08°30W

Away from the coast, the Algarve is gently hilly, with only one range of hills which come close to being mountainous. This is the Monchique range in the north-west Algarve. Many of the species found here are uncommon on the Algarve, although they may occur elsewhere in Portugal, so if you do not intend moving far from the Algarve, Monchique provides the best opportunity to find a good selection of woodland and upland birds. Crested Tits, Short-toed Treecreepers, Great Spotted and Green Woodpeckers are typical and among the more unusual species are Azure-winged Magpie and Subalpine and Bonelli's Warblers. Orphean Warblers have been recorded and may breed. Blue Rock Thrush can be found in the rockier areas.

The highest point is Fóia (902 m), which is somewhat barren, but is good for Rock Bunting. Alpine Accentor has been recorded, but it is unlikely as a regular visitor. Mostly the hills are below the tree-line. Route 266 north from Portimão leads into the hills and is very scenic. Any stretch of woodland along here is likely to yield something of interest. From Monchique town there is a road (the 266-3) heading west to Fóia. It is worth walking the smaller side valleys off these roads, where there is less disturbance. Red-rumped Swallows nest under the bridges, and raptors such as Short-toed Eagle may be seen.

The Serra de Monchique is very picturesque and firmly on the tourist trail, so is best avoided at weekends. Early morning is a good time, especially in spring.

ALVOR ESTUARY
37°05N 08°30W

The Alvor estuary is a semi-enclosed bay with sand bars at its mouth, and is formed by three small rivers which enter the sea either side of a headland between Lagos and Portimão. On the headland is a Christian field study centre and bird observatory which has been set up by the British-based A Rocha trust. As well as a good selection of estuary birds on migration and in winter there are good breeding populations of Stone Curlews, Black-winged Stilts and Kentish Plovers. In winter Caspian Terns and Bluethroats are common. The peninsula has breeding Red-necked Nightjars and Bee-eaters and is good for observing migrating land birds and the three swifts.

Nearby is a reservoir, the Barragem da Bravura, where Orphean Warblers have been recorded nesting in the wooded area near the car park, Red-rumped Swallows nest at the dam, and Short-toed Eagles hunt over the wooded ridge to the east.

Leixão da Gaviota is a small coastal islet close to the mouth of the Arade estuary in nearby Portimão. There are some 200 pairs of Cattle Egrets there and around 50 of Little Egrets. At Lagos the Ponta da Piedae has an even more accessible and spectacular egretry on the rocks, with some 600 pairs of Cattle and 70 pairs of Little.

TIMING

There is a ringing programme throughout the year at A Rocha observatory, with peaks of interest during the spring and autumn passage periods.

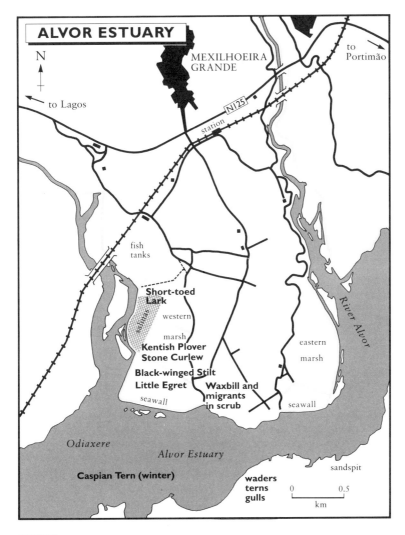

SPECIES
- ◆ *Resident* Little and Cattle Egrets, White Stork, Stone Curlew, Kentish Plover, Hoopoe, Fan-tailed and Dartford Warblers, Waxbill.
- ◆ *Breeding season* Black-winged Stilt, Little Tern, Red-necked Nightjar, Pallid Swift, Bee-eater, Golden Oriole.
- ◆ *Passage* Gannet, Little Bittern, Purple Heron, Black Stork, Spoonbill, Osprey, Honey Buzzard, Griffon Vulture, Short-toed and Booted Eagles, Marsh and Montagu's Harriers, Avocet, waders, Mediterranean and Little Gulls, Great Spotted Cuckoo, Wryneck, Tawny Pipit, Subalpine Warbler.
- ◆ *Winter* Spoonbill, Booted Eagle, Hen Harrier, Caspian Tern, Bluethroat.

ACCESS
The A Rocha centre is south of route N125 along a track opposite the turn to Mexilhoeira Grande. There is a right turn marked 'Cruzinha', where the centre can be visited by appointment on Thursdays (tel. 082 96380), and can

provide bird reports and other useful information. The main track leads on to the salinas. There are various paths on the headland, and visitors should keep to them in order to avoid disturbance.

The Barragem da Bravura is 9 km along the N125-9, which leaves the main N125 at Odeáxere, 6 km west of Mexilhoeira Grande.

RIA FORMOSA

37°00N 07°55W

The most important wetland on the Algarve coast is the Ria Formosa Natural Reserve and the surrounding area. Herons and egrets are well represented here, with mixed colonies supporting Little Bittern, Purple and Grey Herons, Little and Cattle Egrets, the last three remaining through the year. White Stork is also resident. Greater Flamingos and Spoonbills winter along with Ospreys and over 30,000 shorebirds. In total, the wetland extends to some 18,000 ha: 214 bird species occur regularly, as well as the odd rarity.

At the western end is Quinta do Lago, a holiday resort which is rather less of an eyesore than most Algarve tourist traps. Somehow it was built within the Natural Park, but there is a very good nature trail with hides and English-language leaflets, set up by the resort itself. This is at the southern end of the São Lourenço golf course and is perhaps the most reliable place in Portugal for Purple Gallinules. With patience they can often be seen at the edge of the reeds in the small pools here. Also there are Little Bitterns and Water Rails, and a good selection of wildfowl including Red-crested Pochard.

The pine woods which surround Quinta do Lago are home to good numbers of Azure-winged Magpies and chameleons, whose European distribution is limited to this area and one or two sites in southern Spain.

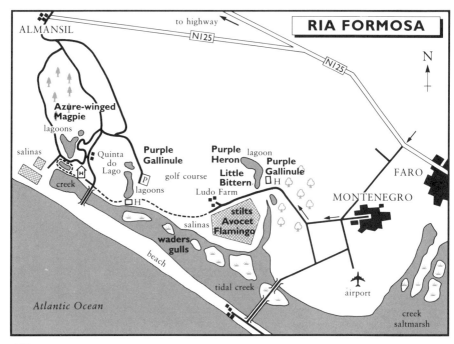

Another good area is near Ludo farm, between Quinta do Lago and the airport. The saltpans here are best at high tide, when shorebirds such as Avocets, Black-tailed Godwits and Little Stints are shifted from the mud-flats. Avocets, Kentish Plovers and Flamingos are particularly fond of the saltpans for feeding and, in the case of the first two, for breeding. Spoonbills are regular visitors on migration and, occasionally, in winter.

A brackish creek is overlooked by a tower hide, giving good views of Purple Gallinules, Night and Purple Herons and often the globally threatened Marbled Teal, which breeds along the coast at Coto Doñana in Spain.

East of Faro, is a new interpretive centre at Quinta de Marim, south of the main road 1 km east of Olhão. There are saltpans, lagoons and coastal scrub which attract migrants in spring and autumn, and shorebirds, gulls and terns throughout the year. Mediterranean Gulls are found here from late autumn to spring, Caspian Terns in winter and Little Terns in summer.

East of Olhão, this outstanding wetland becomes a thin strip of intertidal marsh and sand dunes stretching almost to the Spanish border. At the right season, migrant waders abound, and wintering Bluethroats, Flamingos, Caspian Terns, Dartford Warblers and Stone Curlews can be seen.

TIMING
This area is a year-round holiday resort, but pressure from the package trade lessens slightly in October and November, and February to June, which happen to be excellent times for birdwatching in the area.

SPECIES
- *Resident* Little and Cattle Egrets, White Stork, Flamingo, Red-crested Pochard, Marsh Harrier, Avocet, Black-winged Stilt, Stone Curlew, Kentish Plover, Hoopoe, Dartford Warbler, Azure-winged Magpie.
- *Breeding season* Little Bittern, Purple Heron, Black Kite, Pratincole, Little Tern,Great Spotted Cuckoo, Red-necked Nightjar, Pallid Swift, Bee-eater, Red-rumped Swallow, Tawny Pipit, Rufous Bushchat, Black-eared Wheatear, Great Reed Warbler, Golden Oriole.
- *Passage* Gannet, Night and Squacco Herons, Spoonbill, Osprey, Honey Buzzard, Black-shouldered Kite, waders, Gull-billed, Black and White-winged Black Terns, Wryneck
- *Winter* wildfowl, Black-shouldered Kite, Hen Harrier, Merlin, Little Bustard, Mediterranean Gull, Little Gull, Caspian Tern, Great Spotted Cuckoo, Bluethroat, Penduline Tit.

ACCESS
Quinta do Lago is reached by turning left off the old road (not the new highway) in Almansil, which is 13 km west of Faro. The road through the resort takes in six numbered roundabouts; a right turn at roundabout 2 leads to the Ria, or estuary, itself. This stretches east to become the Praia (beach) de Faro an overcrowded resort area which nevertheless affords good views behind the sands over the estuary. A chain of sand bars continues for almost 40 km, sheltering a complex of lagoons, marshes and creeks to landward. The São Lourenço golf course and trail is reached by turning left at roundabout 5 or by walking from the car park beyond roundabout 6.

Ludo farm is within walking distance of the golf course, or can be reached by car from the airport road. A right turn a kilometre before the airport, followed quickly by another right along a good track, leads to an area of saltpans and creeks. In theory, a permit must be obtained from the Ria Formosa Natural Park Offices (at Quinta de Marim, Quelfes, 8700 Olhão), but often a speculative visit to Ludo farm will suffice. The saltpan workers do not usually object to birdwatchers, but a cheerful greeting would help.

Boat-trips around the wetland are available from Olhão harbour: it is best to get up-to-date information from either Quinta de Marim or the tourist office in Olhão. Access to the eastern end can be gained by cutting through the resort area of Pedras de El Rei, at Santa Luzia, just west of Tavira. The lagoon is sheltered by sand dunes, which are reached across a pontoon boardwalk – itself a good vantage point over the salt-marsh and mud-flats.

CASTRO MARIM
37°12N 07°26W

The eastern edge of the Algarve is marked by the Guadiana river and the border with Spain. There is another good wetland area here, at Castro Marim, which consists mainly of saltpans and halophytic scrub. Like the other Algarve wetlands, this area can produce good numbers of shorebirds in spring and autumn, although Castro Marim has a particular reputation for variety if not quantity. In addition to the species that pass through in bulk – Little Stint, Ruff, Black-tailed Godwit, Dunlin – there is always a selection of shanks such as Spotted Redshank, Greenshank, Green and Wood Sandpipers. The rare Marsh Sandpiper is regular. There are often Flamingos present, sometimes in good numbers: 1200 have been counted in spring. There are two large Spoonbill colonies over the border, and they are seen in Castro Marim at any time of the year, with numbers ranging from one or two to 200 or more. Slender-billed Gull is an occasional visitor, usually in spring and autumn. In the saltpans in early summer there will typically be a profusion of Little and Black Terns, shorebirds and Black-necked Grebe.

Spectacled Warbler is found in the scrub around the saltpans. This bird is particularly common in the large complex north and east of Castro Marim, although like most *Sylvia* warblers it stays in cover and requires patience. Summer also sees Collared Pratincole, Black-winged Stilt, Short-toed and Lesser Short-toed Larks breeding here. There is some good woodland to the north of the area, at Azinhal, where Azure-winged Magpies are common.

TIMING
Towards mid-summer heat haze becomes a real problem after about 10 a.m. and bird interest decreases until the return of the first shorebirds in late August. Autumn is good for small migrants, guided by the Guadiana valley.

SPECIES
- *Resident* Little and Cattle Egrets, White Stork, Flamingo, Red-crested Pochard, Marsh Harrier, Avocet, Black-winged Stilt, Stone Curlew, Kentish Plover, Hoopoe, Lesser Short-toed Lark, Dartford Warbler, Azure-winged Magpie.
- *Breeding season* Black Kite, Pratincole, Little Tern, Great Spotted Cuckoo, Red-necked Nightjar, Pallid Swift, Bee-eater, Red-rumped Swallow, Tawny Pipit, Rufous Bushchat, Black-eared Wheatear, Great Reed Warbler, Golden Oriole.

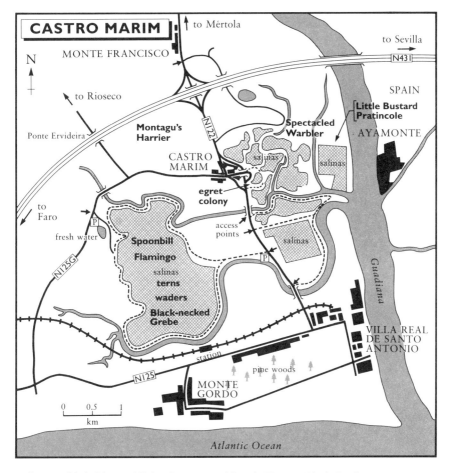

- *Passage* Little Bittern, Night, Squacco and Purple Herons, Black Stork, Spoonbill, Osprey, Honey Buzzard, Lesser Kestrel, Little Bustard, waders, Gull-billed, Black and White-winged Black Terns, Red-throated Pipit.
- *Winter* Glossy Ibis, wildfowl, Griffon Vulture, Bonelli's Eagle, Hen Harrier, Merlin, Little Bustard, Mediterranean and Little Gulls, Caspian Tern, Short-eared Owl, Great Spotted Cuckoo, Bluethroat, Penduline Tit.

ACCESS
The main area is south of Castro Marim and west of Vila Real. A new highway links the Algarve with Spain. Leave the highway at São Bartolomeu and take the N125-6 towards Castro Marim. Before the village a right turn, before a bridge over a small river, down a track to the saltworks follows a channel.

The area north and east of Castro Marim is reached by passing under the new highway and taking a right turn marked *transito local*. This track doubles back under the highway bearing left into some saltpans.

The new highway means that it is now realistic to include Castro Marim and Ria Formosa in an itinerary based on southern Spain, or vice versa. Good birdwatching spots over the border are at Isla Cristina (10 km), Huelva marshes (38 km) and Coto Doñana National Park (121 km).

MADEIRA

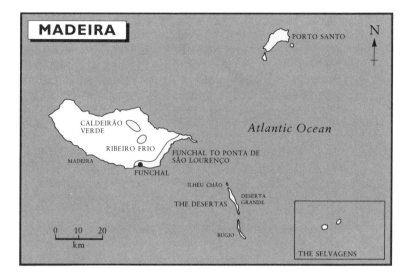

The two Portuguese Atlantic island groups share with the Canaries the typical characteristics of oceanic archipelagos. They are rich in endemic life-forms, but somewhat impoverished in terms of the number of species. Thus, for the birdwatcher they are speciality destinations: there are species (and many subspecies) found nowhere else in the world; there are huge concentrations of seabirds; but you should not expect to come away from the Azores or Madeira with a bird list anything like as long as can be achieved on the Portuguese or Spanish mainland.

Madeira is only 550 km from the Canary islands and 600 km from Morocco. It consists of four groups of islands: Madeira itself, green and forested; the much drier Porto Santo and its nearby islets; the Desertas, comprising three uninhabited islands and the Selvagens, distant uninhabited islets close to the Canaries. Madeira's importance lies in its rich seabird communities and in its laurel forests. The latter are home to the endemic and globally threatened Madeira Laurel Pigeon (also known as Long-toed Pigeon), as well as several very distinct subspecies such as the Madeiran forms of Firecrest and Chaffinch.

Among the seabirds are two globally threatened petrels. They have only recently been considered as distinct species, closely related to the Soft-plumaged Petrel of the southern hemisphere. One, *Pterodroma madeira* appears to be almost extinct, and nests in a single known locality in the world. This site, needless to say, cannot be included in this book. There may be as few as ten breeding pairs: 1993 was the best breeding season since records began, with eight young fledged. The fact that they have not become extinct in the face of predation by rats and disturbance is almost solely thanks to the efforts of two of Madeira's general practitioners, Drs Alex and Frank Zino. In recognition of Alex Zino having first described the species and his son Frank's efforts to keep it on the planet, it has been named Zino's Petrel. The closely related *Pterodroma feae*, Fea's Petrel, is hardly more common. There are about 120 pairs in the Desertas, and perhaps a similar number in Cape Verde, West Africa. There are also about 3500 pairs of Bulwer's Petrel, 20,000 pairs of Cory's Shearwater, 5000 pairs of Little Shearwater, 2–3000 pairs of Madeiran Storm Petrel and, on the distant Selvagem islands some 20–30,000 pairs of White-faced Petrel. Madeira is also home to the three Macaronesian endemic land birds: Canary, Plain Swift and Berthelot's Pipit.

Funchal is served by direct scheduled flights and charters from London during the high season. A TAP flight also operates from Frankfurt via Faro. Otherwise, a change at Lisbon is required. There are also flights from the Azores and the Canary Islands. Cars can be hired from both international and local firms on Madeira.

BIRDWATCHING SITES

RIBEIRO FRIO
32°44N 16°53W
The most readily accessible laurel forest is on the ridge of the island above Funchal, in the region of Ribeiro Frio. This is cloud forest similar to that found on the some of the Canary Islands. Cloud is one of the main factors governing birdwatching success, since to seek out the Laurel Pigeon it is best to overlook as wide an area of forest canopy as possible.

The laurel forest of Madeira makes up about one-seventh of the island, and is almost entirely within the Madeira Natural Park, although the protection afforded by this designation is fairly loose. Some of the forest areas have stricter protection as Nature Reserves. Like all oceanic islands, Madeira has its fair share of endemic invertebrates, and one of the forest's claims to fame is the extraordinary diversity of its land snails: over 200 species of which three-quarters are found nowhere else in the world. More noticeable is the endemic Madeiran speckled wood butterfly, which holds territory wherever there is a break in the forest canopy and a ray of sunlight breaks through.

The Madeiran Laurel Pigeon is most easily seen by finding a look-out point and waiting for the birds to fly across the forest canopy below. The look-out at Balcões is usually rewarding, as it overlooks a large area of forest with one of the densest pigeon populations on the island. At first light it is often possible to see the birds at closer range, especially if one chances upon an overnight roost.

The Firecrest is one of the most distinctive small birds in the forest. Its markings are slightly different from mainland forms. It is worth a good look

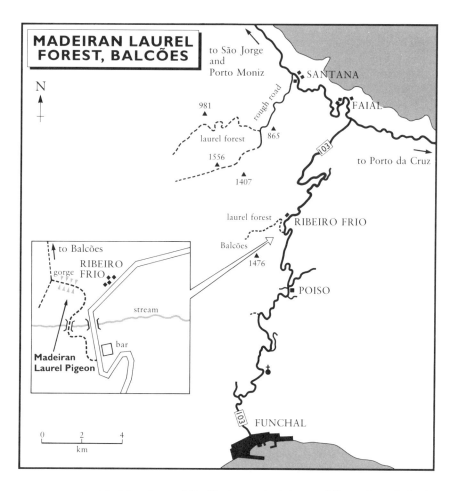

at the Madeiran form of Chaffinch, too, for it is very different from the birds on mainland Europe. Indeed, its generally grey-blue appearance and lack of pink coloration carries more than a suggestion of the Blue Chaffinch of the Canaries.

TIMING
For the most part, there is little to choose between seasons, although in summer Manx Shearwaters nest in the forest. They can be heard returning to their breeding grounds at night but are easier to see at sea (*see* below).
SPECIES
◆ *Resident* Sparrowhawk, Buzzard, Madeiran Laurel Pigeon, Plain Swift, Robin, Blackcap, Firecrest, Chaffinch.
◆ *Summer* Manx Shearwater (February–July).
ACCESS
The road over the island from Funchal, the 103, passes through Poiso and on towards Ribeiro Frio. Just after the sign at the start of the village, but before the village itself, there is a timber-built café – 'Victor's Bar' – on the right.

Park here; opposite there is a wide footpath leading into the forest signposted 'Balcões'. After about three minutes there is a stone bridge over a small stream. The track passes through a cleft in the rocks resembling a miniature gorge before emerging at a point overlooking the road and the village. Balcões is a further 15 minutes' walk away, *turning right* where the track forks.

CALDEIRÃO VERDE
32°46N 16°58W

The best laurel forest is on the north of the island, and an example can be found at Caldeirão Verde, reached via Santana on the north coast. There is a turn off the main road at the western end of the town, by a supermarket, signposted Queimadas. The road gets rough, and the last 3–4 km to Queimadas are best covered on foot. There is a picnic area at Queimadas, and a mossy track along the levada to the right can yield many pigeons as well as the other forest species on the walk to Caldeirão Verde. A route easier on the car is to drive from the eastern end of Santana along the EN101-5, which runs from a Shell garage towards Achada do Teixeira. The car can be left at the picnic area at Pico das Pedras, from which the *levada* mentioned above leads to Queimadas and thence to Caldeirão Verde.

Santana is famous for the traditional A-shaped thatched cottages which, once common throughout the island, are now rarely found away from here.

FUNCHAL TO PONTA DE SÃO LOURENÇO
32°44N 16°42W

The south-east corner of Madeira contains several interesting elements, including Funchal harbour, the coast at Caniço and Santa Cruz, and the São Lourenço peninsula, which is an IBA. The lighthouse island off the rocky headland has colonies of Bulwer's Petrel, Cory's and Little Shearwaters, Madeiran Storm Petrel and Common Tern. Roseate Terns breed in small numbers and more occur on passage. This is also the best place on the island for Rock Sparrow, and Spectacled Warbler can be seen in scrubby areas, especially when there is little or no wind. Migrant passerines and the occasional rarity are often recorded in March–April and October.

Funchal harbour can be interesting, especially during migration, when occasional rarities can turn up. The gull flocks on the harbour buildings are worth scrutinizing; Ring-billed Gulls have been recorded on several occasions. Common Terns feed in the harbour throughout the year, and Roseates occur on passage. Running through the town is a stream which emerges in the harbour between the Marina and the Cais Novo. It is rather unsavoury, but attracts waders in autumn and spring. In October American waders can sometimes be seen: no doubt if there were more resident birdwatchers on the island vagrants would be better documented.

The best sea-watching on the island is immediately in front of the airport, at Ponta de Santa Caterina. Cory's Shearwaters pass by all day, and spend the day feeding in the bay to the east. Bulwer's Petrels and Manx Shearwaters can be seen from here towards dusk, and the occasional *Pterodroma* during windy days. Cory's Shearwaters nest south of Caniço, to the east of a large statue and can be heard here at dusk and into the night. The figure of Christ at Garajau is in another good area to listen for Cory's.

TIMING

For seabirds, *see* under the Desertas, below.

SPECIES

◆ *Resident* Buzzard, Kestrel, Rock Dove, Spectacled Warbler, Linnet, Goldfinch, Rock Sparrow (all local or Macaronesian subspecies).

ACCESS

The 101 coast road east from Funchal passes Caniço, then runs south of the airport to Caniçal from where a small road runs to São Lourenço point.

PORTO SANTO

33°02N 16°20W

Porto Santo is the only other inhabited island in the Madeiran archipelago and is very much drier than the main island. Its bird interest lies primarily in the three islets off its south-east, south-west and north-west corners. These are, respectively, Ilhéu de Cima, Ilhéu de Baixo and Ilhéu de Ferro. However, landbird interest includes species less easy to see on Madeira island: Spanish and Rock Sparrows, Hoopoe and Berthelot's Pipit.

Bulwer's Petrels, Cory's Shearwaters, Little Shearwaters, Madeiran Storm Petrels and Common Terns nest on the islands and Roseate Terns occur on passage. The straits between the main island and the smaller islands, especially Baixo, can be easily watched from the main island, with good sightings of at least some of the breeding seabirds likely around dusk.

The most used passenger boat between Funchal and Porto Santo is a covered hydrofoil; therefore birdwatching from it is less than ideal. However, a window seat will often afford views of Little Shearwater and the ubiquitous Cory's in season. *Pterodromas* have been recorded from this trip, although the speed of the craft makes it a frustrating way of seeking out two of the world's rarest birds! It may be possible to travel on the bridge, with permission, but this seems to be seldom granted. The *Madeirense* plies the same route, taking three-and-a-half hours, and it is possible to sit out on deck.

Spanish Sparrow

THE DESERTAS

32°32N 16°31W

The Desertas islands are visible from Funchal and the summits of Madeira and even from this distance their differing character can be guessed at. The Ilhéu Chão clearly lives up to its name – flat island – and looks like a low tablet of rock rising from the sea. Since 1970 Ilhéu Chão has had none of the problems caused on the other two islands by goat and rabbit grazing and has recovered its lush grassland vegetation. To the south is Deserta Grande, large and with a deep valley at its northern end, while farther south still is Bugio, an inaccessible ridge of rock rising sheer from the ocean to the peaks of its rugged, razorback crest.

The Desertas form part of the Parque Natural da Madeira and are important seabird islands. In addition, they are home to an isolated population of the highly endangered monk seal. The southern part of Deserta Grande and the whole of Bugio are strictly protected, with restrictions on fishing and other activities. Deserta Grande north of the line Doca–Fajã Grande is also protected, but certain fishing practices and leisure activities are permitted under licence in their waters. Landing is permitted but no-one must wander more than 10 m from the water's edge. Bugio is the only place in Europe, and one of only two places in the world, where Fea's Petrel nests. Landing on the island is prohibited.

Some of the craft sailing out of Funchal have landing permission for Deserta Grande, but it is not necessary to land, for the birds are most easily seen at sea. Occasional seabird rarities have been reported by reliable non-birdwatchers who sail these waters regularly, including a Southern Giant Petrel and Red-billed Tropicbirds.

Bulwer's Petrels, Cory's Shearwaters and Madeiran Storm Petrels can usually be seen from boats between the Desertas and Madeira at the right time of year. Cory's Shearwaters are always in evidence between late January and late October. Little and Manx Shearwaters are less common but not usually difficult; Madeiran Storm Petrel is difficult due to its tiny size and the fact that it comes inshore later in the day. It may be seen at dusk in the vicinity of the Desertas.

The best reason for taking a boat into these waters is to see *Pterodromas*. Unfortunately, the two species are indistinguishable at sea and although some birdwatchers may claim otherwise, they are kidding themselves. A *Pterodroma* in late autumn is more likely to be Fea's, and statistically the more likely at other times of the year, simply by virtue of being commoner. *Pterodromas* are delightful birds to watch in flight: they are wont suddenly to launch themselves on an updraft off a wave which may take them 50 m or so into the air, and often they will sail for long distances at this height before returning to sea level; and all without a single wing beat. Windy days seem better for seeing these birds.

Some 80 per cent of monk seal sightings have been at high tide and calm weather is best, although boats are rightly barred from coming close inshore and definitely from entering their nesting caves. Any offers from boatmen to do so, however tempting, should be met with resolve. Dolphins are common in these waters and will almost certainly be seen on any boat trip. Turtles and flying fish are also often encountered.

TIMING
Seabirds have their seasons, roughly as follows: Bulwer's Petrel, May–October; Little Shearwater and Madeiran Storm Petrel, all year; Cory's Shearwater, January–October; White-faced Petrel (rare away from the Selvagens), December–July; Zino's Petrel, April–October; Fea's Petrel, June–January.

At present boat-trips to the Desertas are erratic. From July to the end of October the Costa do Sol company (tel. 38538/224390) has run trips from the Funchal Marina. This and other companies run game fishing trips which allow non-fishermen along. Other private owners run occasional charters or periodically set up an organized trip. Hotels and travel agents in Funchal often have information about these (the hotels seem better informed than the agencies). Trips west from Funchal are also available but are less rewarding for birdwatchers.

THE SELVAGENS

30°09N 15°52W

These outlying rocky islands are included mainly for completeness, because their remoteness and the lack of any practical means of getting there makes it unlikely that they will be visited by birdwatchers in the foreseeable future. They are, in fact, much closer to the Canary Islands than to Funchal. The two islets, of 245 ha and 20 ha, Selvagem Grande and Selvagem Pequena, are of great importance for seabirds, most notably their 20,000 pairs of White-faced Petrel. Sooty Terns have bred and are regularly observed by the Madeira Natural Park authorities, who manage the islands. There are at least 13,500 pairs of Cory's Shearwaters, along with Madeiran Storm Petrels and, it would seem, Swinhoe's Petrels which have been caught here by researchers on a few occasions.

All this would hardly be worth mentioning were it not for the fact that there *are* possibilities for enjoying this great richness. Some cruises call in at both Madeira and the Canaries, passing by the Selvagens. This must provide opportunities for some outstanding deck-based birdwatching in some style. Furthermore the car ferries to the Canary Islands from Cádiz pass through these waters.

AZORES

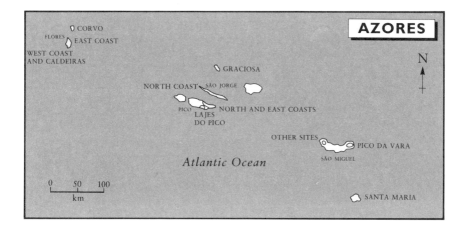

The Azores are remote, mid-Atlantic islands, spread out over 600 km of sea. The nearest island to the European mainland, São Miguel, is over 1400 km away. The Azores are *par excellence* seabird islands, and hold perhaps 80 per cent of the world's Cory's Shearwaters, some 500,000 pairs. The 600 or more pairs of Roseate Terns make the Azores the stronghold of this species in the north-east Atlantic. Fea's Petrel (see above) has twice been recorded, and a new colony may yet be found. There is one endemic landbird, the critically endangered Azores Bullfinch or Priôlo, which is widely regarded as a distinct species, *Pyrrhula murina*. Other interesting landbirds include the Canary and several distinct Azorean forms of familiar species such as Chaffinch and Goldcrest. Typically, many landbirds have expanded their ecological niche in ways which would surprise the visitor from the continent. Grey Wagtails, for instance, are *the* insectivore and are to be found everywhere.

There is undoubtedly much to be discovered about the Azores and their birds. Their proximity to America offers exciting possibilities for autumn rarity-seekers, and the few birdwatchers who have gone at this time have not been disappointed. Some American birds seem to have taken up residence: Black Ducks apparently breed and there are said to be several Great Blue Herons, presumably non-breeders, scattered about the islands. The seabirds are the best-studied group, and the University of the Azores has collaborated with the RSPB and Amigos dos Açores, the main conservation group, over several projects. Even so, there must be surprises in store here, too. Are Red-billed Tropicbirds regular breeders or was the 1993 case an isolated event? Do White-faced Petrels breed ...?

The islands are in three groups: eastern (São Miguel and Santa Maria), central (Terceira, São Jorge, Graciosa, Pico and Faial), and western (Flores and Corvo). Inter-island flights are relatively straightforward and although still relatively inexpensive, the regional airline, SATA, has increased its prices substantially in recent years. Ferry services link the islands within each group, but flying is the only realistic way to get from one group to another. The Azores are just beginning to attract package tourists and charter flights are likely to become more common. At present flights are generally via Lisbon or from Madeira.

Many of the seabird colonies are on inshore islands, which can be viewed from the shore. Many fishing vessels will take on paying passengers, or even make tailor-made trips. However, they often land illegally on the islands or go too close to sensitive tern colonies. The best bet is to enquire at the *Capitania* in the main town of each island. This is the local marine authority who can advise as to which vessels are licensed to land on the islands and are accustomed to working with seabird researchers. This way any disturbance problems should be averted. *Capitania* staff often speak English. Corvo is the only island without a *Capitania* office of its own, and is handled by the Flores authority.

BIRDWATCHING SITES

PICO DA VARA, SÃO MIGUEL
37°48N 25°15W

São Miguel is the largest and perhaps the most varied of the islands. Its lush green appearance tends to hide its volcanic origins. In fact, it is geologically several islands which have grown together in relatively recent times.

At the eastern end of the island is Pico da Vara, at 1110 m its highest point. The two peaks and the valley that separates them contain the best-preserved area of laurel forest in the Azores, although even this is threatened by the encroachment of exotic plant species and commercial forestry. There are plans to create a nature reserve, however, and this may help to save one of Europe's most threatened species, the Priôlo or Azores Bullfinch. It is a little-known species which has been the subject in recent years of a research project funded and supervised by the RSPB. There are believed to be about 45 pairs, and it is found nowhere else in the world. Its large size, dull plumage and lack of white on the rump have led to a growing number of scientists regarding it as a distinct species.

TIMING
June to August is the most reliable time in terms of weather, which is a decisive factor in seeking out the Priôlo.
SPECIES
◆ *Resident* Buzzard, Woodcock, Woodpigeon, Grey Wagtail, Blackbird, Goldcrest, Canary, Chaffinch, Priôlo (all Azorean endemic forms).

ACCESS

The terrain on Pico da Vara is very inhospitable, but fortunately, the Priôlo tends to be readily visible from the road, and it is unnecessary and inadvisable to wander into the forest. It is a matter of waiting, and listening for the call, which is rather similar to that of the European Bullfinch.

The village of Povoação, on the south-east coast, is about 60 km east of Ponta Delgada, the main town on the island, along the EN1-1a road. This road continues round the coast to the village of Nordeste. However, just beyond Povoação the EN1-2a branches off, also in the direction of Nordeste, but over the hills. There is a sharp right turn at the highest point, where there is a viewing point or *miradouro*. From here back down the road for a couple of kilometres is the most likely area for seeing Priôlos.

SATA and TAP fly into Ponta Delgada from Lisbon and the other islands, and cars can be hired at the airport. There are plenty of hotels in Ponta Delgada, and a few in the east of the island, such as at the spa resort of Furnas.

OTHER SITES ON SÃO MIGUEL
37°48N 25°40W

As with all the Azorean islands, very little suitable habitat exists for shorebirds, so the rock-loving Turnstone is generally the commonest wader. However, there are small beaches and the one at Ribeira Grande on the north shore, as well as the rocks offshore there, is worth checking.

The most famous natural area on the island is at the westernmost end, at Sete Cidades. The breathtaking view of the crater lakes here is worth making the trip for, birds or no birds. There are sometimes gulls loafing about here, and like all the crater lakes in the Azores, undoubtedly it attracts transatlantic visitors such as Ring-billed Gulls and American ducks from time to time.

The rocky shoreline at nearby Mosteiros has attracted American waders along with the small groups of Palearctic migrants which seem to congregate there in autumn.

SANTA MARIA
36°56N 25°10W

Santa Maria is the oldest, driest and sunniest of the Azores archipelago. It is distinctly an island of halves: a flat, dry plain in the west, separated from the green, hilly east by a mountain ridge running north to south down the centre of the island.

The main seabird breeding area on the island is at the south-westrtn tip, near the airport at Vila do Porto. There is an islet offshore here which has retained its rich flora, including four endemic plants, despite the presence of a handful of goats. Here and on the mainland opposite there are a few dozen pairs of Bulwer's Petrels, 150 pairs of Little Shearwaters and 100 pairs of Madeiran Storm Petrels. There is also a colony of Roseate Terns, whose size fluctuates but can reach over 200 pairs. Sooty Terns are now regular breeders and in 1993 Red-billed Tropicbirds bred.

The varied countryside of Santa Maria has all the typical species of the Azores, including Canaries. The flat western plain is dotted with small pools and marshy areas which attract migrants from both sides of the Atlantic.

TIMING

Cory's Shearwaters are found almost all year round, but the best time for the other species is May to September.

SPECIES

◆ *Resident* Buzzard, Quail, Long-eared Owl, Canary.

◆ *Breeding Season* Manx, Little and Cory's Shearwaters, Madeiran Storm and Bulwer's Petrels, Common, Roseate and Sooty Terns.

ACCESS

The Ilhéu da Vila do Porto is off the south-western tip of the island, south of the airport. Fishing boats out of Vila do Porto are worth trying, via the *Capitania*, in order to explore these waters, but the headlands south of the town are also worthwhile sea-watching points.

Santa Maria can be reached by air from the other islands, and by boat from São Miguel. Hotel accommodation is sparse, with the airport hotel the only one offering tourist facilities.

INTER-ISLAND CROSSINGS

38°30N 28°00W

Ferry crossings anywhere in the Azores can be outstanding sea-watching experiences, but it is in the central group that the longest and most varied crossing can be made.

An inexpensive eight-hour journey unites Terceira with Faial via São Jorge and Pico. Cory's Shearwaters are abundant throughout these waters in summer. Manx Shearwaters, though less abundant, should present no problems. Little Shearwaters are much less frequently seen, but one or two at least per trip can be expected in summer. Bulwer's Petrels are also recorded on these trips, but their smaller size and fast, direct flight makes them hard to pick up. In September, Great Shearwaters are seen in good numbers along with small numbers of Sooties. Arctic Skuas are recorded in autumn and spring, along with the occasional Pomarine.

The Azores are famous for whales and, until 1970, whaling. Sightings of Bottle-nosed and Common Dolphins are frequent from aboard the ferries, and the occasional Sperm Whale rears its head to add variety to the wildlife watching.

The ferry can be picked up at Angra do Heroismo (Terceira), Calheta, Velas (both São Jorge), Madalena (Pico) and Horta (Faial). The short legs between Pico and Faial, or between Pico and São Jorge are particularly rewarding. There are no restaurant services on board, so it is advisable to take food.

GRACIOSA

39°10N 28°00W

Graciosa is the lowest of the islands, and the sunniest (or least rainy) of the central group. There are two important seabird islets. The Ilhéu de Praia is off the east coast at Vila da Praia (São Mateus), and is grass-covered with rocky shores. Over 100 pairs of Roseate Terns breed there in a good season along with Common Terns. There is a clifftop track to the north of Praia from which the narrow strait can be watched. The beach attracts waders, including breeding Kentish Plovers and Western Sandpipers on passage.

Off the south-east tip of Graciosa is the Ilhéu de Baixo which, with the adjacent headland, has breeding Little Shearwaters (450 pairs) and Madeiran Storm Petrels (300 pairs). The road south from Praia skirts the caldeira of the island's volcano towards the Ponta da Restinga, opposite the island. From the restaurant at the nearby spa of Termas de Carapacho, a mixed colony of Roseate and Common Terns can be watched on the offshore islet below.

Graciosa is reached by air and sea from the neighbouring islands. Santa Cruz, the capital, has plenty of *Residentiais*, small, reliable hotels.

LAJES DO PICO
39°00N 28°00W

Pico, with its great volcano, is the highest of the islands, one of the largest, and one of the best for the birdwatcher. It is here that most sightings of transatlantic vagrants have occurred. There are few good wader sites anywhere in the Azores, but there are usually gatherings of migrant waders on the *lajes*, flat areas of lava where tidal pools provide some feeding for waders, gulls and occasional herons and egrets.

The village of Lajes do Pico is named after one such area, and is perhaps the best known. Western, Semi-palmated and Spotted Sandpipers are among the waders seen there on occasions. Blue-winged Teal and Snowy Egrets are occasional visitors and almost certainly other American ducks and waders will show up from time to time if only more people went there to find out.

TIMING
September is the best month for American waders but spring passage must also be worth sampling.
SPECIES
◆ *Resident* Little Egret, Teal, Yellow-legged Gull (*atlantis* race).
◆ *Passage* Turnstone, Curlew Sandpiper, Knot, Sanderling, Greenshank, Whimbrel, American waders and ducks.
ACCESS
The charming Lajes do Pico is the capital of the island, although Madalena is the main entry point by both air and sea. Car hire firms operate at Madalena, although Lajes is easy to get to by bus. Accommodation is available both here and at Lajes.

NORTH AND EAST COASTS OF PICO
39°00N 28°00W

The old whaling station at San Roque is worth a visit. The tuna processing factory there is a Mecca for gulls, and Ring-billed is almost assured (indeed, this species is not uncommon throughout the Azores and any group of gulls should be checked). The *atlantis* race of Yellow-legged Gull is the common gull of the Canaries, Madeira and the Azores. With luck, other American species might be seen. In late summer and autumn there should be skuas around, and in winter, they will be joined by wintering Puffins and Little Auks.

The eastern tip of the island, at Ponta da Ilha, is a renowned whale-watching spot in late summer and is good for seabirds.

NORTH COAST OF SÃO JORGE

29°50N 38°50W

São Jorge is essentially a mountain ridge rising from the ocean, with its northern slopes plummeting steeply into the sea. Below these tall cliffs, there are hamlets set on small coastal plains – *fajãs* – but the highlands are virtually uninhabited.

The seas of the north shore are one of the principal wintering grounds for Puffins and Little Auks, and they can sometimes be seen inshore, especially after storms or during onshore winds. Severe gales will often produce dozens washed up dead, or wandering about exhausted on the beach.

One of the most spectacular walks in the Azores is between two *fajã* hamlets: Fajã dos Cubres and Fajã dos Tijolos. This stretch of coast seems particularly good for auks. Both *fajãs* have fresh-water lagoons which often have Black Duck and other American visitors on them.

Fajã dos Cubres is 3 km east of Norte Pequeno, which is on the EN1 from Velas. A track leads down to the hamlet and on along the coast to Fajã dos Tijolos. If you drive yourself, you need to double back, making for a long hike of some 20 km. However, most of the islands' taxi drivers are familiar with this popular walk and can drop you on the EN2 east of Ribeira Seca at a track leading to Fajã da Caldeira and Fajã dos Tijolos. A taxi can then be arranged to meet you in Norte Pequeno or, after a rather easier 10 km, at the church in Fajã dos Cubres.

EAST COAST OF FLORES

39°25N 31°12W

The rocky coastline of Flores, with its cliffs, islets and stacks supports the richest concentration of seabirds in the Azores. The north-east coast, between Santa Cruz and Ponta Delgada has some 200 pairs of Roseate Terns, half of which nest on the tiny island of Baixa do Moinho, a few hundred metres north of the airport. This can be viewed from the *miradouro* where the coast road comes closest to the sea at Lagoa.

There is a small reservoir above the nearby village of Fazenda which has occasional Black Duck, presumably wanderers from the caldeiras (see below), as well as regular, and possibly resident, Ring-necked Ducks. The wooded slopes of the Ribeira da Badanela, along a cobbled trail above the reservoir, are good for Canaries, which are not as common in the western group as on the other islands, as well as the other resident birds, most of which are endemic Azorean subspecies.

TIMING
Flores is the wettest, cloudiest and most humid of the islands and therefore June to August are the best months. This is good for seabirds but a little late to see much of the resident landbirds.

SPECIES
◆ *Resident* Grey Heron, Quail, Kentish Plover, Woodcock, Grey Wagtail, Blackcap, Goldcrest, Canary.
◆ *Breeding Season* Manx and Cory's Shearwaters, Common and Roseate Terns.
◆ *Passage* Gannet, Black Duck, waders, rarities.

ACCESS
Flores is served by air from the other islands by SATA to Santa Cruz, where there is accommodation and car hire. Buses and taxis reach all the interesting parts of the island.

WEST COAST AND CALDEIRAS OF FLORES
39°250N 31°40W

There are perhaps 25,000 pairs of Cory's Shearwaters in the vicinity of Ponta do Albarnaz, Ilhéu da Gadelha and Ilhéu de Monchique, but land access to these north-western localities is extremely difficult. However, farther south along this coast is Fajã Grande, which is reached easily by bus or car (along the EN2-2a) from Santa Cruz. This village makes a good base for the west coast, since the lava flow here is frequented by migrant waders and is a good sea-watching point.

The EN2-2a from Santa Cruz passes the four caldeiras which once produced these flows. There are paths alongside the lakes which now fill their craters. Caldeira Branca, the most northerly, has resident Black Ducks, which are almost certainly breeding, and occasional Ring-necked Ducks.

CORVO
39°50N 31°07W

The smallest and least developed of the Azorean islands, Corvo is a short and exciting ferry hop to the north of Flores. The sea can be rough here, but the Risso's dolphins, occasional sperm whales and abundant seabirds make the trip a must for visitors to the western group. This ferry (the *Familia Augusto*) leaves Santa Cruz for the 90-minute trip and returns in the evening. The one town on Corvo, Vila Nova do Corvo, has little to offer the tourist, and no accommodation to speak of: nor are there car hire facilities. However, the rocks at the southern tip of the island, close to the town, are good for resting terns and waders. A taxi ride to the caldeira may reward the effort, with vagrant waders, ducks and passerines possible, especially in late summer and autumn.

FURTHER READING

de Juana, E., *Donde Ver Aves en España Peninsular*, SEO, Barcelona, 1993

Finlayson C., *Birds of the Straits of Gibraltar*, T. and A.D. Poyser, London 1992

Grimmett, R.F.A, and Jones, T.A., *Important Bird Areas in Europe*,. ICBP Technical Publication No. 9, Cambridge, 1989

Rufino, R., *Atlas das Aves que Nidificam em Portugal Continental*, CEMPA, Lisbon, 1989

Stieglitz, A., *Landscapes of the Azores*, Sunflower, London, 1992

Various, *Espacios Naturales Protegidos de España*, Editorial Incafo, Madrid, 1992

USEFUL ADDRESSES

Sociedad Española de Ornitologia (SEO/BirdLife España)
Cra. Húmera 63–1
28224 Pozuelo de Alarcón
Madrid
Spain

Liga para a Protecção da Natureza
Estrada do Calhariz de Benfica 187
1500 Lisbon
Portugal

Spanish National Tourist Office
57–58 St. James's St.,
London SW1A 1LD
tel. 0171 499 0901

Portuguese Tourist Office
22–25a Sackville St.,
London W1X 20E
tel. 0171 493 3873

Gibraltar Tourist Board
Arundel Great Court
179 Strand
London WC2R 1EH
tel. 0171 836 0777

INDEX OF PLACE NAMES

Only principal towns, tourist centres, provincial capitals and towns mentioned as offering accommodation are listed.

INDEX OF BIRD NAMES

Figures in *italics* refer to illustrations

NATURAL HISTORY BOOKS

A complete range of Hamlyn Natural History titles is available from all good bookshops or by mail order direct from the publisher. Payment can be made by credit card or cheque/postal order in the following ways:

BY PHONE
Phone through your order on our special *Credit Card Hotline* on **01933 414 000**. Speak to our customer service team during office hours (9 a.m. to 5 p.m.) or leave a message on the answer machine, quoting your full credit card number plus expiry date and your full name and address. Please also quote the reference number NATHIS 4.

BY POST
Simply fill out the order form below (photocopies are acceptable) and send it with your payment to:
Cash Sales Department,
Reed Book Services Ltd.,
P.O. Box 5,
Rushden,
Northants, NN10 6YX

NATHIS 4

I wish to order the following titles:

	ISBN	Price	Quantity Total
Hamlyn Guide to the Birds of Britain and Europe	0 600 57492 X	£8.99	.... £.......
Photographic Guide to Birds of Britain and Europe	0 600 57861 5	£9.99	.... £.......
Where to Watch Birds in Britain and Europe	0 600 58007 5	£12.99	.... £.......
Behaviour Guide: Birds of Prey	0 540 01277 7	£14.99	.... £.......
Where to Watch Birds in Eastern Europe	0 600 57976 X	£16.99	.... £.......
Add £2.00 for postage and packing if your order is worth		£10.00 or less	£.......
		Grand Total	£.......

Name _____ (block capitals)

Address _____

_____ Postcode _____

I enclose a cheque/postal order for £ _____ made payable to Reed Book Services Ltd
or
Please debit my ☐ Access   ☐ Visa   ☐ American Express   ☐ Diners

account number ☐☐☐☐ ☐☐☐☐ ☐☐☐☐ ☐☐☐☐

by £ _____ Expiry date _____ Signature _____

SPECIAL OFFER: FREE POSTAGE AND PACKAGING FOR ALL ORDERS OVER £10.00, add £2.00 for p+p if your order is £10.00 or less.

Whilst every effort is made to keep our prices low, the publisher reserves the right to increase the prices at short notice.
Your order will be dispatched within 5 days, but please allow up to 28 days for delivery, subject to availability.
Registered office: Michelin House, 81 Fulham Road, London SW3 6RB.
Registered in England no 1974080.

If you do not wish your name to be used by other carefully selected organizations for promotional purposes, please tick this box ☐